Ch
in F

printed
d paper

Stanley Dunham (signature)

Church and State in France, 1870–1914

John McManners

HARPER TORCHBOOKS ◆
Harper & Row, Publishers
New York, Evanston, San Francisco, London

This book was originally published by S.P.C.K, Holy Trinity Church, Marylebone Road, London, NWI, England in 1972. It is reprinted here by arrangement.

First HARPER TORCHBOOK edition published 1973.
LIBRARY OF CONGRESS CATALOG CARD NUMBER: 72–12245
STANDARD BOOK NUMBER: 06–131768–3

Contents

Foreword

The conviction that there was once a golden age of the Christian
faith, from which the present is a radical decline, still attracts many
church historians. But, as Professor McManners suggests, what may
seem a sudden decline in religious practice may be less a change of
faith than a chance of circumstances. "To understand the dechristianization of rural society", he writes, "it is important to
abandon the myth, dear to conservative churchmen, of an earlier
epoch that was 'Christian'". Research into English history is as
yet insufficiently advanced to show how far this may be true of
English religious life, but there is certainly some evidence to suggest
that the alienation of the labouring class from the Church not
merely antedated the Victorian religious revival but was largely
unaffected by it.

Even so, the situation of the French Church in the nineteenth
century was very different from that of any other European country.
It was not merely conditioned by its long past history but by the
particular circumstances of French history after 1815, by the intense
emotions which church-state relations could arouse, by widespread
anticlericalism, and by the number of areas where the process of
dechristianization appeared already to be complete. "Religious
observance declined in most European countries . . . but in France
the decline was perhaps more marked than most", Mr Larkin has
written, ". . . as far as the urban proletariat is concerned, it has
often been pointed out that this class was not dechristianized—it
was born and reared outside the Church".* The story of the
relations of church and state between 1870 and 1914, so dramatic
in its episodes, so paradoxical in its effects, is told here with
fascinating insight into the problems and personalities by Professor
McManners. Like the author's previous book in this series, *The
French Revolution and the Church*, this is a notable contribution
to our understanding of European history of the period. Some might
add that in the curious conjunction of sacrificial action, intellectual

---

* M.J.M. Larkin, "The Church and the French Concordat, 1891 to 1902"
English Historical Review (1966) p. 738.

blindness, and basic conservatism, which seemed so often to typify the French Catholic attitude, there is to be found an object lesson for the Church itself.

V. H. H. Green

A List of Dates

1. THE FRENCH REVOLUTION

1789

4 May	Procession and Mass for opening of Estates General
19 June	Vote of the Clergy to join the "General Assembly" (i.e., they abandon the Nobility)
2 November	Church property "at the disposal of the nation"

1790

13 February	Decree on Monasticism (i) Inmates of monasteries can take their freedom (ii) Contemplative and mendicant orders to be abolished (iii) Taking of religious vows in future forbidden
12 July	Civil Constitution of the Clergy voted (i) Dioceses to coincide with civil Departments; chapters abolished (ii) State salaries for clergy (iii) Bishops to be chosen by electors of Departments; *curés* by those of Districts (N.B. There was no consultation with ecclesiastical authority)
27 November	Decree imposing oath to the Civil Constitution on the clergy

1791

2 January	Taking of oath begins (in the end, half clergy refuse)
4 May	The Pope publishes his condemnation of the Civil Constitution of the Clergy

1792

April	War
10 August	Fall of the Throne
August	Abolition of all religious congregations
2 September	September Massacres begin (of 1,400 victims, there were 3 Bishops and 220 priests)
20 September	*État civil* laicized and divorce legalized

1793

March	Rising in the Vendée
September	Dechristianization begins
7 October	Revolutionary Calendar adopted
10 November	Festival of Reason in Notre-Dame (Note: During the Terror many priests were executed, and many more imprisoned or otherwise persecuted)

1794

7 May	*Culte de l'Être Suprême*
28 July	Execution of Robespierre
September	End of clerical salaries

1795

21 February   Decree of Boissy d'Anglas (3 ventôse, year III)
Separation of Church and State; no "exterior signs of religion allowed"; "the Republic does not recognize and does not pay for any religion"

December   The Bishops of the Constitutional Church, led by Grégoire, lay down a new system of church government by Presbyteries

1796

Beginning of Theophilanthropy—a cult of deism and humanistic morality (The Directory enforces the patriotic official ceremonies of the *décadi*)

1797

September   The coup of Fructidor—renewed persecution

1799

29 August   Death of Pope Pius VI in French captivity at Valence

2. NAPOLEON I

1799

November   *Coup d'état* of Brumaire
Bonaparte becomes First Consul

1800

14 March   Conclave of Venice
Election of Chiaramonti as Pope Pius VII

November   Negotiations for a Concordat begin

1801

September   Ratification of Concordat
     (i) Renewal of episcopate (the Pope to ensure resignations. Some bishops of the *ancien régime* refuse the Pope's order to resign. This is the beginning of the schism of the *"Petite Église"*)
     (ii) New bishops nominated by First Consul
     (iii) Ecclesiastics take oath of obedience to government
     (iv) Church recognizes the sale of ecclesiastical property
     (v) Bonaparte adds the "Organic Articles"

1802

12 April   Easter celebrations in Notre-Dame
Chateaubriand's *Génie du Christianisme*

July   New episcopate completed (for a reduced number of dioceses)

1804

The *Code civil*—includes liberty of conscience, lay control of the *état civil*, marriage as a civil contract, divorce
Decree of 3 Messidor, an XII, reaffirming the revolutionary laws against religious congregations (but exceptions are allowed, e.g. the Frères des Écoles chrétiennes for education. By 1814 there are 12,400 nuns in France)

2 December   Coronation of Napoleon as Emperor in Notre-Dame in the presence of the Pope

1805

April   End of Pius VII's stay in France—the country has shown enthusiasm for him

1806

Creation of the Université, a potential State monopoly of education, though bishops are on its central Council and church schools are allowed
Imperial Catechism of 1806 includes duties towards "Napoleon I, our Emperor"

1808

2 February   French occupy Rome

1809

17 May   Papal states united to the Empire
6 July   Pius VII kidnapped
August   Pope to captivity in Savona

1810

January   Napoleon's divorce pronounced by the Church Court of Paris
March–April   Napoleon marries Marie-Louise of Austria in religious ceremonies

1811

Numerous dioceses are vacant because the Pope refuses Napoleon's nominations

16 June   Council of the French Church
8 July   Napoleon dissolves this Council (the bishops have shown loyalty to the Pope)

November   Only one ecclesiastical school allowed in each Department

3. THE BOURBON RESTORATION, 1814–30

1814

24 May   Return of Pius VII to Rome
The Charter of 1814 states Catholicism is the "religion of the State" (i.e., not just of "the great majority of Frenchmen" as in the Concordat). But guarantees of religious toleration are given and assurances to those who have bought Church property

18 November   Sunday a day of rest again

1816

8 May   Divorce struck out of Civil Code

8 November   Five bishops of the "Petite Église" make submission to Rome (a further blow to the Gallican tradition)

1817

11 June   A new Concordat (essentially a return to that of 1516) signed. But it is withdrawn as the Pope will not accept reservations to preserve the Gallican liberties. Thus, the Concordat of 1801 and the Organic Articles remain in force in France
Thirty new bishoprics are created
Great success of the first volume of La Mennais, *L'Essai sur l'indifférence en matière de religion*—the State should support the true faith

1818

M. Vianney becomes *Curé* of Ars
A limited religious revival in France—growth of religious congregations, work of "missions"

1819

Joseph de Maistre, *Du Pape*—in support of papal infallibility, and against the Gallican tradition

1820

January   The Chamber asks the king to fortify religion "by a system of Christian and monarchical education"

13 February   Murder of the duc de Berry
Extremist royalist and Catholic feeling rises

1821

15 December   Ministry of Villèle. The Ultras and the *Chevaliers de la Foi* now have great influence

1822

17 and   Press laws. Newspapers attacking religion can be sup-
25 March   pressed

1823

La Mennais' attack on the godless Université in *Le Drapeau blanc* (in fact, Mgr Frayssinous is giving the clergy great power within the Université)

20 August   Death of Pope Pius VII

1824

Rising anticlericalism. Since 1817 12 editions of Voltaire and 13 of Rousseau have been published. Béranger and Paul-Louis Courrier active

16 September   Death of Louis XVIII; accession of Charles X

1825

20 April   Sacrilege Law—death for profanation of Host (the law is passed but cannot be enforced—"the only victim was the dynasty")

24 May	Houses of nuns need no more than administrative authorization
29 May	Coronation of Charles X at Reims with the old ceremonies

1826

February	Montlosier, *Mémoire à Consulter*—a Gallican attack on the Jesuits

1828

January	Fall of Villèle. More moderate royalists take over
16 June	Ordinances to oust Jesuits from education and to limit Little Seminaries to clerical pupils only

1829

	La Mennais, *Les progrès de la Révolution et de la guerre contre l'Église*—Ultramontane, and for the alliance of Catholicism with liberalism; for freedom of education and of the press. "Pope and People" instead of "Pope and King"
10 February	Death of Pope Leo XII In 1829 there were 2,350 ordinations (as against 1,400 in 1821 and only 715 in 1814). Of the 90 episcopal appointments since 1814, 70 have gone to aristocrats. The *budget des cultes* has been increased threefold under the Restoration

4. THE JULY MONARCHY, 1830–48

1830

July	Fall of the Bourbons, Monarchy of Louis Philippe Churchmen unpopular; priests wear lay attire
29 July	Sack of the palace of the Archbishop of Paris
16 October	First number of *L'Avenir* (La Mennais, Lacordaire and, very soon, Montalembert) For "Dieu et la liberté"; the separation of Church and State, liberty of education, of the press, of association
30 November	Death of Pope Pius VIII

1831

	Charter of the new Government Catholicism is "the religion of the majority of Frenchmen" The Ordinances of 1828 against the religious Orders are enforced, and the *budget des cultes* is decreased
2 February	Election of Pope Gregory XVI
14 February	Sack of Church of Saint-Germain-l'Auxerrois (where mass for the duc de Berry is being said)
9 May	Montalembert and La Mennais open a school in defiance of the Université; legal proceedings against Montalembert ensue in the Chamber of Peers
May	Death of Grégoire, leader of the Constitutional Church during the Revolution of 1789. The Archbishop of Paris refuses a religious burial but the Government provides one

September	Rome rules that Louis-Philippe may have the title of "*Roi Très Chrétien*"
25 November	The Liberal Catholics of the *L'Avenir* group appeal to Rome against the ecclesiastical hierarchy
30 December	La Mennais, Lacordaire, and Montalembert arrive in Rome

1832

15 August	Encyclical *Mirari vos*: Gregory XVI condemns the separation of Church and State and other ideas of *L'Avenir*. Submission of the Liberal Catholics fortifies ultramontanism in France 6th volume of Auguste Comte's *Cours de Philosophie Positive* appears (first volume in 1830)

1833

28 June	Guizot's Education Law. "Primary instruction necessarily involves moral and religious instruction". Ecclesiastics can teach in State schools Ozanam founds the charitable organization the *Conférences de Saint-Vincent-de-Paul*

1834

30 April	La Mennais, *Paroles d'un croyant*. Liberty and Catholicism are mutually exclusive. "Providence sent Gregory XVI to show the world to what depths the human part of a divine institution can sink" Villeneuve-Bargemont, *Économie chrétienne* (beginning of a Christian socialism of the Right)

1835

15 March	First of the *abbé* Lacordaire's sermons in Notre-Dame

1838

	Bishopric of Algiers created

1839

	Dom Guéranger founds Benedictine abbey at Solesmes
April	Lacordaire revives the Order of Dominicans Allignol, *De l'état actuél du Clergé de France*—a complaint against episcopal despotism over the lower clergy (the lower clergy turn to Rome for support against the bishops)

1840

	Dom Guéranger, *Les Institutions liturgiques*. Recommends adoption of the Roman Liturgy (but in the next eight years only six bishops abandon their diocesan liturgies) Buchez founds *L'Atelier* (a Christian Socialism of the Left)

1841

	Episcopal attacks on the Université and its educational monopoly

1842

December	Louis Veuillot becomes editor of *L'Univers*

1843

Anticlerical attacks upon the Jesuits, especially from the Université (Michelet, Quinet)

Montalembert, *Du devoir des Catholiques dans la question de la liberté d'enseignement* (urges forming a Catholic political party to win over public opinion and take a lead in establishing liberties)

1844

Dupin's Gallican manual of ecclesiastical law published. In spite of the Government, most bishops protest against it

1845

Thiers urges the Government to apply the laws against the Jesuits

23 June   The General of the Jesuits says the French houses of the Order will close (to avert anticlerical rage)

1846

17 June   Election of Pope Pius IX (reputation as a "liberal")

The French legislative elections—146 candidates returned who have signed engagements to Montalembert's *Comité pour la Défence de la liberté religieuse.*

1847

Guizot's speech—the rights of families and of believers have priority in educational policy

Ordinations reach 1,300 this year (had been 1,100 in 1841, but 2,350 in 1829)

There are now 3,000 regular clergy (there had been 70,000 in 1789, there were to be 17,700 in 1861)

Of the 72 bishops nominated since 1830, only 18 were nobles

5. SECOND REPUBLIC, SECOND EMPIRE, 1848–70

1848

22 February   Revolution in Paris. Fall of Louis-Philippe. Churchmen accept the Republic. (Veuillot in *L'Univérs*: "Gallican theology consecrated the divine right of kings ... Roman theology ... the divine right of peoples")

10 March   Montalembert's circular to the bishops—urges concerting efforts to return candidates for the elections to the Constituent Assembly

15 April   Lacordaire, Maret, and Ozanam found *L'Ère nouvelle* (the first French "Christian democratic" type of movement—for the Republic and social reform, including profit sharing and the "right to work")

23 June   Renewed Parisian rising a threat to the "social" order

25 June   Mgr Affre, Archbishop of Paris, killed on the barricades

Catholics now mostly on the side of reaction (Lacordaire says that the attitude of the Catholic press means that "in the next rising the attack will fall on priests and churches")

24 November   Pius IX flees from Rome

25 November	Election manifesto of Louis-Napoleon Bonaparte (he will protect religion and give to the Church liberty of education)
10 December	Louis-Napoleon President (5,454,000 votes against, 1,448,000)

1849

13 May	Legislative elections—conservative majority
July	French troops under Oudinot take Rome from the men who have ousted the Pope
	Dupanloup and Pie both elevated to the episcopate in this year

1850

15 March	Vote of the "Falloux Law"

      (i) Schoolmasters supervised by mayor and *curé*
     (ii) Church can open schools freely
    (iii) Bishops to sit on the *Conseil supérieur de l'Instruction publique*
        Republicans angry at these concessions to the Church
        Père Alzon creates the Assumptionist Order

1851

2 December	Louis-Napoleon's *coup d'état*
20 December	Plebiscite approves this
	The Pope, the bishops, and Catholics generally accept the coup

1852

31 January	Decree: congregations of nuns can be authorized by simple decree (great increase in numbers of nuns follows—also, unauthorized congregations of monks begin to multiply)
	Montalembert, *Des intérêts catholiques au xixe siècle*—warns Catholics against forgetting liberty and accepting the Empire

1854

Crimean War. Clerical support for Emperor
Pius IX promulgates the doctrine of the Immaculate Conception without reference to a Council

1858

Foundation of *La Revue Germanique* to spread the German biblical criticism
The "Mortara affair" (a three-year old Jewish child taken from parents by the authorities in the pontifical States because baptized by a servant; outcry in France)

1859

May	France and Piedmont go to war with Austria
December	*Le Pape et le Congrès*—a pamphlet sponsored by Napoleon III arguing that Pius IX should not cling to his temporal power

1860

28 January	*L'Univers* publishes a papal encyclical urging the bishops to press for the conservation of the Pope's temporal power

18 September	Castelfidardo. The Piedmontese army defeats the papal *zouaves*. The Pope loses most of his dominions

1861

There are now 17,700 monks and 89,200 nuns in France (in 1851 had been only 3,100 and 34,200 respectively)

1862

Quinet, *La création*
The Bishop of Tarbes authorizes the cult of Notre-Dame de Lourdes

August   Aspromonte. Italian forces prevent Garibaldi seizing Rome

1863

First congress of Malines. Montalembert declares that the Church demands liberty for all, and accepts democracy
Victor Duruy, Minister of Education (multiplies primary schools and tries to get secondary education for girls)
Peyrat says, "*Le cléricalisme, voilà l'ennemi*"

24 June   Renan, *La Vie de Jésus* (10 editions within a year)

1864

By now, 80 of the 91 dioceses have adopted the Roman liturgy

15 September   Convention—French will evacuate Rome, Italy will respect the integrity of the Holy See

8 December   The Encyclical *Quanta Cura* and the Syllabus of Errors (the lay state, the separation of Church and State, the sovereignty of the people, liberty of conscience and of the press etc., are condemned by implication)

1865

January   Dupanloup, *La Convention du 15 septembre et l'encyclique du 8 décembre*. Makes the Syllabus respectable by differentiating thesis from hypothesis

March   Darboy, Archbishop of Paris, affirms in the Senate that the Organic Articles are legitimate (he is censured by Pius IX)

1866

By now 20·9% of primary school boys are in State schools (had been 15·7% in 1850); girls, 55·4% (instead of 44·6%)

23 October   Jean Macé founds *La Ligue de l'Enseignement*
French troops pull out of Rome towards end of the year

1867

New, cheap edition of Voltaire

3 November   Mentana—Napoleon III's expeditionary force stops Garibaldi from taking Rome

December   Rouher tells Senate Italy will "never" be allowed to take Rome

1869

In the course of the Second Empire, a dozen new dioceses (including colonial ones) have been created, and the five dioceses of Savoy and Nice have also been maintained

The *budget des cultes* has risen from 39½ millions to 45½ millions

In this year there were 1,753 ordinations (i.e. 500 more than deaths). The total number of priests has risen from 46,000 to 56,000

Controversy about papal "infallibility" in France; Dom Guéranger supports it, while Montalembert complains that France has become the "backyard of the antechambers of the Vatican"

December   Opening of the First Vatican Council

1870

January   Napoleon III puts in a government of clericals
                A commission under Guizot studies to give Church more
                freedom in higher education

18 July   Proclamation of Pontifical "infallibility"

September   Sedan

4 September   The end of the Second Empire

20 September   Italians occupy Rome

6. THE CRISIS OF CHURCH AND STATE, 1870–1914

1871

February   Elections to National Assembly—"Royalist" majority

18 March   Civil war of Commune of Paris begins

2 April   Commune decides on separation of Church and State

5 July   Comte de Chambord's manifesto insisting on his flag

1872

27 July   Conscription law exempts ecclesiastics

1873

8 September   Pastoral Letter of Archbishop of Paris against Italian occupa-
                tion of Rome

1875

January   The Wallon Amendment (the "Republic")

July   Law allows Catholics to set up universities
                The *budget des cultes* is now 53,500,000 (seven years ago it
                was only 45,500,000)

1876

February   Legislative elections—Republican victory

16 May   The *seize mai* coup

October   Legislative elections—Republican victory

1878

                The *abbé* Bougaud publishes *Le grand péril de l'Église de
                France* (there were 1,582 ordinations last year)

20 February   Election of Pope Leo XIII

1879

5 January	Elections renew a third of the Senate—Republican victory Resignation of MacMahon
15 March	Jules Ferry's Education Law brought forward
4 August	Encyclical *Aeterni Patris* (on Thomism)

1880

9 March	Article VII of the Education Law rejected by the Senate
29 March	Decree of expulsion of congregations
29 June	Expulsion of Jesuits
12 July	Law suppresses obligation of Sunday rest
September	Collapse of project of a declaration by the congregations
19 September	Fall of Freycinet
October– November	Expulsion of congregations
2 December	Law for secondary education of girls

1881

	Albert de Mun elected to Deputies—henceforward Social Catholicism represented in Parliament
16 June	Law—primary education to be free

1882

29 March	Law—primary education to be obligatory and "lay"

1884

8 February	Encyclical, *Nobilissima Gallorum gens*
24 July	Law—divorce allowed Meetings at Fribourg of German and French Social Catholics

1885

October	Legislative elections—great gains by conservative groups
November	Encyclical, *Immortale Dei*
November	De Mun abandons idea of a Catholic party

1886

	Drummont publishes *La France juive*
March	De Mun founds the *Association catholique de la Jeunesse française* (ACJF)
14 July	Review at Longchamps; enthusiasm for General Boulanger
30 October	Law to laicize the teaching profession

1887

	Conversion of Paul Bourget
30 May	Rouvier takes office with Royalist support
September	First Catholic trade union

1888

11 August	Boulanger's telegram to *La Croix*—he will not persecute religion

1889

January	Boulanger at height of his popularity
1 April	Boulanger flees
June	Ferry tries to reassure Catholics
15 July	Law—seminarists to do a year's military service
Sept./Oct.	Legislative elections
December	Leo XIII discusses conciliatory policies towards the State with the Archbishop of Paris

1890

October	Cardinal Lavigerie at the Vatican
12 November	The "Toast" of Algiers

1891

May	Encyclical *Rerum novarum* on social problems
2 October	The affair of the French pilgrims at the tomb of Victor Emmanuel

1892

June	Conversion of Huysmans
September	Panama scandal breaks

1893

20 May	First congress of *cercles d'études ouvriers* at Reims
June	Loisy's farewell to the Institut Catholique
Aug./Sept.	Legislative elections
November	Encyclical *Providentissimus* on the Bible
1 November	The *Libre Parole* announces arrest of Dreyfus

1894

	Marc Sangnier founds journal, *Le Sillon*
3 March	Spuller promises *"un esprit nouveau"*

1895

1 January	Brunetière's article in the *Revue des Deux Mondes* ("a morality is nothing if not religious")
March	Ribot's legislation on the *droit d'abonnement* (to be paid by congregations)

1896

29 April	Ministry of Méline
24 August	First clerical congress at Reims
November	"Christian democrat" congress at Lyon

1897

	Publication of the *abbé* Klein's *Vie du Père Hecker* and of René Bazin's *De toute son âme*
December	Another Congress of Christian Democracy at Lyon

1898

January	Zola's article "J'accuse" in the *Aurore*
May	Legislative elections—attempt at a Catholic Electoral Federation
14 June	Fall of Méline
14 September	Dreyfus Case officially reopened
3 November	French recall Marchand from Fashoda

1899

	Marc Sangnier begins *cercles d'études* of *Le Sillon*
22 January	Leo XIII condemns "Americanism"
21 June	Ministry of Waldeck-Rousseau
September	The military judges declare Dreyfus guilty "with extenuating circumstances" Dreyfus pardoned

1900

24 January	Dissolution of the Assumptionists
September	Clerical Congress at Bourges

1901

18 January	Encyclical *Graves de communi* (on Christian Democracy)
July	Law on Associations
September	*Le Sillon* founds its "Guard"

1902

	Publication of Loisy's *L'Évangile et l'Église*; Houtin's *La Question biblique*; and the *abbé* Calippe's *Moine d'après demain*
April	Legislative elections—victory of anticlericals
7 June	Ministry of Combes
20 October	Parliamentary commission to examine proposals for separation of Church and State
2 December	Combes claims to nominate bishops without discussions with the Vatican

1903

March–June	Rejection of congregations' request for authorization
4 August	Election of Pope Pius X
4 December	Condemnation of five books by Loisy

1904

17 May	*L'Humanité* publishes Merry del Val's note concerning President Loubet's visit to Rome
7 July	Law excluding members of congregations from teaching (to be fully effective within ten years)
30 July	End of diplomatic relations between France and the Vatican
August	*Semaines sociales* begin at Lyon

1905
            Conversion of Péguy
18 January Fall of Combes
March   Sangnier at Roubaix says that the wage-earning system is
            doomed
11 December Promulgation of Law of Separation

1906
February   Riots against the inventories
May   Legislative elections
30 May   Plenary assembly of French episcopate
12 July   Dreyfus declared innocent
10 August   Encyclical *Gravissimo*

1907
2 January   Law—annual declarations required for holding church
            services
February   Foundation of the "*plus grand Sillon*"
28 March   Law—annual declarations not now required
8 September Encyclical *Pascendi* against "Modernism"

1908
13 April   Law on repairs to church buildings
April   *Le Sillon* decides to put up candidates for Parliament

1910
25 August   Pius X condemns *Le Sillon*

1913
            Only 825 ordinations this year; but ACJF has 150,000
            members

7. FROM WORLD WAR I TO WORLD WAR II, 1914–39

            THE WAR
            A *Union Sacrée* against the invader. Catholics collaborate
            in the government and in propaganda. The clergy distinguish
            themselves in action (4,608 priests killed)

1914
2 August   Circular of Minister of Interior suspends measures against
            congregations
3 September Election of Pope Benedict XV

1917
1 August   Note of Benedict XV to the powers (disowned by many
            French Catholics because supposedly favourable to the
            Central Empires)

1919

Les *Équipes sociales*, a Catholic organization combining students and workers
La *Vie spirituelle* (periodical) founded

November   First annual meeting of the committee of the French cardinals and archbishops
Formation of the *Conféderation des Travailleurs Chrétiens* (at the 1920 Congress 140,000 workers represented)
Legislative elections—victory of Right and Moderate Republicans

1920

Papal Secretary of State writes to Bishop of Nice approving the work of Sangnier
Dom Lefèbvre, *Missel Vespéral et quotidien* (beginning of a liturgical revival)
Alsace-Lorraine incorporated into France under the 1801 Concordat (the State pays the clergy; the Church enjoys the Education Law of 1850)

16 May   Canonization of Joan of Arc

November   Chamber votes credits for restoration of embassy to Holy See

1921

May   Briand sends ambassador. Rome sends nuncio to Paris and promises that the French government will be given a chance to make "political" objections to proposed candidates for bishoprics

1922

6 February   Election of Pope Pius XI

1923

June   Pius XI calls for the evacuation of the Ruhr. Catholic deputies in the Chamber disavow this

1924

Beginning of *La Jeunesse Ouvrière Chrétienne* (JOC) in Belgium

May   Legislative elections—victory of Radicals and Socialists

18 June   Encyclical *Maximam gravissimamque* accepts the *associations diocésaines*, a revised form of the old *associations cultuelles*. Each to consist of 30 members, who elect a directing council of five from a list of eight prescribed by the bishop, and the bishop is to preside
The French bishops reluctant to accept the conciliatory line of Pius XI

17 July   Ministerial declaration of Herriot's cabinet (Radicals); will suppress the embassy to the Holy See, complete the measures against congregational schools, bring Alsace-Lorraine under the "lay" legislation, and bring in the "*École unique*" in France generally

August   Catholic protest meetings in Alsace-Lorraine

August   *Ligue des Religieux Anciens Combattants* formed

1925

18 February   82 diocesan groups federate under General de Castelnau's
                   Fédération nationale catholique

17 April   Ministry of Painlevé. Promises to drop Herriot's proposals
                   Georges Bernanos, *Sous le Soleil de Satan* (Mauriac also
                   carries on the tradition of the Catholic novel)

1926

                   First JOC mass meeting in France
                   The *Figaro*'s questionnaire to the Academy of Science (the
                   old "scientific" opposition to religion is fading)

5 September

24 December   Pius XI condemns the *Action française*

1927

                   JOC affiliates to the ACJF
                   P. Lhande, *Le Christ dans la banlieue*—a book that revealed
                   the dechristianization of the suburbs

1928

                   La Vie intellectuelle (periodical) founded

5 June   Roman decision rejects the complaint of industrialists against
                   the Christian trades union movement (published in 1929)
                   Poincaré proposes to allow missionary congregations to set
                   up their headquarters in France (passes Chamber, but never
                   brought to Senate)

1929

                   Formation of the *Jeunesse Étudiante* and the *Jeunesse
                   Agricole* (affiliated to the JOC)

1930

                   L'Oeuvre des Chantiers (to build churches in the suburbs)

1931

                   Bergson, *Les Deux sources de la morale et de la religion*
                   Gabriel Le Bras publishes his first writing on the sociology
                   of religion

1934

                   The *abbé* Couturier's "Octave of Prayer for Christian Unity"
                   (many ecumenical initiatives follow)

1936

                   Meetings of the *Professeurs Catholiques de l'Université*
                   begin
                   JOC and Christian trades unions active in the strikes of that
                   year

1937

                   Papal legate received by the Popular Front government and
                   preaches on the Christian vocation of France

1938

                   1,350 ordinations. By now the religious orders (though not
                   authorized to do so) teach 15% of the children in primary
                   schools and 47% of those in secondary education
                   Pius XII lifts the interdict on the *Action française*

8. WORLD WAR II AND AFTER, 1939–51

1941

October   The Vichy regime gives limited financial aid to Catholic primary schools
Religious instruction authorized in State primary schools
Religious congregations allowed to return

1942

La Mission de France—founds seminary at Lisieux to provide priests for dioceses with poor recruitment

1943

Daniel and Godin, *La France, pays de mission*—shows bourgeois priests have little contact with workers (the idea of the "Worker Priests" is implicit). Catholics active in the *RESISTANCE* (the ACJF denounces the German labour conscription; Georges Bidault becomes head of the National Council of the Resistance; the *Cahiers Clandestins du Témoignage Chrétien* published)

1945

Declaration of the cardinals and archbishops—some meanings of *laïcité* are acceptable
Success of the *Mouvement Républicain Populaire* (MRP) in the elections (practically all its leaders are Catholics, from *Action Catholique* or the Christian trades unions)

1949

Decree of Holy Office forbids collaboration with Communists

1950

January   Sixth Congress of the MRP at Nantes demands State aid for church schools

1951

The Marie Law (passed 408 *v.* 208) and the Barangé Law (passed 313 *v.* 255). These laws give government scholarships for pupils at private secondary schools and *per capita* grants to schools outside the State system. The subsidies were increased in 1955, and once again, by the Debré Law, in 1959

NOTE

Sections 1–4 and 7–8 have been added to enable readers unfamiliar with French history to put the crisis years of 1870–1914 into the wider context of the nineteenth and twentieth centuries.

1 Rome and Paris, 1870-71

On 18 July 1870, the bishops of the Roman Catholic world, assembled in St Peter's at Rome, voted the constitution *Pater aeternus*, declaring the Pope preserved from error when he speaks *ex cathedra* in matters of faith and morals. Fifty-five bishops, the so-called "inopportunists", many of them French, were absent. As the others cast their votes, the summer sky was blackened by a thunderstorm and the great basilica was plunged into darkness, intermittently illuminated by lightning flashes. According to an ultramontane journalist from Paris, some interpreted these natural phenomena as a backdrop to the obsequies of the Gallican tradition, others as the volcanic signs of a new revelation from Sinai.

"When has definition of doctrine *de Fide* been a luxury of devotion, and not a stern, painful necessity?", Newman asked. The historian has no criteria to assess such decisions, luxuries, or necessities. But if the friendship of other churches and the possibility of justifying the faith to an increasingly sceptical world mattered, the definition was indeed "inopportune". Already, in the Syllabus of 1864, Piux IX had startled the modern world by condemning propositions which seemed self-evidently true to liberally minded men; henceforward, in theory (though not, as Dupanloup, Bishop of Orléans, had brilliantly argued, in practice) Catholics were forbidden to deny the necessity of having Catholicism as the exclusive religion of the State, to ask for religious toleration for immigrants entering Catholic countries, or to imply the right of the individual to chose his own religion, guided by his reason. However "unofficial" or ambiguous the Syllabus might be, and however limited the definition in *Pater aeternus,* in the eyes of other Christians and unbelievers the Church of Rome was irretrievably set on the path of absolutism in ecclesiastical government and, by analogy and from the experience of the present pontificate, of reaction in matters social and political.

On 19 July, the day after the vote of the First Vatican Council,

1

France declared war on Bismarck's Prussia. Within six weeks the Prussians had triumphed. Napoleon III surrendered at Sedan on 1 September. It was only five months since an overwhelming majority of French voters had approved a new and genuinely parliamentary constitution; now all was ended. Three days after Sedan a Parisian uprising overthrew the Second Empire.

For ten years past a detachment of French troops had been stationed in Rome to preserve the papal city from the envious intentions of the new kingdom of Italy. In this way the Emperor had pleased churchmen at home and lost himself a potential ally abroad. When war came, the detachment was withdrawn, and once the Prussians were victorious, the Italians marched in, meeting only token resistance from derisory papal forces. The white flag of capitulation was run up on the Castel Sant' Angelo on 20 September. Pius IX now ruled only over the Vatican palace and its gardens, and here he declared himself a "prisoner". 1870 had been a year of decisive and paradoxical events. The Second Empire had collapsed shortly after its permanence had been solemnly affirmed in a national plebiscite; once France had achieved a genuine parliamentary regime the Chamber, in its new independence, had thrown the country into a ruinous war; two months after his spiritual authority had been so majestically vindicated, the Pope's temporal sovereignty was annihilated.

A new Government of National Defence, inspired by Gambetta and the old republican spirit of 1793, fought on in France, hopelessly. Paris held out against Prussian siege until the end of January 1871. The country at large passed judgement on Parisian heroism in the elections to a National Assembly in February: of the men of the Republican left who had inspired the continuation of resistance to the invader, only forty were returned. The vote was "a plebiscite for peace". The new Assembly and Thiers, its Chief of the Executive, soon blundered into a disastrous clash with the population of the capital. Paris was armed, embittered at the surrender to the enemy and at the result of the elections, and stirring from below with passions of social equality; it was out of touch with the nation and reality. Thiers was ready, as most of the possessing classes were ready, for a confrontation. On 18 March civil war began, the terrible seventy-two days of the Commune of Paris. Both sides were merciless. Amid burning buildings, corpse-strewn streets, and lakes of blood on the barrack squares, men suddenly saw revealed the viciousness that seethed beneath the surface of society. In this land humiliated by defeat, racked by civil war and class hatreds, and newly entering into the freedoms and tensions of democracy, what part had the Church to play—as a traditional national institution and as a unit within the world-wide Roman Church of the Syllabus and the First Vatican Council?

2 The Concordat and the "Religion of the Majority"

The alliance between Church and State in France was based upon the Concordat of 1801. When originally signed, it had been a precarious treaty, a bridge thrown across a divided nation, a monument to the authoritarian genius of Bonaparte and the far-seeing patience of Pius VII. Only essentials were defined. Roman Catholicism was described as the religion of "the great majority of French citizens"; the clergy (some of them) were to be paid by the State, while the Church reciprocated by renouncing all claim to the ecclesiastical property sold during the Revolution; the head of the State would nominate the bishops, to whom the Pope would give canonical institution. To these provisos, Bonaparte unilaterally added his so-called "Organic Articles" under the guise of "police regulations", a code of ecclesiastical law in seventy-seven articles reviving the restrictions of Gallican days. During the First Empire and the regimes that followed, either side could have made the Concordat unworkable. Rome could have looked askance at changes of government; the rulers of France could have asked in what sense the majority of citizens were Roman Catholics. The Organic Articles had been imposed, not accepted, and in 1865 Pius IX administered a stinging rebuke to Mgr Darboy, Archbishop of Paris, who had defended them in the Senate. What if the State used its power over the purse-strings to coerce the clergy? The *budget des cultes* could be reduced, and the salaries of individual priests who intervened on the wrong side in politics could be suspended.

Yet the Concordat survived. The Church believed in an alliance with the State on principle, and anticlericals and many other Frenchmen were glad to see ecclesiastics bridled by specific agreements. In an essay on liberty of conscience (1868) Jules Simon, philosopher, republican, and deist, observed: "If we were suddenly to renounce the Concordat . . . it would be handing over France to the absolute domination of Catholicism." Both sides had an interest in making the agreement work and preferred not to push disputable

4

points to an outright issue. In nominating bishops, the State stood to the principle (formally reiterated in 1862 by Rouland, Napoleon III's Minister of Religious Affairs) that Rome could not insist on preliminary consultations, and could not refuse canonical institution. True, consultations took place and the Pope occasionally stood firm against a particular nomination; at the fall of the Second Empire the colonial bishopric of Guadeloupe remained vacant because the Vatican had accepted unfounded gossip about the morals of the government's candidate. The most galling regulations of the Organic Articles had fallen into disuse. Priests were rarely cited before the Conseil d'État for "exceeding their jurisdiction", the Gallican Declaration of 1682 was no longer taught in seminaries, and papal letters were freely published in France without permission, though the government expected to receive a copy for the record. Clerical salaries, while remaining modest, had increased, canons of cathedrals had been added to the payroll, a pension fund had been established, and maintenance grants were provided for 3,800 seminary students. By 1870 custom and compromise under successive regimes had filled the interstices of the original Concordat until the structure had acquired a venerable air, hallowed by time and seemingly irreplaceable.

When the Second Empire crumbled, the Concordat remained. Roman Catholicism was still "the religion of the majority of French citizens". But how true was this assumption now, seventy years after its original proclamation? How true was it likely to be in the coming generation? Official statistics of the 1870s record 35,000,000 people as Catholics, as against 600,000 Protestants, 50,000 Jews, and only 80,000 free-thinkers. Convenient as these figures were for apologists, they had little significance. Many of the 35,000,000 accepted no obligation beyond making their Easter communion, many merely attended mass occasionally, or came to church to be married or were brought there to be buried, many were nominal Catholics whose allegiance did not extend beyond the census forms. In certain areas, fixed in essentials by the beginning of the eighteenth century and more sharply defined during the fratricidal strife of the French Revolution, a majority of the population was devoted to Catholicism. This was so in Brittany, Normandy, Maine, Anjou, and the Vendée (with islands of dechristianization in the Finistère and the Côtes-du-Nord), in the Massif Central, and in the east, Alsace, most of Lorraine and Franche Comté. In the rest of France the Church's influence was exercised over only a minority of citizens, in some areas with the good will of the rest, in others (as, for example, the Aube, the Corrèze, and part of the Creuse) there was a preponderance of anticlericals and unbelievers.

Within these broad geographical generalizations, the pattern of religious practice was complex, and at present we know it only in fragmentary fashion. In 1879 the Bishop of Soissons noted that his people were anticlerical in the south of the diocese, infrequent at church but glad to see him around Laon, and fervent in the Vervins area; he hinted at a connection with the elevating qualities of the excellent Vervins cider, though he was no doubt aware also that in the departments around Paris faith generally revived in proportion to the increase of the distance from the capital. Sometimes there was a line of local demarcation between religion and irreligion running along the banks of a river (which suggests that the origin of the difference goes back far into the past); sometimes it runs along the obsolete boundary between two dioceses of the *ancien régime* (suggesting differences of more recent origin). There are enclaves of unbelief among concentrations of workers in a particular trade, such as bargees, and enclaves of religious practice among others, such as deep-sea fisherman. Oases of Catholic loyalty are likely to be found in places were Protestantism had once been strong and challenging. Little country towns could be favourable to religious conformity. Statistics of Easter communions in the mid-century suggest that the *arrondissements* of Pithiviers and Montargis (Loiret) were irreligious, yet the actual towns of Pithiviers and Montargis themselves were haunts of churchgoing—no doubt because there were efficient church schools, an educated clergy, and a big enough complex of believers to resist the social pressures of anticlericalism. There were then, enclaves and exceptions; even so, allowing for complexities, statistics on the broad scale and generalizations by well-informed contemporaries give a picture of large areas of France in which the claim to be the religion of the majority was untenable, and was becoming progressively more unreal with every year that passed.

The grim events of the Commune had revealed the alienation of the Parisian working class from religion. The next thirty years were to see a new generation of workers in the capital alienated in a new way, less by hatred than by isolation and ignorance. The population of the diocese of Paris rose from 1,953,000 in 1861 to 2,411,000 in 1877 and 3,849,000 in 1906. As the government did not endow new parishes and as there were no arrangements to encourage the movement of priests from one diocese to another,[1] the traditional parochial system could not expand to meet the need. In 1861 there were 134 parishes and 661 priests; in 1877, 159 "parishes" (i.e. including new chapels) and 723 priests; in 1906, 185 "parishes" and 866 priests. And the population increase had been concentrated in the XII and XX *arrondissements,* where parishes of 50,000 souls became the norm. A whole generation grew up out of touch with the routines and realities of organized religion. In the 1880s the analogy was drawn between the new districts of the capital and heathen lands afar. "Our suburbs", said *curé* Soulange-Bodin, "in theory peopled with baptized persons, have become part of the mission field (*vrais pays de mission*)".

This picture of parochial breakdown in Paris is confirmed by Canon Charpin's researches into statistics of religious conformity in Marseilles. Here, 47% of the eligible population made Easter communions in 1841; sixty years later, though the absolute number had slightly increased, the proportion had fallen to 16%. The "normal" period of delay before children were brought to baptism (a good test of fidelity to ecclesiastical rules) fell in the course of the century from three days to eight. Allowing for this changing norm, between 1861 and 1901 the proportion of families exceeding the currently admissible delay had risen from 56% to 76%. The explanation lies in the rapid increase of immigration into the city, which came to a peak in the years 1872–76. Even before the peak, in 1866, only 43% of the inhabitants had been born within the commune. The collapse of religious practice took place chiefly in the new mushroom suburbs. "Old families generally good," noted the *curé* of Saint-Barnabé in 1873, "the new population shows little interest." And something like what was happening at Marseilles was happening in rapidly growing industrial centres such as Lille, Saint-Étienne, and Lyon. Anticlericals, who for long had struggled against arguments drawn from the unthinking religious conformity of the past, were glad to appropriate for their propaganda arguments from the unthinking irreligion of the new age of urban concentration. In a study of *Le Présent et l'avenir du Catholicisme* (1892) the *abbé* de Broglie argued that these inferences were illegitimate. The Church was being defeated, he said,

---

[1] Though dioceses "imported" seminarists in 1887. The diocese of Meaux was indebted to other dioceses for 68% of its numbers.

not so much by scepticism as by administrative breakdown under the sheer weight of numbers. This was true enough, but the fact of a continuing disastrous loss remained.[1]

"We are witnesses of a strange *volte-face;*" Renan wrote in 1875, "Catholicism, for so long upheld by the peasant, has lost his support." Outside the deeply Catholic areas there were whole tracts of rural France where the *curé* was sullenly regarded, or passed by with indifference. In the Charente and the Charente-Inférieure the forced conversions of Protestants in the seventeenth and eighteenth centuries had left a legacy of hatred and bitterness; the archives of the Lazaristes of Saintes for the 1860s and 1870s record parishes around Saint Jean-d'Angély, Angoulême, and Cognac without a communicant, and in which half the marriages have no religious ceremony. Statistics of Easter communions about this time show the plains around Montpellier, Nîmes, and Aix and the enclave around Mâcon were areas of poor religious observance. On the North coast the Redemptorists of Boulogne refer to such places as Flers (the Orne) and Villers-Bretonneux (the Somme) where hardly a single man came to confession, a remissness they ascribed to guilty consciences about birth control—"the ravages of onanism". And above all, it was in the departments around Paris where rural dechristianization had proceeded furthest. Statistics from the diocese of Versailles and neighbouring areas suggest that most country folk had given up religious practice early in the century; the records of the Ministry of Religious Affairs in 1859 speak of the empty churches of the dioceses of Evreux, Beauvais, and Meaux; rather later, the Bishop of Châlons-sur-Marne reports that the peasants of the Champenois ask *"A quoi sert le curé?"* and even their wives for the most part stay away from church. In 1851 a group of ten parishes in the department of the Loir-et-Cher are described in the report of a pastoral visitation.

> In every place you find the same backsliding: to whit, an excessive attachement to material interests and, as a result, habitual

[1] The argument from population growth needs careful statement. Broad-scale statistics do not show a correlation between the decline of religious practice and the size of towns or their rapidity of expansion. (F. Boulard and J. Remy, *Pratique religieuse urbaine et régions culturelles* (1968), pp. 45–8, 50–2.) It is not urban living that threatens practice, but the fact of not being integrated in society. (See G. Cholvy, *Géographie religieuse de l'Herault contemporain* (1968), espec. p. 411.)

working on Sundays, a great ignorance of the eternal verities and of Christian duties . . . and abstention from Easter communion by practically all the men. Nevertheless, they generally wish to receive the sacraments before dying.

A report of the *procureur-général* in 1860 would extend this verdict to the whole department—"the spirit of the masses can be summarized in two words, indifference or hostility to the clergy". For the diocese of Orléans we have some detailed statistics (very full, though not absolutely complete) for the mid-century. In 1852 only 3.8% of males over twenty years of age came to Easter communion, as against 23% of those under twenty; of females over twenty years of age, 20%, as against 67% of those under twenty. Mgr Dupanloup's efforts improved the situation in the next fifteen years, but the figures fell again in the crisis years 1869–71. There were more boys and young men and just as many girls and young women still coming to the altars, but once they reached the age of twenty, the vast majority came no more. In 1872 there was a slight improvement, though confined to a single archdeaconry; after this, the decline set in decisively.

Anticlericals liked to explain the dechristianization of so much of rural France by the advent of railways, newspapers, education, and the widening of peasant horizons. Mlle Marcilhacy has recently suggested a different—at least an additional—explanation. The commonly accepted obligation to "practice" under the *ancien régime* had masked indifference and ill-will; after the Revolution, the peasant had grown up in fear of clericalism—involving, perhaps, the restoration of tithe; the identification of the Church with political reaction had made it unpopular. Once the official and social pressures that had supported religious conformity weakened, the peasants—from the mid-century—openly abandoned a Church which had never won their true affection. "Gregarious religious practice has collapsed: personal religion has not yet begun." The devotion of rural France touched the lowest point in its history. The explanation is too sweeping, too harsh in its comparative assessment of the spirituality of routine, conformist generations. And Mlle Marcilhacy is referring especially to the diocese of Orléans, which she concedes is not necessarily representative, and certainly is very different from dioceses in the clerical areas. Even so, to understand the dechristianization of rural society, it is important to abandon the myth, dear to conservative churchmen, of an earlier epoch that was "Christian". The Church had given western Europe its civilization at the risk of its own soul; "Christian Europe" was a social–intellectual–cultural complex and not a concentration of converted believers, and with all its magic and grandeur its decline was necessary to enable the true mission of converting the world to begin again at the point where gregarious conformity ended and individual decision became obligatory again, as in the Apostolic age.

The well-educated groups in French society were divided on the religious issue in a complexity of gradations. It has been said that the aristocracy rediscovered religion as a result of the French Revolution and the *bourgeoisie* after the June days of 1848 and the Commune of 1871. Outward solicitude for religion, naturally enough, could be connected with fears of social overturn, though such a broad, crude statement tells us little. In the clerical West whole departments were subject to what André Siegfried has called "the condominium of presbytery and *château*". In the Mayenne their joint rule was unequal, for the clergy themselves were satellites of the great landed proprietors who exerted pressure on their tenant farmers to vote for the conservative side and to respect religious observances. Elsewhere in France, even if the rest of society was anticlerical, the provincial aristocracy and many local notables, army officers, and magistrates often enough inclined to Catholicism and royalist politics, while doctors and notaries generally were expected to be unbelievers. But in these strata of the population the problem of the quality of the allegiance becomes especially difficult. These are people more capable than most of individual decision, and at the same time more responsive to social pressures and intellectual fashions, the lure of political advantages, and the spur of personal ambition. They might believe more than they said they did, or their devotion might be hypocrisy, for as Anatole France observed, "Catholicism is still the most acceptable form of religious indifference". In the cities the churchgoing of the educated and of the masses may reasonably be considered in isolation;[1] in the countryside anomalies in detail on the map of religious practice might be attributable to the links between classes—the

[1] In the parish of Saint-Pothin at Lyon between 1870 and 1914 the upper class parishioners stayed aloof, and the life of the parish centred in its *œuvres populaires*. (E. Pin, *Pratique religieuse et classes sociales dans une paroisse urbaine* (1960), pp. 57–8.)

relations of landowners and tenants, richer peasants and landless labourers, doctors and patients, notaries and clients and, above all, to the pervasive influence of the growing numbers of government officials and schoolmasters. Much political manoeuvring between 1871 and 1877 was concerned with keeping control of the bureaucracy out of anticlerical hands, and both sides in the war over education after 1878 were well aware of the role the schoolmaster could play in the beliefs and religious attitudes of the village.

Statistics are a poor guide to the quality of a religion, but institutional religious loyalty (a very different thing) can sometimes be clearly assessed. The juxtaposition of statistics of religious practice with those of voting in national elections is revealing. Whenever the country had a chance to pronounce on the anticlerical policies of its governments, it endorsed them. True, the issue was never clear-cut; even so, the voting could not have consistently gone this way unless there had been large numbers of "Catholics" of various kinds who refused to put institutional loyalty before what they regarded as the best overall decision for the political administration of the country. Sometimes the effect of their refusal can be plotted precisely on the maps of electoral geography: M. Goguel draws attention to one of the "bastion areas" of Catholicism, the eastern dioceses of Nancy, Saint-Dié, and Besançon, voting Left for the first thirty years of the Third Republic. "The people rise *en masse* in demonstrations competing for the honour of manifesting . . . their religious convictions", complained the Archbishop of Rennes in 1881 about one area of his diocese, "but if tomorrow they are called to the ballot box they will vote for candidates hostile to religion." The same phenomenon was noted—from the opposite point of view—in reports of the prefects of the Vosges, the Doubs, the Puy-de-Dôme, the Haute-Garonne, the Dordogne, the Finistère; sometimes they emphasized that the population was at once devoted to religious practice and anticlerical as well. "The peasants", wrote the prefect of the Dordogne in 1879, "are assiduous in church attendance, but fear and detest the rule of the parish priests." Clearly, Catholic belief was not incompatible with an anticlerical outlook; Clemenceau, indeed, regarded a combination of the two as a fair description of the attitude of most of his countrymen—"*La France, qui a des habitudes cultuelles, mais qui a en horreur le gouvernement des curés*". In 1886, when Mgr Freppel, Bishop of Angers, pointed out to the Chamber of Deputies that parents rushed to send their children to the schools of religious orders, M. Rivet interrupted: "How then do all these fathers of children come to vote for the Republicans? That's what I don't understand." "Nor do I", the bishop sadly replied. Had he not been a royalist in politics, he might have seen an explanation.

3 Anticlericalism

> We think of the dead as lifeless dust beneath our feet; in reality, they are all around us, they oppress us.... When great ideas, great passions surge, listen for their voice: it is the dead who speak.... They had convictions ... and we have none, yet they compel us to proclaim them. Not only do they speak, but they hate and do battle.... Here is the insoluble problem of our national life.

So say the characters of the *vicomte* Melchior de Vögué, novelist, literary critic, and Catholic sympathizer, in *Les Morts qui parlent* (1910), looking back on a generation of warfare between clericals and anticlericals in France. The alliance between Church and State, they reflected, had been destroyed by 580 politicians debating in wrath and bitterness, unconscious of the fact that the unseen legions of the dead were dictating their every gesture, every word.

There was an apologetical purpose in the novelist's insistence on blaming the past for present feuds; in this way anticlericalism could be made to appear an anachronistic passion, and the failures of the contemporary Church omitted from the reckoning. It was tactically convenient to encourage hostile critics to focus on the Inquisition, the revocation of the Edict of Nantes, and the condemnation of the Civil Constitution of the Clergy rather than on the nearer Syllabus of 1864, the "infallibility" decision of 1870, and the collaboration of churchmen with antirepublican politicians. Yet Melchior de Vögué's myth of ghostly motivation was a pointer to a truth contemporaries were reluctant to admit. The Vatican and French Catholics had been deluding themselves with the fading dream of a Christian nation, with a treaty of alliance between Church and State from which the spirit of honest collaboration was departing. On their side, the opponents of the Church had been driven on by anticlerical passions and suspicions that were excessive, incommensurate with the realities of the contemporary situation, and incomprehensible without taking into account the influence of the past, without listening for *les morts qui parlent*.

By 1870 anticlericalism was an established feature of French life. It resembled Catholicism in so far as there was a determined core of committed men and a wide outer circle of occasional conformists and nominal adherents. The spheres of nominal Catholicism and nominal anticlericalism overlapped, Catholics who resented clerical domination and right-wing politics being matched by priest-haters who accepted the routine gestures of religion at births, marriages, and deaths, very often because their wives insisted.

The roots of anticlericalism go far back into the Middle Ages; the phenomenon, indeed, is probably an instinctive reaction to the existence of any organized priesthood. Clergy are there to be loved or hated; they are not to strive for the quiet social acceptance that is the ambition of ordinary citizens and historians. Given the emphasis of the Roman Catholic Church on discipline, there would necessarily have been a "normal" anticlericalism in French society. According to Taine, the clergy (who had "never been so fervent, so exemplary") were unpopular simply because they claimed to rule the lives of the people, "at table and in bed, at home and in the tavern". The existence of the confessional and its place in the lives of women had always aroused resentment. And these were days when preachers draw the line between vice and things indifferent in an excessively rigorous fashion (even the *curé* d'Ars had spoken of dancing as "the cord by which the Devil drags so many souls to hell"). The parish priest thought of himself as a pastor; outside the clerical areas of France he was often thought of as an officer exercising moral surveillance. In Proust, the monk at grandmother's deathbed watches through his fingers to see if the mourner's grief is sincere, "for in the priest, as in the mental specialist, there is always something of outlook of the examining magistrate". There was, too, the reservation made by so many in their dealings with a celibate caste. It was not just the crude fact of sexual scandals avidly seized upon (Guérolt's *L'Opinion nationale,* with the connivance of the government, had made a speciality of reporting cases of clerical immorality under the Second Empire). More seriously, there was the opinion that the celibate and, more especially, the monastic life were in defiance of the principle of utility and derogatory to the institution of the family. Parents were entitled to enjoy their children's company: when his daughter entered a convent, the baron de Ponnet wrote to his friends on black-edged notepaper. Men without children of their own, without a stake in the country and uncommitted to society ought not to direct the consciences of women and the minds of schoolboys. To these four-square arguments, novelists added a *frisson* of sensibility. In George Sand's *Lélia,* Gautier's *La Morte amoureuse,* Octave Mirabeau's *L'abbé Jules,* and on to Anatole France's *Thaïs,* the theme of the futility of asceticism and its betrayal of the highest emotions of humanity recurs. *"Ô lâche! tu l'as vue et tu as craint Dieu!"*

So far, anticlericalism was traditionally motivated, a blend of practicalities and sullen resentments passed on from the Middle Ages, sardonic comments from Renaissance jest books, and the literate, intelligent hostilities of the Enlightenment. By the mid-century, Michelet, the greatest of Romantic historians, had drawn together these themes into his history of France. He turned against the medieval centuries he had loved to reveal their cruelty and superstition, he pilloried the abuses of the confessional and the political manoeuvres of the Jesuits, and reminded his countrymen of their Gallican tradition of hostility to Roman encroachments and the Protestants among them of the sufferings of their ancestors. These historical memories vibrated through the faction fighting of the Third Republic. Hatred of the Jesuits was uncompromising and anachronistic, old-fashioned Gallican arguments were the stand-by of parliamentary debaters, and many politicians who played a part in anticlerical legislation were from Protestant backgrounds. The central tradition of French history, lay, satirical, humane, and tolerant, Michelet argued, is summed up in three great personalities —Rabelais, Molière, and Voltaire. This great tradition reached its heroic period in the days of the Revolution, and its crowning glory was the Declaration of the Rights of Man and the Citizen. This view of the French Revolution, messianic and *bourgeois,* was perpetuated in the latter part of the century by Republican historians, especially by Aulard, who brought Michelet up to date with superior scholarship and inferior prose.

The Michelet–Aulard version of the national history won wide acceptance. Obscurely, though at this distance of time not very logically, Frenchmen felt it was important to have no enemies on the left, since the Revolution had freed their lands from tithe and enabled their ancestors to acquire ecclesiastical property. More directly, they were moved by the story of the generous Declaration of 1789 incongruously allied with the epic of unparalleled military victories and domination over Europe. Michelet's writings became a patriotic Bible whose contents resembled a bloodstained and triumphant Old Testament story, with Aulard and his school of historians as exegetes and commentators. Against the Catholic myth of a Christian France had arisen the counter-myth of a revolutionary France, the standard-bearer of liberty.

There was an odd discrepancy between the doctrine of "scientific history" which the professionals of the *Université* were establishing and their optimistic, unproven assumption about the direction in which history was moving. On his own confession, Aulard wrote Republican propaganda in text-books and reserved his impartiality for his research publications. But what could Christians do when "scientific history" turned its sceptical techniques upon the Gospels? From 1858 to 1865 the *Revue Germanique* ran, propagating the findings of current German scholarship—doubts about Christology and chronology, miracles and particular texts, about the historicity of certain writings, notably the Fourth Gospel. Until 1863 churchmen could afford to scoff at the tribe of Dryasdust; then came Renan's *Vie de Jésus*. Erudition, sympathetic imagination, and literary skill combined to present the magic of the human personality of the prophet who was "resurrected" by the love of his disciples; the supernatural elements, the divine incursion were banished from the story. Quinet had appealed to French ecclesiastics to reply to the German critics to save the national honour. No reply came beyond reaffirmations of fundamentalism. Renan's book ran into edition after edition. Anticlericals rejoiced in the deadly dilemma he posed: "A single error proves that the Church is not infallible; a single weak link proves that a book is not revelation."

The reverence once accorded to the pronouncements of theologians was now revived, but transferred to those of scientists, and from "science" something resembling a new "religion" was born. In 1862 a French translation of Darwin was published with a preface denying the Christian doctrine of creation. Darwin was read optimistically, in the light of the idea of progress, of Goethe's serene vision of a universal order in which nothing is lost, and of Hegel's powerful teleology. To this sparkling mixture of hopeful ideas was added a harsher, peculiarly French ingredient, the philosophy of Positivism. In essence, Positivism was the assertion that science provides the model for all knowledge, so that everything we claim to know must be susceptible of empirical verification. Here was a doctrine with corrosive force when used in criticism of Christian belief. Yet, curiously, it went on to help to produce a substitute religion. Intermixed with the Hegelian and Darwinian elements—a process beginning with Comte himself and continuing in Taine and Renan—by 1868 it had become what Renouvier called "a kind of pantheism and fatalism animated and developed by the hypothesis of continuous and universal progress". In Quinet's *La Création* (1862) and Laugel's *Les Problèmes de la vie* (1867) there is a vision of the universe as a supreme harmony to which our individual lives contribute, as one immense living organism which defies death even as we all die. Nature, said Renan, was deceiving us with hope, religion, and love, to make us serve her ends; a new species will arise, but we shall live on "in the memory of God".

These pale moonlight dreams of vicarious immortality were the weakest point of the new "religion"; in the end, Renan himself lost his faith a second time and fell into irony and despair. The challenge to Christian belief came elsewhere. For long apologists had argued that, without the Church, society would have no moral foundations and selfishness would reign. But in the 1850s and 1860s books with such titles as *La Morale de l'Église et la morale naturelle* (by Boutteville, 1860) were being published. Havet ascribed all good in Christian morality to the Greeks, Jacques Denis found the moral codes of all religions equally useful, Vacherot looked forward to the day when democracy would give up the code of an authoritarian Church and institute its own programme for moral education, Renouvier wished to replace the doctrine of love by the nobler doctrine of justice. Most extreme of all was Boutteville himself, who accused Christians of teaching immoral doctrines (Original Sin, hell fire, intolerance) and recommending immoral conduct (humility, neglect of the body). All agreed in rejecting the Christian doctrine of salvation as the best way of persuading mankind to accept the life of unselfishness.

This confidence in the possibility of a purely lay morality and the quasi-religious belief in science and progress runs like a bright thread through the anticlericalism of the later nineteenth century, and distinguishes it from the anticlericalism of earlier ages, from the voice of *les morts qui parlent,* and from the sardonic folk-lore still surviving in the pages of *Le Canard enchaîné.* Many of the opponents of the Church had a reluctant admiration for the system of moral influence they were proposing to destroy, and a vision of a faith to replace it. It was not *écrasez l'Infâme,* but a different sort of bitterness, compounded of attraction and repulsion, a love–hate relationship. This combination of a "religious" view of life with hatred of Catholicism was not confined to the educated. In 1877 Corbon, speaking for the élite of the working class, described how a new religion of progress, with work in place of prayer, was taking over:

> France is being decatholicized, as everyone can see, ... but it is not being dechristianized. ... Modern society, although it is not religious in your fashion, is more deeply, more generally Christian than that inspired by ultramontanism and Jesuitism.

Catholic controversialists rarely did justice to the sober purpose, the "religiosity" of some of their opponents. Instead, they had a theory of a conspiracy centring in the Masonic movement. True, under the Third Republic the lodges became centres of anticlerical feeling and Republican politicians discussed plans against the Church more conveniently at their meetings than in cafés or at private dinner parties. Yet the allegations against Masonry are not an explanation; they describe only one aspect of the superficial mechanism of propaganda and political action. If any conspiracy existed, it was an open one. In a sensational speech in the Senate on 19 May 1868, Sainte-Beuve enumerated its component groups —significantly, many of them bearing names indicating a religious quest that had turned its face towards illuminations other than Catholicism.

> There is, gentlemen, another great diocese [outside the Church], with no fixed boundaries, extending over the whole of France, over the whole world ... which continually increases its membership and its power ... which embraces minds in various stages of emancipation, but all in agreement on one point—that above all else they must be freed from an absolute authority and a blind submission—which counts in their thousands deists and adherents of spiritualistic philosophies, disciples of natural religion, pantheists, positivists, realists, sceptics and seekers of every kind, the devotees of common sense and the followers of pure science.

In so far as anticlericalism had a single unifying conviction, Sainte-Beuve here defined it in a sentence: "above all else they must be freed from an absolute authority and a blind submission". There was one document in which opponents of the Church found this demand for blind submission embodied in its purest form— the Syllabus of 1864 which accompanied the encyclical *Quanta*

Cura. Of all the propositions condemned in this disastrous manifesto, the one drawing the most attention was the recommendation
that the Roman pontiff should reconcile himself to "progress,
liberalism and modern civilization". "In this enigmatical form,"
said the *duc* de Broglie, "it seemed to embrace in the same condemnation the press, railways, telegraphs, the discoveries of science. . . .
While believers were lost and baffled, the unbelievers raised a
tremendous shout of triumph." For the whole of the next generation, anticlericals continued to rejoice. Like Clemenceau (speaking
in the Senate in October 1902) they compared "the spirit of the
French Revolution, expressed in the Declaration of the Rights of
Man" with "the counter-revolution of the Roman Church, whose
formula is the Syllabus".

The inherited fears of centuries, distrust of confession and of
celibacy, love for the ideals of the Revolution and hatred of blind
submission, the dream of a humanistic morality and the illumination of a new "religion" of science combined to create the anticlerical temper of the latter decades of the nineteenth century. Yet
its sense of urgency, its desire to transpose distrust and hatred into
immediate legislation still needs explanation. In fact, for political
action there was compelling political motivation. By 1870, in the
minds of Republicans, Catholicism was identified with reactionary
politics. The fatal moment came on 2 December 1851, when Louis
Napoleon seized power by a *coup d'état*. The Pope and the French
Catholics (with a few exceptions) threw in their lot with the "man
of order". "These few months of dictatorship", writes Maurain,
"fixed for long the position of Catholics in French political life."
Montalembert, who had welcomed the new regime at first, soon
came to see that the advantages of collaboration would be precarious. The Church, he said bitterly, works on the principle,
"When I am the weakest I ask you for liberty because it is your
principle: when I am the strongest I take it away from you because
it is my principle". The leading Catholic newspaper, the *Univers,*
had ridiculed the fallen Republic. If the Republic returns, Montalembert warned, you will not get another chance—"the Church will be
the dupe, then the accomplice, then the victim of its alliance with
despotism". In September 1870 the Second Empire fell. The
Church had been its dupe and its accomplice. Would it now have
to pay the penalty for its opportunism? Would it soon be the
victim?

4 The Church of France
Strength and Weakness

In the 1860s, Taine toured the provinces as an examiner, and was amazed to find the clergy so powerful. "We have no idea of this at Paris. We live in a circle of witty sceptics, we do not see the public at large, the mass of France." Of the "moral, mystical and artistic" side of religious life he professed he had seen little evidence; to his acute but limited vision the Church appeared as "a temporal institution, a machine of government" whose power he had been underestimating.

At first sight, statistics about the clergy, like the census figures for the general population, seem to confirm Taine's impression of a strong mesh of ecclesiastical influence over provincial France. There was a diocese corresponding to most departments (seventeen archdioceses and sixty-seven dioceses), with the bishop enjoying formal precedence over the prefect. Altogether, there were 36,000 parishes, on the average one to every thousand inhabitants. Each had its *curé* or *desservant* (priest in charge), and some had *vicaires* or other assistant clergy—a total of 51,000 priests engaged in the parochial ministry. This army of pastors was supported by 4,000 other secular priests who were canons, directors of seminaries, or schoolmasters, and there were numbers of regular priests closely connected with parish life, especially as preachers. Though the Concordat had not provided for the return of the religious congregations, they had come back, traditional orders such as the Trappists, Benedictines, and Dominicans, and a multitude of new organizations reflecting the ideals of the century and the idiosyncrasies of local life and individual initiative. Without formal legal standing (except in five cases), congregations of men had increased from fifty-nine in 1856 to 116 (embracing a total of about 30,000 professed) in 1877. Among them were the Jesuits, active again as schoolmasters in spite of a decree of the Restoration period prohibiting them from teaching; they now had sixty houses and 2,000 members. Congregations of women, most of them enjoying authorization under the provisions of a law of 1825, had extended and multiplied earlier and more rapidly, so that by 1875 there were over 127,000 nuns, that is, one to every 280 of the population.

As we have seen, certain provinces were strongholds of Catholicism. Churchmen themselves jested about the regional nuances of devotion—Normans were supposed to be respectable, Angevins spiritual, Bretons and Vendéans fanatical, and the diocese of Rodez had the trick of producing bishops for all the other dioceses of France. In these areas, with their rich variety of religious sentiment, bishops were the oracles of their dioceses ("You are a *seigneur* of the Middle Ages!" wrote the Bishop of Châlons-sur-Marne to his brother-prelate of Rodez, after a visit in 1873), the *curés* ruled their parishes as they had for generations, the ceremonies of religion were respected, even by those who did not attend mass, and the French Revolution was remembered in terms of Republican atrocities and Catholic martyrs. As anticlericals knew, their propaganda was wasted here. In one of his short stories about his boyhood home, the Vendée, Clemenceau describes how an atheistical doctor left his fortune for the adornment of the parish church, so that the peasants would contrast ecclesiastical wealth with their own misery; a golden chalice was bought and its glitter served only to increase the devotion of the faithful.

Outside the recognized clerical areas, for complex reasons and in patterns often unpredictable, the grip of the parochial system on the population was weakening. But throughout the country, the Church still enjoyed a huge advantage, the right to set up its own schools to educate the rising generations. The Falloux Law of 1850 allowed the formation of church schools subject only to marginal State inspection, and the letters of obedience of a member of a recognized congregation counted as equivalent to a teacher's certificate. Until the Second Empire stopped the practice, local authorities could hand over their own schools to the charge of religious orders, and since monks and nuns required no salaries, thrift had often overcome anticlericalism in the deliberations of rural councillors. By 1870 church schools of various kinds were teaching not far short of 40% of the nation's children. In more than 300 *collèges* and in eighty or more "Little Seminaries" there were 70,000 pupils, as against 116,000 in lay establishments of secondary education. The sons of the aristocracy, magistrates, and army officers were sent to the *collèges,* especially to those of the Jesuits, who specialized in training young men for the Polytechnique and the naval and military academies. In primary schools kept by the teaching congregations roughly 1,500,000 of the nation's 4,000,000 children received their education. Three-fifths of all the girls were taught by the sisters of 500 different congregations. There was a widespread belief, even in anticlerical areas, that nuns should be in charge of feminine education. Under the Second Empire an attempt had been made to set up State secondary schools for girls, much to the alarm of Dupanloup, who pointed out that many of the teachers would be men, some irreligious and some even youthful, and the project had collapsed when clerical journals published the names of the girls attending. Ordinary State schools with exclusively lay personnel were still very much under ecclesiastical influence. The day began with prayers, there were crucifixes on the walls, the bishop sat in the Conseil Académique of the Department, just as there were representatives of the episcopate on the Conseil Supérieur de l'Instruction Publique. The village schoolmaster did well to conform. In some parishes of the diocese of Orléans he was the only communicant—*"sa place vaut cela"*.

Though the age had saints and heroes, it is not one rendered attractive by a delicate spirituality, intelligent apologetics, or an art in tune with the mysteries of the infinite. Yet behind the strident tones and weak arguments of ecclesiastical controversialists, the architectural pastiche, the gaudy lithographs and hideous *bric-à-brac* of devotion, the superstitious and hysterical overtones of popular piety, was a faith that deserved more elevated forms of expression, more intelligent defenders, and a leadership less politically partisan. The 1870s and 1880s were the great decades of mass pilgrimages. The Augustins de l'Assomption, founded in the mid-century, set the pattern by negotiating cheap railway fares, printing song sheets, and publishing a newspaper, *Le Pèlerin*. Crowds of up to 50,000 surged off the trains to visit Chartres, Notre-Dame de Pitiée in the Vendée, to observe the cult of the Sacred Heart at Paray-le-Monial, to bring sick relatives to implore for healing at Lourdes. As far as Rome and the Holy Land French pilgrims carried their banners. These were crowded, brash excursions, far removed from the quiet, haunted intensity of Péguy's walk to Chartres to intercede for his son, but they were spiritual excursions none the less, not to be snobbishly dismissed as the wakes and fairs of the underworld of the new industrial society. Zola himself came to treat them with something near to respect. In 1892 he went by sleeping-car in the Pyrenees express to study the arrival of the pilgrim trains at Lourdes for his next novel. There was the smell of sweat, dirt, and incense, the sharp night wind from the mountains, the vast candlelit processions through the darkness, the "death rattles and communions", the bureau where cures were proved and registered—even if miracles cannot happen, he reflected, the deeps of human nature still cry out for them.

Though the nation was half dechristianized, we must remember that dechristianization is "news" for the historian, while traditional routines of parochial sociability and individual charity can too easily be taken for granted. This was a France honeycombed with innumerable charitable works, committees of Saint-Vincent de Paul, diocesan associations of Saint-Joseph and the like, the main support, both in personnel and money, of the overseas missions of Catholicism—maintaining Lazarist schools in Constantinople and the Holy Land, hospitals of the Sisters of Saint-Vincent de Paul in India, China, and Korea, the newly established Pères Blancs in Algeria, the later Franciscains Missionnaires de Marie in China and innumerable other good works. It was a France that was to produce the Eucharistic Movement and Saint Theresa of Lisieux, who on the feast of Trinity 1895 discovered the vocation of total love only two years before she died.

In the long run, the depths of spirituality in the French Church were its guarantee of survival and of the revival of its influence in a new form in the national life when the old trappings of prestige and material benefits were finally taken away. In the short run, however, for effective political warfare against anticlerical governments, the sort of factors Taine had been observing would be decisive, and on closer examination we can see how, in his enthusiasm for discovering the provinces, Taine had greatly exaggerated the power of the Church as a temporal machine. The parochial and diocesan network, the State subventions, the numerous clergy, the multitude of congregations and their schools, the clerical provinces serving as fortresses and recruiting grounds,[1] the colourful and ostentatious manifestations of piety, the whole impressive display of connection and influence was a façade of power rather than a reality. The Church was undefeatable in the sense that the faith of its converted inner core was beyond the accidents of time. Its structure and outlook were, perhaps, well suited to a ministry to

[1] Not always as recruiting grounds. Gadille has recently shown that the proportion of seminarists to youthful population did not always correspond to the traditional "religious" affiliations of particular regions. (*La Pensée et l'action politiques des évêques français . . . 1870–83* (1967), I, p. 198.)

committed believers. But it was not fitted to face the challenges of unbelief and anticlericalism, to reach out to win the world or to change society, nor was it fitted to fight the political battles of the future. Under a conservative, monarchical regime it might have continued to enjoy the fruits of alliance with power, to keep the Littrés out of the Academy and deprive the Renans of their chairs. But in democratic politics it could not translate nominal allegiances into votes even at the direst crises of its fortunes, nor could it deflect the attacks of enemies by convincing demonstrations of intellectual integrity and political neutrality.

Ecclesiastical France had no central organization to co-ordinate the activities of the dioceses or discuss common policies. Nothing had replaced the Assembly General of the Clergy of the *ancien régime,* and after Napoleon I's dubious Council of 1811 there had been no more plenary meetings of the episcopate. The Concordat had been negotiated by the Pope alone; presumably, if the Church of France was to speak as a unity, the lead would have to come from the Vatican. This necessity was not entirely pleasing to the French episcopate. Not that much remained of the old Gallican spirit. Something like 40% of the bishops had been reluctant to have the "infallibility" issue raised in 1870, but only twenty-two individuals had felt strongly enough to leave before the final vote, and only eight or nine of these can be described as "Gallican" in theology; after the event, all had submitted. The point was, they had practical grievances concerning the administration of their dioceses; they complained of Roman interference with their rights of visitation over monastic establishments and to discipline erring clergy, and of the Congregation of Rites' success in forcing acceptance of the Roman Liturgy in place of cherished diocesan variants. In 1871 there was a great scandal at Montpellier, when *Père* Alzon, Vicar-General of Nîmes, founder of the Assumptionist Order and one of the leading ultramontanes, appeared in a parish church in violet stole (symbol of the grant of extraordinary episcopal powers) to read a Roman decree cancelling measures of Bishop Le Courtier against a religious community of his diocese.

There were, it is true, some bishops who were passionate ultramontanes and, more significantly, others who acted as if they were because their lower clergy were all of this persuasion. Indeed, the ghostly Gallicanism which lingered on in the episcopal palaces after 1870 had long since been exorcized from the presbyteries. The French bishops possessed unreasonable powers over their lower clergy, and sometimes had exercised them unreasonably; under Pius IX the Roman Curia consistently lent a sympathetic ear to complaints by French priests against episcopal tyranny.

> This attitude of Rome [writes J.-R. Palanque] did more for ultramontanism than the works of Joseph de Maistre or of the theologians: in twenty years, from 1845 to 1865, the great majority of clergy completely abandoned the old Gallican spirit and committed itself wholeheartedly to the Holy See.

They were encouraged in doing so, and brought into unity with the ultramontane members of the laity by the principal Catholic newspaper, Louis Veuillot's *L'Univers,* implacably, with masterly verve, denouncing Gallicans and Liberal Catholics and preaching allegiance to the Chair of Peter. The *abbé* Frémont, who described Veuillot's genius as consisting, like Hugo's in "ceaseless repetition of the same things under new forms", summarized these habitual themes. Two are unexceptionable: "Without the Church we can do nothing", "the Church is the remedy for all our ills"; two are wildly partisan: "Dupanloup and his school are the ruin of Catholic hopes", "Pius IX losing the Romagna is Jesus at Calvary". Widely read in country presbyteries, the *Univers* encouraged the clergy to be uncompromising towards potential allies and divided amongst themselves. When serving as *vicaire* in the parish of Fay-aux-Loges, the *abbé* Gibier (a future bishop) ridiculed the newspaper in the presence of his *curé,* and henceforward the two priests had to take their meals in separate rooms.

The parish priest who preferred the fulminations of the *Univers* to the instructions of his bishop was acting on instinct rather than on principle. There was no longer a social gulf between the lower clergy and the episcopate; of the 167 holders of episcopal office between 1870 and 1883, only twenty-one were of noble origin, fifty-six were from *bourgeois* or rich peasant families, and ninety were from the "people". There was, however, an intellectual and cultural gulf between the hierarchy and the parish clergy, the latter for the most part being men of a rudimentary education, while the bishops were men of intellectual merit, well-educated in the literary and classical disciplines of the age. Of the 167, only eighteen had spent a significant time in the parochial ministry before their elevation; twenty-three had risen through diocesan administration, and over ninety had been teachers in big and little seminaries or holders of academic chairs. With a salary twenty times that of a *curé* and moving in the loftier reaches of the "establishment", a bishop often appeared to those below him as an aloof, superior figure. Only one secular priest in ten enjoyed security of tenure; the others could be moved at will by the bishop and, if they were accused of offences, judged by him without due process. Regrettably, many bishops clung to their arbitrary authority, and a project of Jules Simon in January 1873 to give security of tenure to older *desservants* who had ruled their parishes for more than ten years had to be abandoned. Except in Savoy and the south of the Massif Central, episcopal appointments were not normally made to a candidate's diocese of origin; as a result, a bishop manoeuvring to appease the central government might find his policy disowned by his parish priests—mostly local men and by their very position subject to the pressure of local notables, Legitimist nobles, and the like. As the prefect of the Aisne reported in September 1879:

> Under the influence of ultramontane newspapers the greater part of the lower clergy has become fanatical and intractable. As you go higher in the hierarchy, you find more sense of proportion and reasonableness . . . the bishop is incontestably the most conciliatory of the priests of the diocese.

On the other hand, the head of the diocese himself could be under pressure from local grandees in a world far above that of his clergy; in the 1870s, Kolb-Bernard, president of the Chamber of Commerce of Lille, had to be listened to in the affairs of the diocese of Cambrai, the *duc* d'Aumâle in Beauvais, the banker Thomasset in Lyon, the *duc* de Broglie in Evreux, Gabriel de Belcastel in Toulouse. And there were physical, as well as psychological, obstacles to be overcome if a prelate was to lead his lower clergy. There were 720 parishes in the diocese of Arras, 600 in Cambrai and about 500 in many other dioceses. It was impossible for one man to maintain so many contacts, and suffragan bishops were rarely appointed.

These impressive figures of the number of parishes—so daunting to many bishops—might be supposed to have had the advantage of ensuring continuous pastoral care for the bulk of the population. It is important to remember, however, that the population was not evenly distributed among the parishes—an imbalance not confined to the growing industrial centres. In each of the dioceses of Bourges, Limoges, and Clermont there was something like 600,000 people to about 500 parishes; in each of the dioceses of Albi,

Cahors, and Saint-Claude there were fully as many parishes and only half the population. The diocese of Cambrai with the huge population of $1\frac{1}{2}$ millions had no more than 600 parishes, while the neighbouring diocese of Arras, with half the number of souls to care for, had 720. Even so, in France there was a priest to every 639 inhabitants, and however ineffective the geographical disposal of the work force, it seems strange to hear of the Church being endangered by the approaching collapse of its parochial ministry. Yet such was the thesis of the *abbé* Bougaud's *Le grand péril de l'Église de France* (1878). According to Bougaud, the highest peak in the graph of ordinations had been reached in 1868; from then onwards there was decline, the figures falling within nine years from 1,753 to 1,582. Worse still, recruitment was drying up in the less religious areas, and there was no machinery to move priests to places where they were most needed. In 1870–71, in each of the dioceses of Evreux, Meaux, and Versailles, more than 100 parishes had been vacant, and in only twenty-five Departments did ordinations meet local needs. Bougaud also demonstrated that recruitment had narrowed down socially. The aristocracy and *bourgeoisie* were still interested in the religious orders, especially for their daughters, but their sons were no longer coming forward for the parochial ministry. Nine-tenths of ordination candidates were from the families of peasants and artisans. The ministry was becoming limited in its background of social experience and was declining in social standing. In theory, apostolic poverty ought to win the respect of parishioners, in practice, the low incomes of the clergy helped to depress their status still further in the eyes of many. A *desservant* with his 850 francs had the wage of a *gendarme*; a *vicaire* got less than half as much; a *curé* (and there were only 5,600 of these) could only go as high as a modest 1,500. Vestry boards (*fabriques*) and the local authorities of the commune were allowed to vote a supplement. Those who chose to do so offered meagre sums, sometimes insultingly tied to an annual vote, and the presbyteries, which were maintained by the communes, were often left in dingy ill-repair.

Yet the greatest "peril" of the Church of France lay neither in the decline in the numbers of clergy nor in their depression in social status. At a time when the intellectual foundations of Christian belief were cracking, the educational programme of the seminaries seemed designed to exclude the cultivation of the mind. Most of the day was devoted to meditation and pious exercises. "There is

enough virtue in Saint-Sulpice", said Renan sadly, "to suffice to
govern the world." Enough virtue, but not the intelligence to reply
to half the questions the world was legitimately asking. At the
Sulpicien house of Issy in 1871 the *abbé* Frémont found his ten-
hour work-day contained only one hour devoted to the intellect—
"It is not by reciting the Rosary that Renan . . . can be refuted." In
ancient manuals written in dog latin, seminarists studied theological
courses consisting of fragments of the Scriptures, the Fathers, and
the Councils tacked together. The chronological difficulties of
Genesis were still explained by the theory of *"jours-époques"*, the
millenial "days" of creation, and the implausibility of the Flood
story was overcome by confining it to a segment of the earth's surface. Of Vigouroux's manual of biblical studies adopted by the
Sulpiciens in 1878, the *abbé* Amette (a future archbishop)
observed: "Evidently he writes only for those who believe already
and do not wish to be disturbed." Small wonder that there were
complaints from the parishes of preachers confining themselves to
excessively rigorous denunciations of common pleasures, to the
necessity of the confessional, and animadversions upon man's latter
end and the Last Judgement—a religion of prohibitions and fear.

The failure of seminary teaching reflects the intellectual failure
of the Roman Catholic Church in general in this period. There
were no answers in the seminaries, because there were no answers
to give. "Scientific" unbelief met with no reply worth making. The
literary culture of the bishops did not qualify them to analyse the
problems of modern society, and in the 1870s and 1880s only two
diocesan prelates, Ginoulhac of Lyon and Meignan of Châlons
(then of Arras and Tours) had any first-hand knowledge of the new
German biblical criticism. The leading apologist was Dupanloup,
hammer of freethinkers, expert educationist, the casuist who had
produced the brilliant device making the Syllabus almost respectable by distinguishing between the "thesis" official documents must
proclaim and the "hypothesis" by which men must live in practice.
Yet this great Liberal Catholic, this master of logical controversy,
was eloquently futile when it came to defending the biblical documents. In lectures to his clergy he produced "scientific" facts to
support the Flood and refuted "rationalist" explanations of the
crossing of the Red Sea. His *Histoire de Jésus Christ*, a reply to
Renan, was a mere collection of texts, and he was content to
establish the divinity of Jesus by prophecies—"there is no scientific
or historical fact which rests upon such a collection of proofs".

This was the best Dupanloup could do, so what could preachers in rural pulpits hope to say?

From the most subtle to the most naive, the apologists juggled with unproven assertions and unspiritual arguments from utility—Christian belief is a unity, it is necessary to men's lives and to society; you have to take it or leave it. In his *La Religion* (1869) Vacherot complained:

> To the scholar who asks for the resolution of a textual contra- diction . . . they reply that all things cohere in the monumental structure on which the faith of peoples reposes, and that a single stone knocked out might imperil the whole edifice. To the philo- sopher who cannot reconcile a particular dogma with his reason or his conscience, they reply by pointing him to the great moral and social achievements of religion.

There was no sense of immediacy, of urgency in the apologetics of this period. Whatever offended reason now, it was assumed, would be made clear by God himself in his own good time. This was to ignore the right of the existing generation to receive mental satisfaction up to the limits of possible explanation, and the duty of theologians to abandon comfortable assumptions in the interest of intellectual integrity. Dupanloup himself felt obscurely that the inadequacy of Catholic apologetics was nullifying the effectiveness of the vast educational machine which the congregations provided.

> We have the instrument of victory [he said] but I fear it will only serve to show the greatness of our defeat . . . I fear our *collèges* will turn into refuges for the spoilt children of the upper *bourgeoisie,* . . . their routine of religious practice serving only to give the child a distaste for the Church.

And there were signs already that the "instrument of victory" would not remain in ecclesiastical hands much longer. In 1866 Jean Macé founded the anticlerical Ligue de l'Enseignement to promote the cause of an exclusively lay education, and by 1870 it had the support of the freemasons and leading Republican politi- cians.

In one other major respect the Church of France was failing to rise to the heights of its mission. Dupanloup, with all his generosity and intelligence, may again be taken as the illustration of this blind spot in the collective conscience, the deadly myopia of unimagina- tive kindness. His book on "atheism and the social peril" predicted an attack on the Church as the opening skirmish of a war against property and society. When the Commune came, he claimed his prophecy was verified: 'It is atheistical socialism that burned Paris." He showed no sympathy for the Communards—they were "satanic". What then must a Christian do in face of human misery and the accompanying "social peril"? Objecting to State intervention as prejudicial to liberty and family duty, and to strike action by the workers as improper violence, for Dupanloup there was a single remedy, "charity" in the narrow sense of the word, almsgiving.

Yet France was the land of La Mennais, Buchez, and Ozanam, where the modern theories of Christian socialism had begun. A country in which a third of the industrial labour force consisted of women, and two thirds of it served small masters (those with fewer than half-a-dozen employees) would have been suited to the rise of a reform movement based on moral force, with Catholics supplying the unity and programme. The opportunity was not being taken. The patchwork pattern of Christian almsgiving was not fitted to cope with the new industrial discontent and urban misery. It helped the old, ill, and defeated (and this should never be forgotten), but it was not able to reach out to those who were active and angry, as well as underprivileged. As the *abbé* Naudet was to say, the clergy talked of helping "the workers" when they were, in fact, giving alms to "precisely those who could not work". In Orléans the Catholic charity committee busied itself with church attendance, Sunday observance, orphan apprentices, and libraries—peripheral matters so far as the proletariat was concerned. In Lille where, under the Second Empire, 30% of deaths were from consumption and diseases of the lungs, rickets, and syphilitic debility, the Catholic "Society for Good Books" distributed Mme de Gaulle's *Georges: ou le bon usage des richesses.* Well-meaning Christians, preaching almsgiving as a duty, were at a loss to understand their failure to communicate. "How can we explain the hostility of the worker?" asked Mgr Freppel, Bishop of Angers, in 1876, "We found him eighteen centuries ago in the chains of pagan slavery.... We have solemnly declared him ... our brother in Christ Jesus.... We have nothing to reproach ourselves with in regard to this man." In the following year Dupanloup asked in the National Assembly, *"Qui donc me dira pourquoi ce peuple nous délaisse?"* Corbon, a worker who had been elected to the Senate, replied in an open letter, "Why we are leaving you"; you are allied to the rich, he said, and to the cause of political reaction; you teach resignation to poverty; "hatred of revolution has extinguished the love of God within you. . . . We are leaving you today because you have left us already"; we have turned our faces to a new religion, "the religion of humanity". It did not occur to Corbon that the new religion could possibly be there already incapsulated within the old.

There was, for those who sought it, a "Socialism implicit in Catholicism". The phrase comes from Flaubert, the uncommitted observer, who believed only in art. "I have collected the oddest quotations from the so-called men of progress", he wrote to Michelet in February 1869, "beginning with Saint-Simon and ending with Proudhon. They *all* start from the religious revelation". Flaubert's discovery was one which Christians themselves were tardy in making; they needed to go back to the original sources of their inspiration. True, the spirit of charity was not absent from the Church, and the incomprehension of churchmen before the social problem was the incomprehension of the whole society to which they belonged. What was lacking was an understanding of the magnitude of the need and a new effort to rise to the extreme sacrificial demands of the Gospels to meet it. They did not see the way the world of labour was moving and they lacked the ability to break out of the cocoon of class prejudice. It is surprising, indeed, how few Catholics were aware even of the downright political advantages that could accrue to those who became guardians of working class interests in a democratic society, though the Legitimist Pretender, the Comte de Chambord, dimly perceived them.

The social problem presented the Church of France both with a challenge to its ideals and with an opportunity to extend its influence. But its leaders lacked long-term vision. Anticlericals were able to represent it as an institution kept going by the momentum of tradition, with no new plans for society and only reactionary ones for political government, its old beliefs undermined by science and overlaid by newly invented superstitions, its newspapers ultramontane and monarchist, its supporters massed in backward and peripheral rural areas. The voters who were to go to the polls of the Third Republic would not be thinking of the threadbare *curé* who called when auntie died, the black-shawled old ladies who crept to mass every morning, and other accepted details of day-to-day experience; their minds would be taken over by a stereotype compounded of the Syllabus and the Sacred Heart, intellectual obscurantism and opposition to all progress, antirepublican plots and Roman machinations.

In September 1870, when the Empire fell, this anticlerical stereotype of Catholicism was not fully formulated. This happened, and its currency became widespread and effective in the course of the next seven years, when the conduct of Catholics clinched the proof that the Church was an instrument of reactionary politics. As it was, when Frenchmen cast their votes in February 1871 to elect a National Assembly to wind up the legacy of defeat and confusion, the Church was enjoying an ephemeral popularity. The clergy had distinguished themselves in the war as chaplains and unpaid hospital orderlies, the Catholic gentry by their heroism as officers. Bishops had defied the victorious Germans and denounced their demands for hostages, the Archbishop of Reims insisting on being the first of the sureties they put on trains against derailment. With the collapse of the Empire all who had anything to lose became afraid, and they turned with relief to an institution they regarded as a buttress of conservatism. Except in a few big cities the Republicans had no electoral organization, and the local officials who had managed elections for the imperial government were now helpless —which left the clergy as the only nation-wide pressure group. The system of voting, the shortness of the time available for electioneering, the absence of so many prisoners of war, the ban on public meetings in the forty-three Departments occupied by the enemy— everything conspired to favour the election of local notables. Only in some Departments of the west had the successful candidates formally declared themselves Royalists, and only in Corsica and the Charente were they openly Bonapartist. Mostly they were men of local distinction and, above all else, they were known to be in favour of ending the war. The Republicans had successes in the east and south east and in Paris and other big towns, but elsewhere they had little chance, as in the minds of the peasants they were identified with the continuance of the hopeless battle against the Germans. In circumstances that could not recur and in a vote that was essentially "a vote for peace and a vote for persons", France threw up a National Assembly with a Catholic and Royalist majority. For the moment the Church was safe. Embittered Republicans could not inflict a revenge on the "accomplice" of the Second Empire. The attacks of scepticism and anticlericalism would intensify, but they would be raids and harassing operations only; there would be no breakthrough on the political front.

In the terrifying days of the Commune following the elections, the Church, passively, not by any initiative of its own, gained further lukewarm respect from the possessing classes and was alienated still further from the urban workers. On 2 April the Commune decreed the separation of Church and State and the confiscation of ecclesiastical property. Many church buildings were taken over as clubs, offices, and storehouses. Nuns were charged with murdering their illegitimate children and using instruments of torture (bones under the paving stones of chapels and the leg irons of cripples were collected for evidence). The Archbishop of Paris and more than fifty priests were shot as hostages and in reprisals. Just as the rest of respectable society, the clergy did not protest against the ferocity of the repression, though a *vicaire* risked his life to smuggle Cluseret, the Communard general, to safety. On Sunday, 28 May, when only the fort of Vincennes still held out and the volleys of the execution squads had died away, the National Assembly processed to the church of Saint-Louis at Versailles for a mass of thanksgiving in the presence of the papal nuncio. At the archiepiscopal palace, mourners filed through darkened rooms tapestried with black hangings sewn with artificial pearl-drop tears, and illuminated only by candles in their silver holders, to pay their tribute to the murdered prelate lying in state in the chapel. Paul Bourget, then a young law student, was nauseated by the propaganda the clergy were making out of their martyr and by the brutalities of the forces of order. But in the Place du Panthéon he saw the piles of barefooted corpses and lost for ever the optimistic belief in progress and human nature which was the century's alternative to Christianity.

5 The Failure of the "Moral Order"

After the elections of February 1871 France was ruled by an Assembly dominated by Royalists. Yet the throne was not restored. A quick decision was impossible. At Bordeaux, where the deputies first assembled, all was confusion; at Versailles, where they met again on 20 March, the war against the Commune occupied their endeavours. Besides, they wished to have the peace treaty with Germany signed before they recalled the Pretender, lest the new reign should begin with an act of humiliation. Perhaps the Royalist deputies were unsure of themselves, knowing their majority was ephemeral. "I believe neither in the Republic nor in the Monarchy", *duc* Albert de Broglie told Thiers. "I make you my profession of scepticism ... I believe in the regime the people want provided it is put in the care of honest men."

What did the people want? In the by-elections of July (numerous because of the number of multiple candidatures in February) the Republicans gained 99 of the 114 seats at stake; there were three Bonapartists elected, three Legitimists, and nine Orléanists. These voting figures indicate another problem for the monarchists: there was only one throne, with three candidates to sit upon it. But once the period of initial hesitation was over, there was no insuperable difficulty. Even before the "fusion" of 1873 (the reconciliation of Legitimists and Orléanists), the Legitimist Pretender, the *comte* de Chambord, would have been given the votes of practically all Conservative deputies if his candidature had been formally put forward. This never happened, because Chambord refused to abandon the white flag of the Bourbons for the national flag, the tricolour. "Henry IV said Paris was worth a mass," complained the Pope, "Henry V finds France not worth a serviette." Possibly, under the influence of his wife, who knew herself unfit for regal duties, and of his confessor, the Pretender was taking an indirect way of evading the burden of kingship; possibly, in what appeared to be romantic folly he was making a realistic objective test of the true loyalties of Frenchmen. Months went by as envoys posted back and forth to the villa at Frohsdorf, the headquarters of the court in exile. Meanwhile Thiers, with an ambition and self-confidence age could not dim, remained "Head of the Executive". In this office he delighted to prove his indispensability, and he won the confidence of *bourgeois* France with his speedy negotiation of the peace treaty and his suppression of the Commune. The rule of this sprightly septuagenarian proved it was not necessary to resort to kingship to preserve the conservative social order.

On 5 July 1871 Chambord published the manifesto insisting on his flag. The *Univers* applauded the decision: "A man who aspires to the crown of France ... does not begin with an apostasy." Mgr Pie, Bishop of Poitiers, and some other Legitimist churchmen concurred. Politic Catholics were dismayed. Dupanloup (who himself preferred Orléanism to Legitimism and claimed that "all governments are changeable in form and the Church is not committed to any one of them") took in hand the task of persuading the Pretender to put the interests of religion above personal scruples. To no avail. The prelate who had advised Renan about leaving his seminary and heard Talleyrand's last confession had to admit he had seen something new—"an intellectual phenomenon without parallel. Never has there been a moral blindness so complete as this." In January 1873 he appealed again to Chambord and received a sarcastic reply, part of his own letter being made public without his permission. At Frohsdorf the point of honour was not always so nicely observed as in the flag issue. In February the Pope gave audience to emissaries of Chambord and Mgr Pie and advised the acceptance of the tricolour, and in October the Catholic and Royalist deputy Chesnelong went to meet the Pretender with new suggestions for a compromise formula. Hopes ran high. Liveries had been designed for the royal footmen and seven white horses purchased for the carriage. On 30 October Chambord's reply to Chesnelong was published. "I am the necessary pilot, the only one capable of steering the ship to port . . . I cannot found a strong regime to remedy the errors of the past with an initial act of weakness." It was, said Thiers, "a manifesto of suicide". On 5 November a motion to constitute France formally as a republic was lost in the Assembly by only fourteen votes, and a fortnight later, the law of the Septennate made Marshal MacMahon head of State for seven years. It was an admission that there was no hope of restoring the throne.

The Catholics had shown themselves united in wanting France

to accept a king again, even if they were divided on the flag issue and on the powers and nature of the monarchy if ever it should return. In the eyes of Republicans and, indeed, of all those Frenchmen whose political convictions consisted essentially of fear of reaction, the lessons of the Second Empire were reinforced: the Church was regarded as inextricably linked with right-wing politics. On 31 October 1873, when Chambord's public reply to Chesnelong had ended Royalist hopes, Flaubert rejoiced, for in his view, a restoration would have been the signal for a great onslaught on the clergy. "We'll not have a monarch, thank God," he wrote, "that is to say the churches won't be burnt down and the parish priests won't be killed, which would have been the infallible result of a return to Legitimacy."

If the cathedrals had gone up in flames that autumn, the alliance of churchmen with the politics of reaction would not have been the sole cause; their allegiance to the Pope would also have borne some responsibility for the conflagration. When the Italians had seized Rome and Pius IX had withdrawn as a "prisoner" to the Vatican, excommunicating all who had been implicated in the annexation of his city, the Catholics of France, with touching unanimity, had rallied to the defence of the papal temporal power. Chambord had committed the Royalists politically to the demand they were already formulating as Catholics, that Rome be restored to the Pope. During 1871 the bishops were eloquent on the subject and made a forceful collective petition to the Assembly. This outcry was disastrous for French foreign policy. Defeated and disarmed, without a single ally, the country was being asked to embark upon a quarrel with Italy in which no national interest was involved.

The bishops wanted the Assembly to pass a resolution that would have embroiled us with Italy, [wrote the Legitimist *vicomte* de Meaux in his *Souvenirs*] some measure—I do not know what, no more did they—in favour of the Pope's temporal power. What could M. Thiers do, and what could any of us do at that time? Did the bishops wish to provoke a quarrel with Italy, which Germany would certainly have encouraged? Assuredly they did not, and when they protested their reasonable intentions, they were as sincere as they were illogical. But they did not feel themselves responsible for the country at large and, without enquiring whether they were pushing us over a precipice or forcing us into a retreat, they were content to satisfy themselves and their immediate circle.

It was the Roman question, principally, which lost the Conservatives votes in the bye-elections of July 1871. In the Loir-et-Cher the local newspaper sardonically asked the Legitimist candidate (unsuccessful) whether he stood for compulsory confession and obligatory attendance at church, and if he accepted the manifesto of the bishops "which urges France to re-establish the temporal power of the Pope at the cost of a war with Italy".

Thiers was too judicious to allow the debaters of the Assembly to harass him into provocative words about a foreign nation; supported by Dupanloup he refused to take any action except in concert with all other Catholic powers. "What political Sedans after the military ones", raged the *Univers*. Though the Catholic press and the Ultras in the Assembly failed to force the government into making official representations to Italy, they raised a furore and alienated Italy just the same. Until the autumn of 1873 the Roman question continued to smoulder divisively between the two countries; then, on 8 September of that year, Mgr Guibert, Archbishop of Paris, published a pastoral letter in the *Univers* which fanned the smoke into flame. To Frenchmen the archiepiscopal invocation of divine vengeance upon the governments allowing the occupation of Rome was just another irrelevant outburst. But the Assembly had overthrown the cautious Thiers in the preceding May and elected Marshal MacMahon, a soldier and a Royalist in his stead. In this context and from far-off Rome, both the Italian government and the Papal curia were inclined to regard the pastoral letter as deliberately designed to have political repercussions. On 22 September Victor Emmanuel and his entourage visited Berlin, where Bismarck, who was conducting his own feud against the Catholic Church in Germany, was glad to give the Italians portenteous assurances. The Pope completed the disaster for French foreign policy by condemning Italy and Germany together in a single encyclical and awarding a cardinal's hat to Archbishop Guibert. An Italian politician openly blamed France for the Italo-German *rapprochment*: "isolation will be her condemnation. Clericalism generates solitude."

France still had no permanent institutions: there was the Assembly and the President, but no constitution. It was impossible to go on for ever keeping the way open for the portly middle-aged gentleman of Frohsdorf, who had no intention of coming anyway. An Assembly that still had a Royalist majority found it difficult to swallow the actual title of "Republic". The problem was solved by Henri Wallon, a scholarly Hellenist and pious Catholic who intervened in the constitutional discussions of January 1875 with his deceptively simple amendment: "The President of the Republic is elected by an absolute majority of votes cast by the Senate and Chamber of Deputies united in a National Assembly.... He is named for seven years and is re-eligible." This passed—President, Republic, and references to some useful conservative safeguards all together—by 353 votes against 352, a majority of one. At least one deputy who meant to vote against was delayed on his way to the Chamber, and there is a story about the Royalist who went over to the amendment solely because the *duc* de Broglie mistook him for a footman in the lobby and gave him an umbrella to hold. Yet there was nothing accidental about the coming of the Republic. Wallon, "the father of the Constitution", had added the name to what existed already. The question was: Who would dominate the State under the new Constitution? The Assembly ensured there would be a second chamber, the Senate, indirectly elected in each Department by municipal and district councillors and other delegates under a system heavily favouring the rural areas. For elections to the Chamber single member constituencies and second ballot were introduced, arrangements which were expected to favour the candidature of local notabilities, the sort of man who would be recommended by the landowner and the *curé*. Having made its preparations for the future with a ramshackle constitution (that was to last for sixty-five years), the Assembly dissolved on 31 December 1875. The Republic now existed in name as well as in fact, and the men who would control it were to be elected in the following February. Would they be Republicans?

The elections of February 1876 were decisive. On the first ballot, out of 533 seats 428 were settled, and of these the Republicans got 295—a clear majority of the Chamber to start with. The final score after the second ballot was 340 Republicans and 155 Conservatives. Of the Right, half were Bonapartists and only thirty were Legitimists. The swing to Republicanism was nation-wide, most evident in the rual areas of Languedoc, Auvergne, the Lyonnais, and in the cities, but with some indications even in deeply Royalist and clerical areas such as Brittany.

Why were the elections such a débâcle for the Right? In a sense the question is wrongly put, for the monarchist triumph of 1871 was the accidental, unusual occurrence requiring the special explanation. Only one dynasty could appeal to the imaginations of Frenchmen, and it was not the Bourbons. Legitimism had no mass support. True, many voters wanted guarantees that conservative policies would be pursued, but as was evident now, the safeguards were adequate under a Republic. M. Thiers, a *bourgeois* intellectual, had shot down the Communards; kings and emperors were not necessary for the defence of property. Though the Constitution had been passed by monarchist, Catholic votes (it had finally been accepted by 425 v. 254, with Broglie and the Orléanists supporting it), the country realized these votes were reluctantly given. For stability at home it seemed reasonable to put the working of the Constitution into the hands of the men who really believed in it, to put Republicans in charge of the Republic, and for peace abroad it was advisable to disown the clericalist agitation for the papal temporal power. The Conservatives were weakened in the elections by dissensions in their own ranks. Before it disbanded, the old Assembly had had to elect seventy-five life senators. With astonishing malice, the Legitimists had come to a secret understanding with Gambetta to exclude the moderate Right: sixty Republicans, ten Legitimists, and only five of the Right-centre were eventually elected. This cynical bargain was proof to the electorate that the monarchists were not fit to govern. They had no practical policy to offer; beyond allegiance to Catholicism they had no common ideology relevant to the needs of France; they extolled the virtues of a form of government which they could not implement, and they proclaimed romantic loyalty to a cause while they were demonstrably incapable of showing loyalty to each other. 25% of the electorate stayed away from the polls; for the most part they were Royalists, disillusioned and embittered by the feuds and inefficiency of their representatives.

The electoral defeat of the Right in 1876 ended the halcyon period of Church–State co-operation, five years during which the country had been ruled by an Assembly predominantly Catholic in sentiment. As ever in France, there had been limits to what Catholics in official positions were prepared to do for the cause of religion: the deputies had refused to vote for the papal temporal power, to repeal old legislation restrictive of the growth of religious congregations, or to forbid work on Sundays. But they had made significant concessions, and there had been an air of deference to the Church in the ordinary operations of government. Successive ministers of religious affairs worked amicably with Rome when making nominations to bishoprics. Jules Simon, a deist and a moderate Republican himself, had shown the way in complacency—"he'll be a cardinal before me", said Dupanloup. Under Batbie, Fourtou, Cumont, and Wallon the general system was one candidate from the government list followed by another recommended by Rome. The annual *budget des cultes* which paid the salaries of the bishops and some of the other clergy rose from 49,500,000 livres in 1870 to 53,500,000 in 1876. The conscription law of 27 July 1872 exempted ecclesiastics from the call-up. In July 1875 an old dream of Dupanloup's was fulfilled, for legislation was passed allowing the Catholics to set up their own universities, conferring independent degrees on the verdict of "mixed juries" of their own and State professors. The opportunity was taken immediately, in case the offer did not remain open much longer, and free universities were set up at Lille, Lyon, Angers, and Toulouse.

These privileges were exasperating to Republicans. Yet they caused less anger and eventually lost fewer votes to the Right than the outcry over the basilica of the Sacré-Cœur at Montmartre. One of the inspirations of the mass pilgrimages of the age was the desire to offer reparation for the sins reputed to have brought on the nation the defeat of 1870 and the horrors of the Commune, and the chief resort for such journeys was the shrine of Paray-le-Monial, where the faithful made "the consecration of a penitent France to the Sacred Heart of Jesus". 150 members of the Right of the Assembly set their names to such a declaration, which was read on their behalf at Paray-le-Monial on 29 June 1873 by Gabriel de Belcastel. But the supreme gesture dedicating the nation to the Sacred Heart was to be the building of a great church on the heights of Montmartre, and a bill was put forward in the Assembly to acquire the site. The Archbishop of Paris and all reasonable Catholics wanted nothing more than the barest legal authorization for the project, but Belcastel fanatically pressed for an expression of homage to the Sacred Heart in the text of the law itself. He failed, as he was bound to do, but the uproar he and his group caused (aided by another foolish declaration on the part of the *comte* de Chambord) enabled the Republicans to present the law as a superstitious gesture humiliating to the pride of a great people, an example of the sort of politics of the sacristy to be expected if churchmen ever managed to get full control.

By the spirit of the Constitution monarchist–clericalist domination ought to have come to an end with the electoral defeat of 1876.
Unluckily for the long-term interests of the Church, the "Moral
Order" continued for a twilight period of nearly three years while
President MacMahon struggled to prevent the Republican majority
taking over control of the Republic. His first expedient was the
ministry of Dufaure, of the Centre-left. The Chamber showed its
teeth by passing a bill taking away from the Catholic universities
the power to grant degrees, a bill which the Senate duly rejected.
Dufaure tried to demonstrate his independence by dismissing
twenty-six "moral order" prefects, and his ministry ended when he
fell out with the President on a clerical issue, the dispute over "lay
funerals". For the past few years enthusiastic Republicans had been
devising a posthumous revenge on the Church by prescribing non-
religious funerals for themselves. In Marseille, a campaign by the
left-wing newspaper *L'Égalité* popularized the new idea and there
were fifteen priestless burials in 1874. In the Finistère, so it was
said, Republicans in a hurry were joining in by "purchasing the
corpses of women and children" for secular interment. The government suddenly became involved when the Minister of War refused
to send the customary military detachment to the funeral of a
member of the Légion d'Honneur because religious ceremonies
were being omitted; MacMahon refused to remove the recalci-
trant Minister, and Dufaure took an early opportunity to resign.

The Marshal's next expedient to keep out Gambetta was a
ministry under Jules Simon. The barriers excluding the anticlericals
from power were collapsing now, yet Catholics unrealistically
treated Simon's government with contempt. At a time when the
international situation was tense, they sent up a great petition
against new anticlerical legislation in Italy, urging the Government
to "use all methods to compel respect for the independence of the
Holy See". "All methods"—these would include war; it was then
Gambetta cried, *"Le cléricalisme, voilà l'ennemi"*, and in less well-
known but more deadly words, "It is rare indeed for a Catholic to
be a patriot". Even Dupanloup was not immune from the tempta-
tions of brinkmanship, and harried the feeble government. "We have
no doubts about the Marshal's clear-sightedness", he wrote in his
newspaper, *La Défense*, "we know he awaits the appropriate day
and hour to declare the experiment finished." So much for even
the moderate Jules Simon's pretensions to rule.

On 16 May 1877, by a hasty and ill-advised intervention, Mac-

Mahon drove Simon to resignation—the *seize mai* coup against the decencies of the Constitution. Broglie took over with a ministry of Legitimists, Bonapartists, and the Centre-right, and the Chamber was adjourned. When it met again it passed a vote of no-confidence in the government by 362 against 158. On 25 June the Senate having given the necessary permission, the Chamber was dissolved and new elections were set for 14 and 28 October, the latest possible legal date—indeed, it could be argued, rather later still. The administration went all out to win at the polls. Bardy de Fourtou, a tough Bonapartist at the Ministry of the Interior, made a clean sweep of doubtful officials, from mayors to tobacco vendors, heavy fines and, sometimes, prison sentences were imposed on newspaper editors who were too enthusiastic in advocting the Republican cause, and the President himself toured the country calling for the election of "men of all parties who will support the principle of order". There was no doubt where the sympathies of churchmen lay, though the Minister of Religious Affairs warned the bishops not to be too obvious in their tactics—even prayers for "good-elections" were inadvisable. Anticlerical rage was not mollified by the tactical reticence of the clergy. "They are silent," said *Le Siècle*, "therefore they are conspiring." Either way, active or passive, they stood to be blamed. Their enemies identified them totally with the coup of the *seize mai*; "*c'est le gouvernment des prêtres,*" said Gambetta of the *duc* de Broglie and his group, "*le ministère des curés*".

The menace of clericalism was the central theme of the highly organized Republican propaganda. There were allegations of a plot to subvert the Constitution and liberty in France, with the clergy as its agents. They were in the conspiracy to obtain rule over the nation, so that they could build many a new basilica to the Sacré-Cœur and engineer a war against Italy to restore the Pope to his temporal possessions. "The coup of 16 May", said Gambetta, "was hatched in the Vatican, where the Pope, complaining of what he chooses to call his 'captivity', has mobilized the French clericals against Italy and Germany. Tell me, peasant, do you wish them to send your sons to their deaths to restore the Pope to a throne?" If the Republicans lost, said Parthenay, the country would have to endure "a government of priests and a second Sedan", clerical rule at home and defeat abroad. Left-wing newspapers made much of the visit of Italian statesmen to Berlin, of gloating articles in papal journals about "the sword of MacMahon", of reports in the German press concerning Bismarck's plans for a preventive war if clericalism came to power in France. Frenchmen went to the polls, Broglie was to complain, like members of an eighteenth-century Polish Diet looking over their shoulders for a signal from the Russian ambassador before they dared to vote: "It is the first time that the menace, supposed or real, of the foreigner has been seen intervening in our internal discussions."

In the elections, the Republicans obtained 55% of the total vote and 315 seats, and the Conservatives 45% of the vote and 199 seats. With all their efforts, MacMahon and Broglie had ousted the Republicans from forty or fifty constituencies, a significant illustration of the role administrative pressure could play in elections, but nothing near what was required to turn the scales of power in the Chamber of Deputies. With a Republican majority of well over a hundred against him and no hope of being granted another dissolution by the Senate, Broglie resigned. MacMahon clung to the Presidency to try to protect the officials who had worked on his behalf in the elections. The Chamber refused to have any relations with the first ministry he commissioned, so Dufaure was called upon once more, this time to form a ministry of Republicans. On Gambetta's advice the new government and the majority in the Chamber proceeded cautiously, while the Republic demonstrated its respectability. Funds were voted to enable MacMahon to preside with dignity over the great International Exhibition of 1878. Tourists flocked to Paris. The France of Sarah Bernhardt and the new Opéra, of Monet, Renoir, and Cézanne, of Flaubert, Renan, and Zola was the centre of civilization, even if the sound of the Marseillaise, banned for so long, was now heard again. Perhaps the nation would soon become more glorious still by regaining her role of standard-bearer of liberty—Liberty, whose statue was an added tourist attraction on display in Paris before shipment to New York. Meanwhile, *bourgeois* citizens were content with the five per cents standing at 111.5. In this period of calm and optimism the by-elections to the Chamber and the local elections of October showed opinion in the country was moving still more to the left. On 5 January 1879 the elections to renew one-third of the Senate were completed; of the eighty-two seats at issue only sixteen fell to the monarchists. Both Senate and Chamber now had Republican majorities.

There were rumours in Paris of a desperate *coup d'état* being prepared, of the Bonapartist Cardinal de Bonnechose, Archbishop of Rouen, calling at the Élysée to urge the Marshal to bring in the generals and send Parliament packing. Instead, MacMahon preferred to depart from the political scene himself. The Republicans had been purging officials, and he found it intolerable when their attention turned to the army. General Ducrot (one of the best corps commanders, an avowed Legitimist who had held a great open-air mass for his troops before they went on manoeuvres two years ago) had already been sacrificed. Faced with a demand for the dismissal of another five corps commanders, the President resigned. In his place the two Houses elected a colourless, crafty, politician, Jules Grévy.

By the end of January 1879 the Republicans controlled the Presidency, the Chamber of Deputies, and the Senate. They could take revenge for the past, establish themselves more securely in the present, insure for the future. All these purposes, it seemed, could be served by action against the Church. As the history of the Second Empire and of the "Moral Order" proved, churchmen were committed to monarchist politics, Catholicism provided the forces of reaction with their unifying ideology, clericalism was the enemy. Three years ago the young *abbé* Frémont, one of the few clergy with Republican sympathies, had vowed to devote his life to preaching the neglected doctrine that "the Catholic Church can live under all forms of political government". And now, he noted sadly, it was too late to avoid disaster.

> Because it has bound up its cause with that of Royalism, the clergy of France has finally convinced everyone who believes in things popular and democratic that between the Church on the one hand and progress, the Republic and the future on the other, there is no relationship possible but the most deadly hatred.

At last the Republicans were in control of the Republic and the policies of hatred were to prevail.

6 Jules Ferry and the Battle over Education 1879-82

Now they were in power, the Republicans intended to reduce the clergy to political impotence. But how could this be done? Perhaps in the end the whole Church–State relationship would have to be severed, though for the moment practical men agreed the Concordat must be maintained. For one thing, there was the old argument in favour of specific limitations. "The Concordat is a treaty devised to limit the authority of the Church", wrote Paul Cambon the diplomat in 1881. "This treaty is essential since the Church obeys a foreign power". Then, as Gambetta declared in May 1877, changes in the Church–State relationship would have to be delayed because of "the moral and social state of the country", a Republican way of admitting that most Frenchmen still respected the Church even if they would not vote for it. It was a question of changing the "moral and social state of the country", and to this there was one obvious answer: if the superstructure could not be demolished, a start might be made on the foundations.

The educational establishments of the Church were the surest guarantee of its continued influence. In them so many young minds were imprinted with a permanent allegiance to religion, or a subconscious residual respect for its practices; at this point, the multitude of monks and nuns (a "multicoloured militia without a fatherland" as Gambetta bitterly called them) could be thrown into the battle for the control of society. The Republicans saw the Catholic schools as an instrument of power. "What does the Church ask for today?" said Eugène Spuller, Gambetta's henchman. "She seeks what she has always sought, to educate mankind, that is to say, to dominate it. This is what she calls procuring its salvation." And he made the blood of Republicans run cold by predicting that within a century the Roman pontiffs would have taken over modern democray as surely as they had taken over the social order of the Middle Ages.

The policy of "laicization"[1] of education was an insurance for the future of the Republic; it also served to unite its supporters here and now. A frontal attack on religion—the ceremonies by which wives set so much store, the consolations available in the hour of death, the *curé* and all his supporters—would have alarmed the provincial *bourgeoisie*; a flank attack on clerical education, on Jesuits, monks, obscurantism, and schools for the children of the privileged classes, was safer electoral propaganda. Except in the clerical areas of France the peasants would be glad of an opportunity of escaping from the tutelage of the *curé*. "The laicizing policy", writes M. Mégrine, "had its roots in the soil. The Church underestimated this movement towards peasant emancipation." There is evidence from the period of the Second Empire that those industrial workers who were politically conscious did not like the religious schools—for an odd assortment of reasons: they were patronized by the upper classes, they administered corporal punishment, allowed military exercises, taught children to admire unrevolutionary mendicant saints, and emphasized unpractical subjects. According to Catholic controversialists, Republican politicians deliberately appealed to the prejudices of the workers to conceal their lack of a social policy, the attack on Catholic schools being an inexpensive substitute for a truly "revolutionary" programme. Later on, Socialists made the same accusation: as Jaurès put it, when Ferry (the chief educational reformer) declared his intention to "organize society without either God or king", he was not proposing to exclude the factory owner.

To break the hold of Catholicism over future generations and to unite the supporters of the Republic: such was the justification of the policy of laicization. Yet it is unfair to the politicians to describe their programme exclusively in terms of its lowest common denominator of self-interest. Some of the leaders of the attack on Catholic schools were inspired by the vision of a new educational order. In 1872 the word *pédagogique* was regarded as a ridiculous Teutonic invention; eight years later the *Revue pédagogique* was founded; in 1882 Félix Pécaut said, "*La France pédagogise*"—the country was in the throes of educational mania. One has only to look at the children's books published by Jean Macé, founder of that anticlerical Ligue de l'Enseignement which struck terror into

[1] *Laïcité* was a neologism first appearing in Littré in the Supplement of 1877. It was used by Renan in an academic discourse in 1875, but it did not appear in the 1878 edition of the Dictionary of the Academy.

Catholic hearts, to see how embarrassingly sincere was his enthusiasm.

> I have already recounted to you, in the *History of a Mouthful of Bread*, my dear child, one part of your story, that which takes place inside you in silence and darkness. . . . What remains for me to tell is less mysterious. It is about your arms, legs, your little nose, your big eyes that look at me, your ears which listen . . .

and so on from *The Servants of the Stomach;* the *Histoire d'une bouchée de pain* is as unctuous.

And in this new high-minded pedagogical system there was to be a Republican substitute for religious instruction itself. Though the Positivist philosophy had produced no coherent doctrine of education, it had left in the minds of its adherents two conflicting dreams. One was of an education to unify the spirit of the nation. In 1876 Spuller was denouncing Catholic schools for their divisive influence. The State, he said, must have the monopoly of examining for degrees, and he feelingly depicted scenes of the future in the national examination halls, "when, before mingling in the endeavours of life, young Frenchmen would recognize themselves as sons of the same fatherland", competing to forward the progress of culture "under the impartial and benevolent eye of masters of human thought". This enthusiasm for national unity had its harsher side. Both Jules Ferry and Paul Bert, the chief leaders of the laicizing movement, advocated military training for children, and the anticlerical municipality of Paris was to create cadet battalions in schools. France lived in the shadow of the defeat of 1870, lightened only by the pale horizon gleam of the hope of the *revanche*. As early as May 1871, in the *Revue de l'enseignement chrétien* a monk blamed the State schools for the disaster of Sedan. But the argument was soon annexed by anticlericals, and it became a commonplace to compare the pupils of the Jesuits with the more efficient German officer corps, trained in academies which honoured Protestantism and science.

The other Positivist dream, according uneasily with hopes of national greatness, was of a new religion of Humanity. Ferry's two chief educational administrators, Henri Buisson and Félix Pécaut, Protestants who had moved off into sentimental deism, had first become famous by their proposals for such a lay religion. Pécaut, who had tried to set up a liberal Protestant Church in Switzerland, was to open the daily sessions of the new École Normale Supérieure with prayer and meditation. In 1869 Buisson had published a "manifesto of liberal Christianity"—a Christianity freed from obligatory dogmas, belief in miracles, infallible books, and priestly authority, and as director of primary education he was to talk of hymns and ceremonies for a new *"mystique civile religieuse"*.

But on these high matters Republicans were divided. Pécaut's prayers and Buisson's projected ceremonies seemed to some too much like pale imitations of Catholicism. Paul Bert was an atheist and to Ferry the teaching of science, patriotism, and "love of Humanity" was enough. Even so, they were all devotees of progress and believed in their country's mission in the service of mankind. "For them," said Ernest Lavisse, the historian, "modern France was the soldier of Humanity, as the France of the Crusades was, for our ancestors, the soldier of God."

For nearly three years (February 1879 to November 1881) and through three ministries (Waddington's, Freycinet's, and his own) Jules Ferry, as Minister of Public Instruction, was in charge of the Republican reform of education. But for President Grévy's jealousy of greatness this task would have fallen to Gambetta who, by the logic of parliamentarianism, ought to have been called to power once the Republicans were in charge of the Republic. We can see what Gambetta's policy would have been from his brief seventy-two days as Prime Minister (14 November 1881 to 26 January 1882)—an intensified attack on congregational schools, a parade of violent anticlericalism with Paul Bert as Minister for Education and Religious Affairs, but very little practical action, certainly nothing at all to threaten the continuance of the Concordat. The anticlericalism of the great tribune was politic, a multi-purpose device with uses ranging from conciliating Bismarck to side-tracking Socialists, the supreme example of his theorem: "to govern France you need violent words and moderate actions". The spirit and motivation of Ferry's educational policy was very different. To him, the laicization of education was "this great reform which contains within itself all other reforms", the only possible policy for a statesman who believed "in the natural rectitude of the human mind, in the definitive triumph of good over evil, in reason, in democracy". For the long-term interests of the Third Republic it was, perhaps, fortunate that educational reforms were initiated by Ferry's enthusiasm rather than by Gambetta's well-bridled truculence. Amidst the plastering and replastering of

Jules Ferry and the Battle over Education, 1879–82

ministries and the interplay of local pressures and metropolitan corruption, the Republic needed, more than anything else, the leadership of idealism.

In the speech of 10 April 1870 in which he vowed to devote his life to the cause of education, Ferry professed allegiance to the doctrine of Condorcet: he believed in the continuous, inevitable progress of mankind. This, indeed, was his religion. We shall be truly emancipated, he said, when we realize the glorious truth about our place in the universe—

> when humanity appears to us, no longer as a fallen race, stricken with Original Sin . . . but as an endless procession striding on towards the light; then, we feel ourselves part of the great Being which cannot perish, Humanity, continually redeemed, developing, improving; then we have won our liberty, for we are free from the fear of death.

From his other great intellectual inspiration, Auguste Comte, "the founder of the Positivist philosophy", Ferry admits to taking the belief in education as the sovereign instrument of improvement. He liked to think of his own reforms as the foundation of the whole democratic future, and there is more than a hint in his speeches of a desire to emulate the medieval Church, whose schools had been the basis of an entire social order. In the past, the Church had unified society, mitigated inequalities, and taught morality. So too the new lay education would unite Frenchmen in a common patriotism, fitting them for the day when they would challenge the Germans and recover Ferry's homeland of Lorraine; it would help the poor to rise, give women equality with men, and in the factories, where hierarchy was inevitable, it would make inferiority tolerable by creating an equality of dignity. As for morality, at last it could be separated from those "high metaphysical questions about which theologians and philosophers have disputed for 6,000 years", so young minds would see clearly "that true . . . light which, from the beginning of the world (as a great saying has it) has lighted every man".

Behind Ferry's phraseology we can sometimes recognize the schoolboy who won first prize for religious knowledge at the *collège* of Saint-Dié and who "made such a good First Communion". His father and the males of the family were Voltairean free-thinkers; by marriage he had moved into the milieu of Protestantism and riches; his sister, Adèle, who brought him up, was a cripple who

was carried to mass every morning and in her dying letter to him
prayed that her sufferings might work his salvation. Both in his
anticlericalism and in his fervour for a religion of Humanity Ferry
reflected the conflicting worlds in which he had been formed. In
his will he asked to be buried in the same tomb as his unbelieving
father and pious sister, "facing the blue line of the Vosges from
whence the sad complaint of the defeated can reach my faithful
heart. And, of course, I do not wish to have any priest present at
my funeral".

The education law which Ferry presented to the Chamber of
Deputies in 1879 had two objects: to prise the clergy out of influential positions in State education, and to weaken the private system
of education controlled by the Church. Henceforward, ecclesiastics
would be excluded from the national and departmental councils
which supervised the official schools, and the name of "university"
and the right to confer degrees would be limited to public institutions. These provisions could be regarded simply as the cancellation
of secular privileges. But article VII was calculated to deprive the
Church of schools of her own creation, for members of non-
authorized religious congregations were forbidden to teach, whether
in official or in private educational establishments. There was no
secret about the intentions of the legislator: article VII was meant
to ruin the Jesuits.

Nearly a century ago, during the Revolution, Mirabeau had
proclaimed: "Every man has the right to teach what he knows,
and even what he does not know." Ferry was repudiating this
liberal doctrine. The raking up of the question of State recognition
for congregations was a device to deprive certain citizens of their
right to teach; this invention was repudiated by Littré and
Vacherot the leading Positivist thinkers, by Wallon "the father of
the Constitution", by Jules Simon the philosopher of Republicanism, and by Waddington himself once he was out of office.
Indeed, it is something of a mystery why so conservative a cabinet
as Waddington's should have accepted article VII, and we know
from Freycinet's memoirs there was little discussion. True, the law
had to make some mention of non-authorized congregations, lest
it appear to be granting them tacit approval and the mention had
to be unfavourable, as a sort of sop to the Left in the Chamber,
which was inconveniently demanding the prosecution of Broglie
and all concerned in the *seize mai* business. Significantly, out of a
cabinet of ten, five were Protestants, and Protestants, even if non-

practising, had not forgotten the persecutions of the seventeenth and eighteenth centuries.

Ferry's legislative proposal was passed by the Chamber, but in the Senate article VII was struck out by 187 against 103 votes. To out-manoeuvre the Senate, the deputies called on the government to apply the existing laws to the non-authorized congregations. On 29 March 1880, Freycinet's cabinet complied by issuing a decree calling on these congregations to apply for official recognition within three months, except the Jesuits, who would be dissolved. The procedure was dubious, for the Senate's manifest intentions were being flouted, and since the constitutional arrangements of 1830 and 1848 had included liberty of education, the government's citations of precedents from the eighteenth century and from revolutionary laws of 1790 and 1792 looked like sharp practice. And the prefects were to act administratively, thus precluding appeals to the ordinary courts. The Jesuits and monks of other non-authorized congregations stayed in place, leaving the authorities with the odium and ridicule of having to evict them. Bishops, aristocratic ladies, and distinguished laymen kept vigil in monastic chapels and processed out with the inmates when the gendarmes came. Monks who had fought in the war wore their military decorations for the occasion. At Paris the Prefect of Police launched simultaneous dawn raids on eleven religious houses, which he claimed was the biggest co-ordinated operation in the capital since the *coup d'état* of December 1851. According to right-wing newspapers, the Carmelites persuaded the police that their founder had obtained an authorization from Jehu: "Jehu? I don't remember him. But it's not surprising, there have been so many ministries." At Nîmes, egged on by a cheering crowd, 400 soldiers laid siege to a monastery that had been empty for four years. A still larger force went into action at Bellefontaine to expel the Trappists and their supporters, while at Frigolet (Tarascon) General Billot directed operations against thirty-seven monks for which the Catholic press ennobled him with the Napoleonic title of "Duc de Frigolet". Altogether, between 9,000 and 10,000 monks were evicted from 261 houses.

When the furore died down, it gradually became evident that Ferry had succeeded in doing no more than levelling a few outworks of the fortress of Catholic education. Before long many of the evicted monks quietly gathered together again, although the Jesuits were sometimes prevented from reopening their schools by the prosecution of the new headmasters who were put up as camouflage.[1] And, in any case, the schools of authorized congregations remained undisturbed. A law of 16 June 1881 requiring teaching nuns to take the examination for the State certificate of proficiency did not do the damage fervent anticlericals hoped for; the nuns passed easily, which was fortunate for everybody, since there were not enough teachers to staff the State schools without them. Deprived of the title of "university", the Catholic institutions of higher learning carried on successfully as "Instituts Catholiques", their students proceeding to degrees by taking the national examinations.

Churchmen hated Ferry as the initiator of the attack on their schools. Yet his chief success, even as an anticlerical, lay in his less sensational activities, in what he began to build rather than in what he began to destroy. If the religious congregations were to be ousted, the State must take over the responsibility for educating every child in France, and Ferry put up the legislation which made the State system ultimately capable of taking over in every sphere. Primary education was declared to be both "free and obligatory", so the Republic henceforward would have to provide a teacher even in the most isolated commune, even if the whole population preferred an existing clerical school. Up to now most girls had been taught by nuns, whether in State or private establishments. Ferry set out to create a new race of lay schoolmistresses in their place. A decree of August 1879 ordered each Department to set up an École Normale to train them, and in July 1880 an École Normale Supérieure was set up at Fonteney-aux-Roses to prepare the lecturers for these new training colleges. A year later another École Normale was set up at Sèvres to provide teachers for new secondary schools for girls. The project at Fonteney-aux-Roses, with Pécaut in charge of its "spiritual" development was particularly successful; in Capéran's words, it became the "Port-Royal of the Third Republic".

In the debates on Ferry's Legislation, the Catholic deputies did their best to challenge the principle of "free, obligatory, and lay education". They had no established theological position to argue from, since Scripture and the early Church did not afford clear precedents, and until 1917 there was no specific ruling in canon law. They were at a disadvantage too as the educational problem could not be disentangled from the issue of Republic versus reac-

[1] See J. W. Padberg, *Colleges in Controversy: The Jesuit Schools in France from Revival to Suppression, 1815–1880* (1969), pp. 269–72.

tion. It was no good appealing to the vast majority of nominal
Catholics, for in the elections of 1881 (first ballot 21 August,
second ballot 4 September) the Republicans were to win 457 out of
557 seats. Even allowing for the 30% of the electorate which
abstained, there were clearly many Catholics who were not willing
to sacrifice political preferences to register a protest about church
schools. And in any case, whatever arguments were produced, the
Republican deputies were agreed on their strategy and were not to
be deflected from it by vague appeals to liberal theories. What
could be said was well said by Mgr Freppel, Bishop of Angers,
spokesman for the ecclesiastical cause in the Chamber of Deputies. The faithful, he complained, would have to pay twice over, for
maintaining their own children in confessional schools and the
children of other people in State establishments. Why then should
the national budget not contribute to the church schools as it did in
England? If it was true that socialism was evil and free competition
good, why were different educational systems not allowed to com-
pete freely? If free education was to be offered, why not free bread
as well and the whole programme of socialism?

Though these arguments of principle could not move the majority, on issues where the Republican deputies were divided
the interplay of debate could influence the details of legislation.
Ferry's law making primary education obligatory included "moral
and civic instruction" in the curriculum. Mgr Freppel moved an
amendment: to go back to the formula of the Falloux Law, "moral
and religious instruction". Most Frenchman believed in Christianity,
he said, so it was no more reasonable to allow a minority to prevent
the majority of citizens having religious instruction for their children
than it would be to allow Socialists to veto teaching about private
property or determinist philosophers to prohibit theorizing about free
will. There were subjects, French history for example, which lost
their savour if all reference to the Church and its beliefs were
excluded. To keep home and school in separate compartments was
like the judgement of Solomon (had it been carried out), destroying the young mind by cutting it in halves. "To teach a child for
six hours a day for seven years without mentioning God is to press
on him positively the belief that God does not exist, or that he is
not worth bothering about." Freppel's amendment was lost, but in
the Senate Jules Simon succeeded in having "duties towards God
and towards the fatherland" written into the curriculum; this in
turn was thrown out in the Chamber of Deputies. Having won the

battle to exclude religion from the text of the laws, Ferry finally allowed "duties towards God" to appear in the syllabus as drawn up by the Conseil Supérieur de l'Instruction Publique—God as revealed in different forms in different religions, whose laws are known in "conscience and reason". This was not what Catholics meant by religious instruction, and since an administrative decision could easily be reversed, there was no security for the continuance of even this minimum of deistic teaching.

7 New Anticlerical Measures
and Hopes of Compromise
1881-89

With the government under anticlerical control, French Catholics
had to make a painful readjustment of their attitude to the
Church–State alliance. In the snug old days they had assumed that
the spiritual authority was entitled to deference from the temporal,
to support in educational and propaganda activity, and, indeed, to
preferential treatment in ordinary legislation. As Gadille's analysis
has shown, of the 167 bishops of the period 1870–83 only a dozen
were prepared to consider the Church in terms of one association
among others, essentially concerned with the conversion of individuals, and entitled to influence the government solely through the
intermediary of public opinion. These were the liberals of the
school of Maret, Dean of the Faculty of Theology at the Sorbonne;
generally, their concept of the role of the Church in the world was
moulded by their acceptance of the ideals of the French Revolution
and their acknowledgement of the autonomous authority of science
and of reason. By contrast there were, perhaps, ten or so prelates
who were exponents of an extreme "neo-ultramontane" belief in the
right of the spiritual power to give instructions to the temporal
authorities. "In a Christian people", said Mgr Freppel, Bishop of
Angers, "politics is but the ... application of morality to the
government of the country, and morality, according to Catholic
doctrine, is inseparable from religion." The remaining bishops—
the vast majority—avoided Freppel's dangerous confusion between
the spheres of earthly and heavenly jurisdiction, but they expected
the Church to enjoy a unique and favoured position *vis-à-vis* the
government all the same. They belonged, in roughly equal numbers,
to two categories of opinion which have been identified respectively
with Cardinal Pie, Bishop of Poitiers and with Dupanloup, Bishop
of Orléans, though in fact these groups, traditionally set in antithe-
sis, were agreed on fundamentals. In emphasizing the kingship of
Christ and the duty of the State to listen to the Church as a devout

layman listens to his confessor, Pie was, no doubt, going further than Dupanloup; even so, when it came to a crisis, the great bishop of Orléans was as anxious as anyone to have government backing for religion, extending even to the stifling of adverse press criticism. On the other hand, both groups said Catholicism was not wedded to any one form of government; Pie, a fervent and notorious Legitimist, always claimed to be so from strictly practical considerations. The Church could accept Republicanism and democracy, so it was conceded—in theory; in practice, there was a nostalgia for the great days of the medieval papacy. The Republicans were right when they suspected the bishops, even the cautious majority, of yearning in spirit for the success of the *seize mai* coup and the victory of the policy of "order".

Knowing they were suspect, when the policy of "order" had indeed failed, churchmen began to abandon nostalgic dreams and to take seriously the doctrine of the viability of all forms of temporal government. In July 1876 Mgr Guilbert, Bishop of Gap (one of Maret's school) had published a sensational pastoral letter restating the doctrine in uncompromising terms: the early Christians had accepted Nero; "it is our duty to ensure that the altar does not go down with the throne". After the collapse of the *seize mai* manoeuvres, Guilbert's episcopal colleagues belatedly remembered his eloquence, and they now made desperate efforts to show how coexistence with Nero might be possible. Dupanloup produced an impressive memorandum on "The Crisis of the Church" for the conclave to elect a new Pope; he condemned, not only the intrigues of a "politico-religious party", but also the "occult government" of the Church by royalist laymen and right-wing newspapers, to the detriment of the authority of the ecclesiastical hierarchy. These themes resounded in pastoral letters of various bishops during the next four years, and in 1883 Perraud, Bishop of Autun, added a new one in his speech of reception at the French Academy: priests should keep out of political intrigues because the social question called for their full endeavours—"Lazarus is at our gate". It became a commonplace now to emphasize the role of the Church as the conversion of individuals, rather than the christianizing of society by manipulating governments. Lavigerie, Archbishop of Algiers, became the most notable exponent of this opinion.

There are [he said] two methods. The first: to address unbelievers individually to bring them to believe in God and his Son. If you win them, you transform their society. The second: to address the national community (which has forsaken Christianity) and to teach that Christ ought to reign over it. If you fail, you are inevitably cast out. That is what is happening to us.

Lavigerie's first "method", the conversion of individuals, was the policy recommended by the Vatican under the new Pope. Pius IX had died on 7 February 1878, out of touch with the ideas of the modern world and at feud with most of the major powers of Europe. His one consolation had been the France of MacMahon, and the Marshal resigned in January 1879, leaving the Republic in charge of the Republicans. Meanwhile, however, Cardinal Pecci had been elected to the Chair of Peter, taking the name of Leo XIII.[1] The new Pope was anxious to damp down the fires of conflict in France, and he sent to Paris a new nuncio, Mgr Czacki, a diplomat and a realist. Bishops who wrote to the nunciature about tactics in the political struggle found they were advised to concentrate on pastoral work: "We seek only the good of men's souls." Amidst the bitterness of public controversy, Czacki deftly maintained ordinary social relationships with the anticlericals. "I often saw him sitting on a sofa beside Jules Ferry, Freycinet, Spuller or Paul Bert", says Bülow in his memoirs, "smoking a cigarette and engaged in animated conversation." One outcome of these smoking sessions was the continuance of a reasonable understanding over the appointment of bishops. The Church did not lose, and there was some gratification for Republicans to see Guilbert translated from Gap to the important see of Amiens, then to Bordeaux, and Meignan (also of the Maret school) to Arras, then to Tours, and to see "Republican" bishops appointed to Poitiers, Cambrai, and Saint-Claude (The latter two, it is true, renounced their inclination towards the government, once they were safely consecrated, while Bellot des Minières, succeeding Cardinal Pie at Poitiers, was subjected to a campaign of abuse and innuendo which paralysed his brief episcopal career). Another liberal elevated to a bishopric was Lamazou, who began by issuing a pastoral to his clergy of Limoges enjoining complete abstention from politics, even in private conversations: "Preach the Gospel, and nothing but the Gospel."

Given the realistic mood which was beginning to prevail in the episcopate, and the manifest intentions of Rome to seek a com-

[1] For a consideration of the character and aims of Leo XIII, see below, page 68ff.

promise, Ferry's education laws met with no more than verbal resistance—except for the demonstrations when the non-authorized congregations were expelled. In the clerical press proposals for defiance were made: monks and nuns employed in the State schools were to go on strike, and fathers should refuse to send their children to secular establishments. But there was no strike and very little withdrawal of children; indeed, during the outcry there was an attempt behind the scenes to bring together moderate men of both sides. Freycinet, the head of the Government, gave the nuncio a secret undertaking to authorize all congregations making the prescribed application, and the details of the scheme were worked out with Mgr Lavigerie, Archbishop of Algiers. The Prime Minister, it was decided, would be overcome by a fit of collusive anger and publicly accuse the threatened congregations of being allied to parties hostile to the Republic; in reply, the monks would make a common declaration protesting their political neutrality, and the government would accept this declaration as an assurance that the authorizations could safely be granted. Freycinet duly made the "accusations" in the Senate on 25 June 1880, and the declaration was circulated for signature. But on 30 August the plot was revealed in a royalist newspaper. Freycinet, who had acted without consulting his cabinet, was driven to resign, and the eviction of the monks proceeded.

Yet this disaster prepared the way for an understanding between Church and Republic nine years later—the future "Ralliement". Churchmen saw the moderate Republicans would be glad to call off the persecution, provided they could *appear* to be anticlerical, and moderate Republicans saw the Pope and some of the bishops were willing to compromise. To those Catholics who put the interests of religion above their political convictions, the danger of complicity in right-wing politics was revealed. In the last resort, the Royalists would push the Church down to ruin simply to raise up hatred against the Republic. On 20 March 1881, Czacki wrote angrily to Lavigerie: "Here the situation is really bad, for there is a coterie which wishes to play all the cards in the Church's hand after it has lost all the other possible tricks."

The cause of moderation among the anticlericals soon gained an illustrious recruit, for having laid the foundations of Republican education, Jules Ferry himself would have been glad to call a halt. In 1883 he was defending the salaries of the clergy, the Vatican embassy, and the Concordat; "he's making us into ultramontanes",

"le cléricalisme n'est plus l'ennemi", complained the men of the
Left. But Ferry had not carried his programme to a logical stopping
point; in particular, after all the disputes about an appropriate
formula, the precise content of the moral education to be given in
primary schools had still to be defined. Among others, a professor
from Toulouse, the Rector of the Academy of Caen, Paul Bert the
politician, and Lavisse the historian, tried their hands at manuals
of civic education. Lavisse, writing under the splendidly respectable pseudonym of "Pierre Laloi", cheered up the children by printing an article of the penal code at the head of each section, and
encouraged respect for the institution of marriage by adding a
picture of a nuptial chamber with a portrait of the President of the
Republic between the bed curtains in place of a crucifix. Some of
these manuals were put on the *Index,* a number of bishops pro-
hibited children who had read them from attending First Communion, while the government stopped the salaries of parish priests
who enforced the episcopal orders. In 1886 the Goblet education
law rounded off the laicization policy. Henceforward, monks and
nuns could not be recruited into the State schools, which were to be
staffed as soon as possible by an exclusively lay personnel. Catholic
spokesmen were quick to point out that the principles of the liberal
era of the French Revolution had again been affronted, for citizens
were being penalized because they chose to assert their religious
convictions with a peculiar degree of solemnity.

If monks and nuns, prayers and crucifixes were to vanish from
the nation's schools, it was logical to get rid of such traditional
religious observances as still remained in the details of public life.
The laws were therefore amended to allow Sunday work, the posts
of army and hospital chaplains were abolished, mayors of communes were given control of religious processions and the keys to
bell towers, public prayers at the opening of the parliamentary
session were abandoned. By the law of 27 July 1884, divorce was
restored to the Civil Code, whence it had been banished in 1816.
The fashion for "lay funerals" caught on in government circles from
January 1882, when Hérold, Prefect of the Seine, notorious for
removing images and crucifixes from schools ("the laicization of
the furnishings") was given resplendent civic obsequies without
benefit of clergy. In December Gambetta followed him to an un-
blessed grave. "Not a priest, not a whisper of a prayer", wrote
Pelletan. "The Catholic Church yesterday lost something of its
power." Legislation (drafted in 1883, but not passed until four

years later) encouraged citizens to make their own preliminary arrangements to follow these examples. At any time they could make a declaration to ensure themselves a non-religious funeral, and there were heavy penalties on the family in case of infringement, even if there was evidence proving a death-bed conversion.

Much of the anticlerical legislation has a nuance of studied defiance, a hint of Voltairean glee in ridiculing religion combined with a pigheadedness of the Monsieur Homais kind in gratifying personal prejudices. The political overtones sometimes imply insincerity, an exaggerated onslaught to spite the Right, or a sycophantic, routine bristling to convince allies on the Left that all is in earnest, an attempt to appear authentic in the role of heirs of the revolutionary tradition by politicians uncomfortably conscious of their lack of zeal for social reform or popular agitations. But in the outcrop of lay funerals and in the legislation to encourage them there is a more serious undercurrent of principle, and with it a tremor, as if a raw nerve of the mind had been touched. We have not given due weight, in the history of anticlericalism, to the fear of death. At the end, churchmen had hope, none the less real and enviable if, as their opponents claimed, it was illusory. The gibe of Anatole France (in the mouth of the pagan Hippias) that "Christ is the god of the dead . . . the prince of death", was only wounding if the dead are dead for ever, and he himself never heard the *Dies irae* without coming to the verge of tears. In the same year (1876) Renan asked the haunting question in face of which he could offer only the consolations of irony: *"Qui sait si la vérité n'est pas triste?"* Man is the only animal who knows he must die. This phrase of Voltaire and of Anatole France lies behind Roger Martin du Gard's *Jean Barois* (1913), a novel reflecting the secret preoccupation, rarely avowed, of the enthusiastic anticlerical generation which had preceded it. What will a man do in his last hour? Jean broke and confessed as his unbelieving father had broken before him: *"C'est un x si terrible"*. In France's *L'Anneau d'Améthyste,* the doctor, the archivist, and M. Bergeret walk in a funeral procession, free-thinkers all, bitterly reflecting on the one clerical argument to which they have no reply. If you visited the sick every morning, the doctor says, you would understand the power of the *curés,* and M. Mazure, the archivist, is "suddenly stricken with a great desire to have an immortal soul."

By 1887, having laicized education, instituted divorce, removed religion from State ceremonies, and smoothed the way for secular dying, the moderate Republicans felt they had gone far enough. From now onwards it would be prudent to be conciliatory. In foreign policy the Republic could no longer ignore the Papacy, for Leo XIII had restored the diplomatic prestige of the Roman curia and was cultivating good relations with Germany. Only a Russian alliance could rescue France from isolation in Europe, and the Tsar was not likely to throw in his lot with reckless radicals presiding over a divided nation. In the Near East and China French influence depended to some degree upon the protectorate over missions which Rome had conferred and could withdraw. As Gambetta had said, "anticlericalism is not for export". At home there was a delicate web of clerical influence in certain social milieux; blatant priest-haters would not gain the entrée to the more respectable and rarified reaches of high society in Paris, the Academy, inner naval and military circles, or the aristocratic coteries of the provinces. More significant still, it suddenly became evident that the Republicans had been relying too complacently on mass popular support. In the elections of 1885 the conservative groups increased their seats from 100 to 201, and the Republicans fell from 457 to 383. This was the final result on the second ballot; the figures for the first ballot were more frightening still, as the Republicans had then gained only 129 seats outright, as against the Right's 177, and the total of votes cast for them had been 4,327,000 against their opponents' 3,541,000. A *curé* of the Department of the Haute-Garonne had rung his church bells on news of this preliminary victory: *"C'est le glas de la République."* His salary was stopped for "electioneering" and the Republic survived. But the moderate Republicans were shaken. A year or two of economic stagnation, an unpopular venture in colonial affairs, or an excessive show of anticlericalism (these were the reasons given for the débâcle on the first ballot in 1885) and the regime might founder.

There are two ways in which a democratic State can be destroyed by the people: they can vote it out at the polls or stand by and let it be undone by a *coup d'état*. Having been scared by the first possibility during the elections of 1885, the Republicans were confronted with the second in the course of the following year, as France became electrified in a mindless enthusiasm for General Boulanger. Since the passing of the possibility of presidential dissolution after the constitutional crisis of 1877, a spirit of proud irresponsibility was evident among the deputies of the Chamber. Secure in their seats for a tenure of four years, incurably suspicious

of intelligent leadership, and with local rather than national interests in the forefront of their minds, they made politics a game of
intrigue and tried to keep the workings of a modern State under the
day-to-day supervision of parliamentary debates. Ministries were
overthrown and restructured: they changed "like opera scenery" it
has been said, though the comparison is misleading in so far as the
new backdrop was rarely distinguishable from the old. Policies
did not change; they lost their continuity without renewing their
content. The Third Republic had not yet manifested its peculiar
potential for mere survival, the subconscious reflex towards co-
operative action that swept through Republican milieux only when
all seemed lost. Disillusionment with politicians swelled the demonstrations in favour of Boulanger in the summer of 1887, and when
revelations of corruption forced the resignation of President Grévy
in December and there was a renewed outburst of Boulangist agitation in 1888, it seemed to many that the regime was doomed.
During this dark period the moderate Republicans naturally did all
they could to live down their reputation for anticlericalism. It was
vital to persuade Catholics to withhold their support from the
forces cynically massing behind the frivolous and insolent general.

The elections of 1885 had left the political groups in the Chamber
in three main blocks of roughly equal size. In the centre were the
moderate Republicans, the so-called "Opportunists" of the school
of Gambetta and Ferry, about 200 strong. To their left was a
rather larger group, equally divided internally between Radicals
and more extreme opinions; to the right of the Opportunists was
the conservative opposition. Freycinet's ministry of January 1886
was composed of four Opportunists, two Radicals, and two of the
extreme left. Goblet's ministry of December was much the same.
But it was theoretically possible to organize a government with
support from the other side, a combination of centre and right, if
old prejudices could be forgotten. On 30 May 1887, this is what
happened, for Rouvier took office with a cabinet composed solely
of moderates—Boulanger, the Radicals, and the Left being excluded. This ministry owed its inception to an understanding with the
baron de Mackau, who offered Royalist support; in return,
Rouvier, who "refused to treat as enemies part of the representation
of the French nation", promised to halt the policy of lacization.
These six months of right-wing backing for Rouvier are taken by
M. Goguel as peculiarly significant in the history of the Republic,

for they suddenly revealed the possibility of rule by a basic party
of order if a truce could be declared on the religious issue.

As things were, Mackau and some of the Royalists soon changed
their minds and decided to gamble on Boulanger. The most sensi-
tive Catholic politicians refused to follow suit, though the *Univers,*
after calling Boulanger "a vulgar adventurer" asked "why should
we, the oppressed, do anything for the crumbling Republic?" Originally, the general had been an anticlerical, promising to subject
the clergy to conscription, but on 11 August 1888 he sent a telegram to *La Croix* promising never to countenance the persecution
of religion. Wisely, most Catholics refused to trust him, and for
more than one reason. The "protest vote" which gave Boulangism
its power did not represent a swing of French opinion towards
Caesarism; it consisted rather of disillusioned men of the Right in
ephemeral and accidental co-operation with artisans and industrial
workers voting, not for dictatorship, but for a reform of the
Republic. The general's entourage stood for constitutional revision,
not for a *coup d'état,* and the general himself was a cardboard
conspirator whose adventure came to an ignominious end when he
fled to Brussels in April 1889.

Though the danger had passed, the moderate Republicans had
learnt their lesson. With 200 supporters of the Church in the Chamber, said Ferry in December 1888, the policy of anticlericalism
cannot be pressed further. In June 1889 he repeated this assurance.
It was then that Albert de Mun made his sensational, deadly, and
injudicious reply.

> It is too late! . . . There are men from whom we could accept
> advances—from you, never! Everything done against us was
> done by the moderates. . . . The Radicals gave the orders, the
> Opportunists carried them out. Religious war has been the
> cement of your union . . . it is on you like the poisoned shirt of
> Nessus, you cannot escape from it, it is burning you, it will
> destroy you.

8 Leo XIII and the Ralliement 1889-92

The moderate Republicans had gone to extremes against the Church to maintain their support from the Left; the anticlerical tail had been wagging the Republican dog. Yet it would have been wiser for Albert de Mun to refrain from saying so, especially in the year in which the celebrations and counter-celebrations of the centenary of the French Revolution were reinforcing old hatreds. Trampling on Ferry's professions of toleration was not going to make it easier to promote the decline of the alliance between Opportunists and Radicals.

Since hopes of a restoration of the throne had faded, the Right had been groping for a policy. Albert de Mun himself had tried to found a "Catholic Party" on the analogy of the German Centre Party, but few deputies had joined and in November 1885 he accepted instructions from the Vatican to abandon the design. In August of the following year Lepoutre, a Catholic deputy from the Department of the Nord declared his intention to refrain from systematic opposition, while Raoul-Duval, a Protestant Bonapartist, unsuccessfully attempted to create what he called "a right-wing party within the Republic, not against it". About this time a useful word for the phenomenon of accepting the Republic came into currency. In a letter of 7 September 1886 to the *Univers*, a *curé* described how he had "rallied loyally to the Republican principle after the death of Henry V", and a journalist in *Le Matin* took up the theme under the headline of *"Le clergé rallié"*. In the following May the *baron* de Mackau made his offer to Rouvier to allow the formation of a ministry of Opportunists to the exclusion of the Radicals. This new idea of direct co-operation with moderate Republicans was thrown overboard when Mackau, de Mun, and others got involved in Boulangism, an adventure which did the Right no good and probably accounts for the loss of more than forty seats in the elections of 1889. Jacques Piou, another conservative deputy who had been on the Boulangist central committee, tried to regain the lost ground by creating "La Droite constitution- nelle", a party to work for economy in government expenditure and for the delegation of control of education to the local authori- ties. Since Royalism was a dead cause, the objective was to have a conservative programme to put to the electorate within the exist- ing constitutional framework. But before such a new group could hope for mass support, it would have to define its position more clearly. Did it mean to co-operate with the moderate Republicans, getting the best terms it could for religion by a process of com- promise, or did it mean to lurk for ever on the right flank, sniping and threatening? And above all, was Royalism really being abandoned, or was it just being omitted from public announce- ments? As *La France Nouvelle* asked on 24 October 1890, were Piou and his friends "Republicans without saying so, or were they saying they were Republicans when they weren't?"

By the beginning of 1890, in spite of the recent spate of memories of the great Revolution, the political barometer of the Third Republic was set towards appeasement and compromise. Some conservatives were trying to escape the electoral consequences of their monarchical convictions, and some Opportunists were trying to shake off the dependence on the Left involved in anticlericalism. More significant still, there were a number of bishops who wanted to take the Church out of politics to save it from persecution. The affair of the non-authorized congregations in 1880 had been a lesson to them; they had seen how the Royalists were willing to play all the tricks in the Church's hand when there was none left in their own. In December 1880 the *abbé* Frémont noted the existence of "a whole party of clergy" wishing to protect the Church by a *rapprochement* with "the Republican conservative party". Since then he had watched events, hoping to see these clerical moderates come out into the open. In May 1889, in despair at the sight of a reckless pamphlet by Mgr Freppel attacking the centenary celebrations of the Revolution, he once more lamen- ted the silence of the more realistic members of the episcopate: "The day when a bishop says publicly in Parliament, 'I am a Catholic and a Republican', the whole struggle will be trans- formed."

The bishops who wanted to come to terms with the Republic were diverse in their opinions and motives; the one thing they had

in common was political realism.[1] Cardinal Place, Archbishop of
Rennes, and Cardinal Foulon, Archbishop of Lyon, former liberals
of the Dupanloup school, were wary and senior ecclesiastical statesmen. Mgr Fuzet, only recently appointed to a colonial see, was
illiberal in matters intellectual, authoritarian in pastoral relationships, and formally Republican in politics. In 1881 he had published an anonymous brochure proclaiming the duty of the Church
to accept democracy as she had accepted the barbarians at the fall
of the Roman Empire; this brochure he used, through M. Monod,
Prefect of the Allier, to influence the Republican politicians towards giving him a bishopric. "I believe in the possibility of the
alliance of Christianity and democracy", he wrote ". . . and I wish
to work to this goal with the authority an official position would
confer on me". Five other prelates of the party of compromise had
been appointed by Baroche, Minister of Napoleon III, between
1865 and 1867, a time when the government was at feud with the
Papacy. Such is the continuity of French history; the more erastian
episcopal appointments of the Second Empire provided the leaders
for a *rapprochement* with the Third Republic. One of these bishops,
a scholar of distinction, Hugonin of Bayeux, had been brought into
the priesthood under the patronage of Dupanloup, and had subsequently become a friend of Maret and one of the little group in
the French episcopate which had consistently stood for a compromise with the ideals of 1789. Another, Mgr Guilbert, Archbishop of
Bordeaux, "the red archbishop" as Paul de Cassagnac affected to
call him, was of peasant origin, the sort of pastor who was often
seen going round his diocese on foot. It was his pastoral letter of
July 1876, issued when he was Bishop of Gap in the twilight
days of the Moral Order, that had drawn attention to the early
Christians' submission to Nero, though, indeed, to him the Republic
was far from being a Neronic type of government, since he
accepted democracy as a truly Christian concept. Mgr Meignan,
Bishop of Tours, a liberal intellectual who sent his priests to study
the new theological ideas in England and Germany, was inclined
to agree with Guilbert for more subtle reasons; acutely aware of

[1] The list of bishops mentioned here is not meant to be exhaustive. Perraud
of Autun, Turinaz of Nancy, Thomas of Rouen, and others, no doubt, should
be included. We very much need a study of political attitudes among the
episcopate during this period, taking over at the point where Gadille's major
monograph leaves off.

the intellectual difficulties across the path of Christian belief, and of the alienation of the masses from the Church, he saw how slow a business the conversion of the world must be. By contrast, Mgr Isoard, Bishop of Annecy, a reactionary in politics and theology who had a long record of feuds with Republican ministries, was in the camp of compromise through sheer realism.

Finally, of Baroche's bishops, there was Cardinal Lavigerie, Archbishop of Algiers. Ten years ago Lavigerie had conducted negotiations with Freycinet in an attempt to save the non-authorized congregations, and he was still angry at the Royalists who had betrayed him. Not that he had any enthusiasm for the Republic. An Imperialist under the Second Empire, after 1870 he became a Legitimist, and in August 1874 urged Chambord to risk a *coup d'état*; there would be only a limited amount of street fighting, he said. When monarchist hopes faded, Lavigerie turned again to the established—Republican—government. This was partly because he feared socialism and the flare-up of another Commune, partly because he wanted the Church left in peace to reform itself and to educate its clergy and, most important of all, because he wanted to continue to use the money, protection, and prestige of the French State to aid his missionary work in North Africa. In the eyes of this great colonial prelate the work of his White Fathers among the desert Arabs and the suppression of slavery were more important than disputes about prayers in schools and lay funerals. Seen at a distance, from across the Mediterranean, the political affairs of the metropolis fell into a longer-term perspective; however hateful the government in Paris, it was the only accredited representative of French nation, and the Archbishop of Algiers was a patriot.

France, of a certainty, is one of his principal passions [said a government report in 1888]. It would be risky to go so far as to say that he is devoted to the Republic, but without fear of being mistaken one can definitely state that he will never cause difficulties for the government from the political point of view.

If any churchman could intervene effectively as a conciliator between Church and State, Lavigerie was the man. He had the necessary toughness (a cleric who met him for the first time in 1887 compared him in appearance to Hercules and Bismarck), and more than that, he had a firm belief in his vocation to lead the Church in a new direction: "*Il faut un homme prédestiné, et croyez-moi je le–suis.*"[1]

By themselves, a few politic bishops could do little. True enough, many of their colleagues in the episcopate would welcome proposals for an understanding with the Republic, but few of them were likely to be willing to go far enough to make an approach to the Republicans convincing. Perhaps most of the bishops and certainly most of the lower clergy and influential laity in the parishes were monarchist in sympathy, and even those prepared to concede the death of their cause hesitated to accept the inference that they ought to make gestures towards the persecuting Republicans. In any case the French Church had no central machinery for planning a *volte face* in politics, since by the Gallican principles of the State any formal assembly of bishops would have been illegal. We have seen how, after the collapse of the proud independent Church of the *ancien régime* in the French Revolution, churchmen had come to look to Rome for leadership. The "Ralliement" could only have come about with the active support of the Pope. Behind the Herculean Cardinal from Algiers who bore the brunt of the first assault was the frail, waxen-faced figure of Leo XIII, eighty years of age when he faced the great decision which was to bring on him the hatred of so many friends of the Church and the lukewarm and cynical applause of so many of it enemies.

This Pope was an enigma to contemporaries. Great age, slow speech, and hesitancy made him sometimes appear a weakling, the pale figure of Zola's caricature, borne on a sedan chair past the naked marble goddesses in the silent gardens, the effete ruler of a dying institution in a world that was rediscovering the flesh and paganism. Yet no modern pope has made more courageous and revolutionary decisions. Behind all his delays and manoeuvrings he maintained course unflinchingly. Old men may be in a hurry, or sunk in procrastination. Leo XIII was neither. At a leisurely pace his diplomacy moved towards its goal. "My daughter," said the aged pontiff to the nun who expressed the hope he would live to be 100, "why should we set a limit to the bounties of Providence?" Like Lavigerie, but without enthusiasm or recklessness, he was a predestinate.

[1] This comes in a letter to Maret of 3 December 1875, in which Lavigerie describes his mission to "de-Italianize" the Church. (He means opening it to modern ideas and making it capable of working with all governments as well as ending the predominance of the Italian cardinals.)

Contemporaries, friends and foes, came to speak of Leo XIII as a "liberal" pope. The term was appropriate for one who threw the Vatican archives (up to 1831) open to scholars; encouraged seminarists to read Dante, kept in touch with the great issues of the day, and published the encyclicals on politics and society that rescued the Church from the odium of Pius IX's anathemas on "modern civilization". Yet, before his accession the Pope of the Ralliement had been one of the inspirers of the Syllabus; he was to act against writers his predecessor had spared and renew the condemnation of freemasonry. When he spoke of the legitimacy of freedom of the press and liberty of conscience, it was to deny them the status of things absolutely good in themselves; they were allowed for the sake of public peace or other "just cause", and to enable the Church to ensure that no one embraced Catholicism unwillingly. At the end of his life Pius IX had admitted a change of course would be necessary under his successor, and it was a change, not a reversal of course that Leo XIII made. He emphasized neglected aspects of Roman Catholic doctrine, taking care not to say anything incompatible with aspects over-emphasized by his forerunners. Of Rome it can be said, as of the Third Republic, only more truly, for the process was conscious not instinctive, *plus ça change, plus c'est la même chose.*

The Italians soon put the new occupant of Peter's Chair in the category of the *politici,* and in due course the enraged French Royalists were to endorse this verdict. Yet no fewer than twenty-five encyclicals of the pontificate were to be concerned with purely spiritual themes—grace, the Eucharist, mystical union with Christ, the consecration of the human race to the Sacred Heart. Like the "liberal" stereotype, the "political" one is inadequate to describe the complexity of the mind of Leo XIII. True, an explanation of the Ralliement can be given in terms of essentially political motives. A conciliatory policy towards France, following the pattern of similar moves towards Germany and Russia, would strengthen the position of the Roman curia in international affairs, and an understanding with the Republic would save the French Church from further assaults on its schools and on its position in society. Piecing together what was said to various visitors to the Vatican, we can go further and glimpse the political role Leo XIII was designing for the French Catholics once they were freed from the electoral handicap of Royalism; instead of forming a confessional party on the German, Austrian, or Belgian model, they were to become the right wing of a central conservative bloc in alliance with the moderate Republicans.

But these aims, which by themselves provide a respectable explanation of the policy of the Ralliement, ought not to be listed starkly as nothing more than the appropriate rational motives of a politician. If we do this, the pronouncements and encyclicals which preceded the launching of the new design—the letter to President Grévy of 12 May 1883, *Nobilissima Gallorum gens* (February 1884), the brief on the press (November 1884), *Immortale Dei* (November 1885), and *Sapientiae Christianae* (January 1890) fall too easily into place as a sort of doctrinal "softening up" process to prepare for the Ralliement. They were this, but they were more. They stand in their own right as necessary restatements of aspects of doctrine obscured or cheapened by the exigencies of the political battle under the Third Republic. In them Leo XIII affirms the necessity of the "salutary link" between Church and State. God has divided the government of the human race between two powers, each sovereign in its own order "in conformity to its nature and proper end". The Church's end is superior, but this superiority does not convey any right to interfere with the temporal power. Nor does the Church have anything to prescribe so far as forms of government are concerned. It can live with all of them; it accepts the powers that be. There is nothing to be said against the participation of the people in government, and in appropriate forms of constitution this may be a duty for the citizen. But no group acting within the temporal sphere should attempt to impose the pursuit of its temporal ends, however lofty, upon the ecclesiastical power. The Pope and the bishops rule the Church, not ecclesiastical journalists or pious laymen, and it is "an abuse of religion" to "attach the Church to a party or to try to use it as an auxiliary to defeat opponents". A great deal of this doctrinal clarification, of course, is pointedly directed to the condition of affairs in France. But who was being "political", the pope who tailored the cap or the Catholic Royalists whom it fitted so perfectly?

For long the Church had been regarded by its enemies as the propaganda department of the monarchical parties. How could this engrained suspicion be eradicated? How could the Catholics be persuaded to rally to the Republic, and how could the Republicans be persuaded that they had really done so? An additional degree of proof would be required after the Boulangist affair. Rome had

stayed aloof and disapproving, but a few prominent French Catholics had become implicated and others had made it clear they
would shed no tears if the Republic fell. Leo XIII's first scheme to
promote a reconciliation between Church and government was put
to Mgr Foulon, Archbishop of Lyon, and Mgr Richard, Archbishop
of Paris, when they came to Rome in December 1889 to receive
their investiture as cardinals. The idea was to have a declaration
drawn up by the six French cardinals and to circulate it for
signature to all the other bishops. Nothing came of this, for when
the cardinals drew up their statement it proved to be full of complaints against the Republic, and the Vatican hastily suppressed it.
At this point, in April 1890, on the advice of the Archbishop of
Rennes, the Pope decided to call on the services of Cardinal
Lavigerie, who had already been involved in close negotiations
with the moderate Republicans, in 1880 over the affair of the
congregations, and in 1885 over electoral policies. The task
required craft and courage, qualities the Archbishop of Algiers
possessed in abundance, craft supported by an intimate knowledge
of political circles, and courage of his own particular style, enlivened by a flair for publicity and a love of the flamboyant gesture.

The Cardinal did not need to be persuaded; indeed, historians
have asked whether the Ralliement originated in his brain rather
than in Leo XIII's. On 10, 14, and 16 October 1890, Lavigerie
was received in audience at the Vatican, ostensibly on matters
concerning his campaign against slavery. From the start he and the
Pope were in agreement on what should be done; the only disagreement concerned the question of who should do it, for the Archbishop
was acutely conscious of the importance of Royalist contributions
to his missionary work in Algeria.

> The idea of an intervention of the hierarchy was in the air
> [writes Xavier de Montclos]. Leo XIII and Lavigerie both accep
> ted it. But in their conversations there was a subtle manoeuvring,
> neither wishing to assume the decisive role, both desiring the
> other to take the lead. In such a dialogue, the last word would
> necessarily remain with the Pope.

On 17 October Lavigerie promised to do what was required, and
he began with craft by coming to a secret understanding with the
politicians in Paris. Here, Freycinet was in power again, and still
anxious for an accommodation with the Church in spite of the
disastrous failure of another collusive design ten years ago. On 18

October, Lavigerie wrote to Paris, urging the Government to avoid any provocative action, as there would soon be an "explicit adhesion of the French episcopate to the Republican form". Then came the time for courage and flamboyancy. On 12 November, at a dinner in honour of officers of the Mediterranean fleet, the Archbishop proposed the famous "toast of Algiers". "To rescue the country from disaster", he said, there must be "unqualified adherence (*adhésion sans arrière-pensée*)" to the established form of government which "in itself is in no way contrary to the principles which are necessary to the life of civilized and Christian nations". In saying so, he declared he was certain he "would not be disowned by any authorized voice".

At the news of the toast of Algiers, a storm of rage swept over Royalist France. It had been a speech of betrayal, fit to resound over the ruins of ancient Carthage; here was "Punic faith" for the modern era. And Royalist faith was exemplified by the publication of the confidential letter Lavigerie had sent to Chambord in 1874 urging a *coup d'état*. The outcry was more than a selfish outburst of thwarted politicians, more even than the protest of outraged loyalty. In so far as the Ralliement was intended to create a new and influential Catholic line in politics, the monarchists were exasperated by the justifiable fear they were being asked to sacrifice a hopeless cause they loved for a hopeless cause they detested. It was impossible to avoid wondering if the Republicans would aim to split the Catholics rather than to co-operate with them. (Long afterwards it was revealed that Constans had admitted as much to his cronies at the time.) There was also the question which inevitably occurred to all who remembered the Gallican tradition: Was the Pope entitled to give orders in matters of political allegiance? In a sense, the "liberal" Leo XIII was extending the field of operation of the authoritarian tradition of Pius IX. "Ultramontanism exerting itself in favour of the Republic", said *Le Temps* in July 1891 "is no less dangerous than ultramontanism directed against it." At some point the individual had to insist upon his own political judgement; for example, Mgr d'Hulst asked, what would happen if an order was given for everyone to become Royalists? When a secular regime called for allegiance, it got no more than it could verify—an external genuflexion; was it decent for spiritual authority to prescribe such an unspiritual formality on men whose hearts and aspirations lay elsewhere?

No "authorized voice" disowned the toast of Algiers. The

months went by and no authorized voice supported it either. Rome remained silent. "I will always go where the Pope wishes," wrote Eugène Veuillot to Lavigerie on 30 April 1891, "only I must be able to say he does wish it." Of the bishops,[1] only Isoard and Fuzet committed themselves to the Algiers pronouncement; Meignan and Foulon expressed sympathy, but not publicly. "Rabbits in mitres", said Lavigerie. In his cautious fashion Leo XIII gradually informed individuals of his true intentions; in May 1891 he published *Rerum novarum*, his great encyclical on social questions: finally, in February 1892 he came into the open in an interview with a French journalist. "Each individual may retain his personal preferences, but in the sphere of action there is only one government, the government which France has chosen for itself." Would the French Catholics obey? And if they did, would they be accepted into the Republic which, as Ferry told them, had "got along for twenty years without you and against you"?

[1] Guilbert, Archbishop of Bordeaux, had died on 15 August 1889.

9 From the Ralliement to the Dreyfus Case, 1893-99

"They call themselves *ralliés*: I call them *résignés*. They have learned something but they will be the first to recognize they have forgotten nothing. . . . I'm all for them submitting to the Republic: what I ask them is, will they defend it?" It was a searching question. There was a sort of moral ambiguity inherent in the whole idea of "rallying" to a democratically elected government. If, by showing deference to the Republic, conservative groups won a decisive electoral victory, could they then set in motion machinery to change the Constitution? Leo XIII seems to have regarded this secret hope as proper and inevitable. "If you follow my advice," he told Mgr de Cabrières, Bishop of Montpellier, in a private interview, "you will have 400 Catholic deputies in France and you'll establish the monarchy. I am a monarchist myself."[1] This is what the Republicans suspected all along, and since convictions cannot change overnight, how could things have been otherwise? Anticlericals made it clear they were determined not to be duped, and by so doing reinforced the belief of many Royalists that it was useless to rally anyway. Memories of old feuds kept returning. Tempers ran high during the last three months of 1891. A young pilgrim to Rome wrote *"Vive le pape!"* in the visitors' book at the tomb of Victor Emmanuel, the French government banned pilgrimages, the Archbishop of Aix protested and was fined by the courts, and the *Figaro* and the *Univers* raised a much larger sum by public subscription to compensate him. In September 1892, seven months after Leo XIII had declared himself, the Panama scandal broke. By November the country was reading details of the bribes paid to deputies and senators. So this was the Republic of the *ralliés*! *"Elle est belle, leur fiancée"*, said Cassagnac.

If Rome had supported Lavigerie immediately, things might have been different. As it was, for more than a year the Royalists had

[1] We only know of these words because the Bishop told a friend before the obligation of secrecy was imposed, and the friend, long afterwards, revealed what was said. (M. Bruyère, *Le Cardinal de Cabrières* (1956), p. 198.)

been free to decry the Ralliement as merely a personal campaign of
the Archbishop of Algiers, and to argue, as if the problem was
purely hypothetical, about the limits of the papal power to
command in political matters. Some of them had angrily—or
factitiously—reaffirmed their allegiance to the monarchist cause,
leaving no route of escape for themselves when the pontifical ruling
finally came. During this year, the French bishops had grown accustomed to keeping their heads down. In his memoirs, the *abbé*
Dabry, himself a Republican, was inclined to excuse them. "It is
always easier for a politician or a journalist to change his line",
he said, "than for the head of a diocese, who has responsibilities
and obligations and, like everyone exercising government, has to
take account of the wishes of the majority." The "obligations"
refer to the diocesan charities and other organizations dependent on
the good will of Royalist families. When Leo XIII published an
encyclical in French in February 1892, urging the faithful to
accept the established government, many bishops neglected to give
it publicity in their diocesan magazines. Some who did added dubious comments. "It only condemns systematic and insurrectional
opposition to the form of government", said the Bishop of Carcas-
sone. "We must obey, even when we do not understand", observed
the Cardinal Archbishop of Toulouse. "The blinder the submission,
the more meritorious."

If Constans had been plotting to divide the Catholics, he had
succeeded beyond all expectations. Faced with a conflict of duties
they split, sometimes along strange dividing lines. Deeply religious
Royalists such as Keller refused to obey the Pope, while ,cynical
politicians such as the *baron* de Mackau made a virtue of loyalty
to the Vatican. Of the two pious and honourable army officers
who had been leading the Social Catholic movement, Albert de
Mun followed Leo XIII's instructions and René de La Tour du Pin
did not. Eugène Veuillot rallied, taking the *Univers* with him; his
sister Élise, "the Iron Virgin", seceded and founded a new newspaper, *La Vérité française*. There were astonishing differences in
interpreting what "rallying" actually meant. In the Department of
the Nord, the news of the Panama scandal brought out the true
colours of the old Royalist newspapers which had proclaimed their
obedience to the Pope. "If your Republic is not founded on
integrity, let it perish!" said *La Vraie France*, the former Legitimist organ; on the contrary, "the Republic has nothing to do with
all this, ... the form of government is above and beyond these

scandals", said *La Dépêche,* mouthpiece of the Orléanist industrialists. Everywhere, the Catholic rank and file were in confusion. "I knew a convent of nuns", writes Paul-Boncour in his memoirs, "where simple souls prayed for the conversion of the Pope."

In so far as he had specific objectives within French politics, Leo XIII had dreamed of a strong Catholic contingent operating within a conservative bloc. These hopes were fading now. For the elections of 1893 the *ralliés* put ninety-four candidates in the field, mostly belonging to two new political groups led by Étienne Lamy, a sincere Catholic who had been a Republican deputy for fifteen years before the toast of Algiers, and Jacques Piou, the right-wing politician who had tried to found a new party of compromise, La Droite constitutionnelle. Though there were vague references to social reforms and to government by a homogeneous party of "order", the *ralliés* had no convincing programme, and on the burning subject of the laicizing education laws most of their candidates avoided expressing an opinion. Their strategy was to help Opportunists on the second ballot if their own candidate appeared unlikely to succeed, but the Opportunists rarely reciprocated. With old friends denouncing them as traitors and new allies lukewarm and silent, the *ralliés* had little hope of success. Only thirty-six of their number were elected, Piou, Lamy, and de Mun being defeated by Republicans. Many right-wing voters stayed away from the polls in despair, and the Republican share of the total vote rose from the 53% of 1889 to 82%. Even counting the *ralliés* as still belonging to the Right, the conservative groups had lost something like eighty seats. The great gainers from this débâcle were the Opportunists who, with more than 300 deputies returned, were now in a position to govern alone.

Governing alone meant moderate Republicans could now express their true attitude to the Church, free from anticlerical pressure from the Left or from the taint of complicity with the Right. It was important to conciliate the Catholics until the Panama scandal was lived down and the alliance with Russia consolidated. Something also had to be done to enlist conservative forces to confront the rising threat to property. Anarchist bombs exploded in the Chamber in December 1893. Forty-one Socialists had been returned at the elections, and Jaurès' warning was fresh in the memories of politicians: "You have torn the people away from the guidance of the Church. You have interrupted the age-old cradle song that lulled human misery, and human misery has reawakened, crying ...

demanding its . . . place in the . . . sunshine of the world." From the toast of Algiers Spuller had been urging his fellow-Republicans to make some welcoming gesture to the Catholics. Now, as Minister in charge of religious and educational affairs in the ministry of Casimir Périer, he proclaimed (3 March 1894) the end of petty anticlerical vexations and the beginning of a new and tolerant era. There was to be *"un esprit nouveau"*.

Brave ministerial declarations resound in the annals of the Third Republic; the question in the minds of the hearers was: How long can the minister last? The Opportunist majority was an agglomeration of individuals and groups rather than a party, and there was a steady desertion from its ranks towards the Left. This was how, from October 1895 to April 1896, a government of Radicals, supported by Socialists, could come to office under Léon Bourgeois; there were nine freemasons in the cabinet, including Émile Combes in charge of religious affairs and education. And before the Bourgeois ministry afforded this brief preview of disasters to come, the preceding Opportunist ministry of Ribot (March 1895) had provided an illustration of another threat to the *esprit nouveau*. The Royalists were waiting their chance to demonstrate to Catholics that Spuller's gesture of conciliation was a fraud. The Ribot government provided them with the issue they sought. It was a complex question of taxing religious congregations. Though the new *droit d'abonnement* took from them no more than 0.3% of the annual value of their possessions after charitable and missionary obligations had been covered, there was still a question of principle to be fought. Masonic lodges and other lay organizations were not being taxed, and a modest levy, once imposed, might be increased in future. The clerical newspapers (including the *Univers* until it began to suspect a plot against the Pope) and most of the bishops glowed with indignation, and the right-wing press fanned protest into a blaze. In *La Libre Parole* Drumont said that if he was allowed to spit only once in his life this would be the occasion: "My choice is made, I'd spit in the face of Ribot." Mgr Meignan sadly reflected on the folly of his episcopal colleagues who had allowed themselves to be drawn into such an agitation, throwing away the interests of the whole Church in defence of a part, like "the widows of Malabar who burn themselves on the funeral pyres of their husbands". The *ralliés* were miserably divided; five of their deputies voted with Ribot's government, thirteen against, eight abstained, and ten were, quite simply, on vacation. At the end of

1896, with the lessons of the *droit d'abonnement* and the Bourgeois ministry to look back to, the *abbé* Frémont noted in his diary that the initiative of Leo XIII had "almost entirely failed"; it was regarded as "a pontifical *boutade*", a whimsical folly which the next pope would surely disavow.

Frémont's judgement was based on the general course of events rather than on those of the last eight months, for in April 1896 the Bourgeois government had proposed a mild income tax law and had promptly been thrown out for pushing the country "into the antechamber of Communism". With the aid of the *ralliés* and, indeed, of a few Royalists, the moderate Republicans formed a ministry under Méline. A new tolerance towards the Church came in, together with tariffs, economy, and the abjuration of income tax; apart from legislation about industrial accidents, the ideas of social reform dear to some of the *ralliés* were set aside. It was a government in defence of property. "The Right is not voting with us," said Méline, "it is voting against a social revolution."

The new conservative alignment was tested by the 1898 elections. Leo XIII attempted to direct all Catholics into a sort of electoral federation. Étienne Lamy was given the task of bringing together the various newspapers, *La Croix* and *L'Univers*, *Le Peuple français* representing "Christian Democracy",[1] *Le Petit Moniteur* representing the Catholic Republicans, and so on. Two French monks were sent round the bishops with instructions from Rome to vote for Catholic candidates if they were sure to be returned, otherwise support should go to Méline. The algebraic logic of these instructions meant little to Catholic voters. They were being exhorted to play their part in an electoral bargain in which only one side had obligations, for the moderate Republicans had refused to promise any relaxation of the laicization laws and were suspected (rightly, as the correspondence of Méline's Minister of the Interior with the prefects shows) of being unwilling to encourage their voters to support candidates of the *ralliés*. In any case, the hatreds and prejudices of French local politics could hardly be overcome by political bargains in the metropolis. Accustomed to being swindled by deals in the corridors of the legislative assemblies, the voters were unwilling to accept the obligations of compromise in local affairs and at the ballot box. Lamy and Piou

---

[1] For Christian Democracy, see p. 94ff below.

could not give effective orders to their followers in the provinces—
nor could Méline to his.

Thus the politics of the Ralliement had little effect upon the elections of 1898. The existing balance was not dramatically altered.
About thirty-eight *ralliés* got in, the Right lost a dozen seats and
was left with a total of only forty-five, the Socialists gained five
and the moderate Republicans were reduced to 250 or so. Arith-
metically, government by a conservative coalition was still possible,
but psychologically, this was now out of the question. As Poincaré
warned Méline on 20 May 1899, he was in danger of becoming "a
prisoner of a reactionary coalition". The trend of the election
results was ominous. The Opportunists felt they had had enough of
risky dalliance with the Right and the Ralliement. Méline was overthrown, the Chamber resolving that future ministries must be supported by "exclusively Republican majorities".

As a political manoeuvre the Ralliement had failed. If the object
had been, as one of its indiscreet clerical exponents declared, to
board the Republican train with the hope of taking over control
from the engine driver, the scheme had been a fiasco from the
start. If the object had been the more limited one of introducing
the Catholics into a broad conservative bloc to restrain the
Republic from warfare against religion, the collapse of the Méline
ministry marked the end of the dream. Had propitious times
ensued, the experiment might have been renewed, but on 13
January 1898 Clemenceau's newspaper *L'Aurore* published Zola's
J'accuse, and the hopes of conciliation between Catholics and
moderate Republicans vanished in the bitterness of the Dreyfus
Affair.

Yet, while the Ralliement meant different things to different
people, to Leo XIII, its originator and inspirer, these calculations of
immediate political benefits could only have been secondary. He
was forcing upon Catholics the acknowledgement, in practical
terms, of a doctrine already well established in theory—all forms of
government are legitimate so long as they preserve order, respect
morals, and allow the Church reasonable liberty to fulfil its mission.
The immediate conversion of a majority of Catholic Royalists into
Republicans was neither possible nor credible, and by 1898 the
Railliement as a short-term expedient was manifestly a failure.
But Leo XIII had kept the way open for the future; he was thinking
of Catholic participation in French politics two or three generations
ahead. The success of the Ralliement is to be judged, not in terms

of the collapse of Méline, but in terms of Briand's conciliatory gestures in the middle 1920s, and of the contribution of the MRP to French political life after the Second World War. A still more daring interpretation of Leo XIII's motives was suggested by Spuller in an article in the *Revue de Paris* in February 1896, "Has the policy of Leo XIII failed?" The Pope's aims, said Spuller, were not those of the French *ralliés*; he was thinking of all nations, not just France, and of the whole future of the Universal Church. Essentially, he was planning a readjustment of the Church to the aspirations of the future, more especially to the growing and foreseeable demand for social justice. When La Mennais had prophesied the advent of a pope who would lead the Christian nations to new destinies, the young Joachim Pecci had been in Rome preparing his theological doctorate; as Pope Leo XIII half a century later he was steering the Church in the direction La Mennais had indicated.

10 The Church and
the Social Problem

Between Leo XIII and La Mennais two major Parisian insurrec-
tions, massively and mindlessly suppressed, had intervened. The
first of these, the rising of the June Days of 1848, had destroyed
the nascent Social Catholic movement in France by the terror it
inspired among *bourgeoisie*, peasantry, and the possessing classes
generally. But the argument from fear is ambiguous. When the
shooting is over, apprehension may sharpen the zeal of reformers,
rather than setting their faces like flint against all change; more
nobly, the sight of misery in abject defeat may touch the conscience
of the victors with a shadow of personal involvement and
guilt. This is what happened to *comte* Albert de Mun, an aristocratic cavalry officer who was with his troops at Versailles when the
Communard prisoners were brought in. He never forgot how one
of them, dying, cursed the defenders of order—*"Les insurgés, c'est
vous!"* The accusation seemed to echo across an abyss, from
another world. It was the beginning of his "social vocation". In
truth, de Mun and his friend René de La Tour du Pin, both deeply
pious Catholics, had already studied the doctrines of German Social
Catholicism while prisoners of war at Aix-la-Chapelle. But it took
the horrors of the Commune to reveal to them the stark realities of
the underworld of industrialism. Amid the debris of civil war they
saw the guilt of their own class, and clear evidence of the alienation
of the urban workers from the Church. The lesson was driven
home by Maurice Maignen, a priest who ran a club for boys in
the slums, the Cercle Montparnasse. When the two officers called
on him as part of their military duties (investigating the origin of
the Commune for the military governor of Paris), Maignen pointed
them to the blackened ruins of the Tuileries outside his office
windows.

> You yourselves are really responsible [he said], the rich, the
> great, the successful who amused themselves so lightheartedly
> within those broken walls, who passed by the people without

seeing them, without knowing them, who know nothing of their souls, their needs, their sufferings. I live with the people and on their behalf I can tell you that they don't hate you; it's simply that they have no contact with you nor you with them. Go to them with your heart open. . . .

On the following Sunday the youths of Maignen's Cercle Montparnasse gaped at the tall handsome officer in the light blue uniform with silver shoulder knots who had come to meet the people. Social Catholicism was reborn in France.

"Il va au peuple: jamais il ne sera peuple lui-même", said Marc Sangnier—"he goes to the people, but he will never be one of them". De Mun always remained an aristocrat and (though he resigned his commission in 1875) an army officer by temperament. While the Œuvre des Cercles Catholiques d'Ouvriers which he founded had a yearly general assembly, it was oligarchically directed, all power resting in the hands of a general committee of nine which recruited itself by co-option. The workers who joined were treated as the worthy members of a necessarily inferior class, equal no doubt in the eyes of God, but not in the affairs of society. They were to be helped and guided as if they were children. The original prospectus laid down the basis of the movement as "the devotion of the directing class (*la classe dirigeante*) to the working class". Each Circle of the Œuvre had a committee of the "directing class", very often consisting of aristocrats or army officers, which provided a club for workers and ruled over it through the supervisors and chaplain it appointed. There was no question of bringing the workers into partnership; in 1877 the committee of Avalon was censured by headquarters because it allowed the official *Bulletin* of the Œuvre to circulate among them.

In retrospect, it is easy to ridicule this paternalistic institution and its network of clubs in tutelage, what Floquet called "convents of workers". The charades, concerts, gymnastics, billiards, and visits to places of interest provided by the Circles did not attract the militant industrial workers wanting help to fight the factory owner; the applicants who queued at Paris at the four Sunday roll calls for free tombola tickets were, often as not, young men fresh from the provinces who were there on the suggestion of their parish priests back home; the influence of the duchesses and baronesses of the auxiliary organization of the Dames Patronnesses did not extend beyond the fashion trades and the big department stores of the capital. Yet the simple alleviation of misery, even if there are no long-term reforming consequences, is worth more attention from historians than it commonly receives. The intervention of titled ladies helped to spare seamstresses from working at nights and on Sundays, to speed up the payment of bills by careless socialities, and to have stools provided for shop girls to sit down while on duty; the Circles provided companionship and distraction for young men alone in big cities. No doubt the "directing class" should not have been spoken of so openly and so obviously been put in charge, but de Mun had at least set up machinery to bring the rich into touch with the urban poor. In this way he passed on to the privileged the lesson he himself had learned from the *abbé* Maignen, and from the work of his Circles begins a deeper understanding of the social evils of industrialism among the Catholics of France.

The Œuvre des Cercles gave no encouragement to industrial employees to league together to fight their own battles. *Noblesse oblige,* Albert de Mun devoted his life to fighting those battles himself. From 1881 to his death he was a member of the Chamber of Deputies and, after Jaurès, its greatest orator. In the Chamber he supported (not always successfully) the principle of international labour legislation, insurance against industrial accident, unemployment benefit, old age pensions, and limitations on the hours of work of women and children. His most famous speeches gain something of their force and pathos from the precise information gathered by the network of the Circles and, more especially, by the Dames Patronnesses—about the flower seller who died because she had to work immediately after her child was born, about the *veillée,* the vicious system of compelling women to work on all night in the factory without previous warning. The Socialists ridiculed de Mun as the embodiment of what Marx had called "feudal socialism", but they admitted his sincerity and admired him as a man. Yet admiration did not mitigate their anticlericalism. It was not Catholicism or, indeed, Social Catholicism that was spoken of in the corridors of the Chamber, but "the ideas of M. de Mun".

In 1873, at a pilgrimage of the Circles, to de Mun's rage, an uninvited delegation turned up complete with band and led by a massive, bald-headed plebeian figure. This was the beginning of friendship and collaboration between the aristocratic founder of the Œuvre and Léon Harmel, owner of a successful spinning factory at Val-des-Bois, near Warmériville, in the Department of the Ardennes. The workers here were the most fortunate in France. Already they had a savings bank, a co-operative society, medical aid, and other amenities organized by the management; shortly they were to have a factory council of elected workers and a system of supplementation of wages for big families. "A simple visionary," Viviani the Socialist was to say of the master of Val-des-Bois, "but if all the owners acted as he did, the social problem would become insignificant." Harmel's main contribution to Social Catholicism was the realization that paternalism was not enough; the workers must be helped to form their own organizations. "Simple philanthropy", he said, "ends in hatred." Within the Œuvre des Cercles he pressed for a degree of autonomy for the working class groups, and on his tours round France he managed to extend the activities of the Circles in some places by setting up employment exchanges and medical advice bureaux. When the Association Catholique des Patrons du Nord was founded in 1884, Harmel urged his fellow factory owners to reconsider their policy of *syndicats mixtes* (trade unions consisting of both owners and workers); in the end, he predicted, the workers would reject tutelage and would insist on using their full power of collective bargaining. After the law of 1884 legalizing trade unions, Catholic groups in various parts of the country did indeed form *syndicats* of workers alone. Harmel himself led the way in Champagne, Gailhard Bancel formed agricultural groups in the south-east under the banner of *Cruce et aratro*, the Catholic minority among the silk workers of Lyon set up their own organization, and the Frères des Écoles Chrétiennes founded a union of "employees in commerce and industry" in Paris. The power of Christian trade unions, however, was necessarily limited. The mass of workers did not join, and if they had, the unions would have been no longer Christian.

In politics, de Mun was a Legitimist. But whatever the nature of the government, he believed the State had a duty to intervene to help the working classes; as Lacordaire had said, "In the domain of labour it is liberty that oppresses, and the law which sets free". Most of the deputies of the Right voted against the law of 1891 limiting the hours of work of women and children, Mgr Freppel, Bishop of Angers, who was one of them, arguing that owners and workers were bound together by a "contract of wages" freely entered into. To this de Mun replied by denying the existence of freedom in the relationship; it was a contract of serfdom, and the public authorities therefore had to protect the serfs against the caprice of their masters. La Tour du Pin, the theorist of the Œuvre, listed the basic rights to be guaranteed—a living wage for the whole family, opportunity for promotion, a chance to save, security against unemployment and in old age, and a share in the profits of the enterprise. From 1884 he was recommending these ideas to meetings of Social Catholics from Germany and elsewhere held at Fribourg, and in 1885, the "Union de Fribourg" formally condemned the doctrine of *laissez-faire*. During the next five years the idea of State intervention won wide support among Catholics: in 1890 a congress at Liège welcomed the idea with acclamation. When Mgr Freppel (who in his own individualist fashion was a social reformer) held a counter-congress at Angers to support the limitation of State action to the prevention of abuses, La Tour du Pin and his colleagues of the Œuvre des Cercles contemptuously refused to attend to debate such a futile proposition—"You don't shoot at ambulances".

Ideally, the State intervening to help the workers would be the monarchy of Henry V, not the Republic of Jules Grévy, and in the theories of La Tour du Pin the monarchical regime of the future would dispense with the crude electoral machinery of democracy in favour of representation through a system of "corporations". From the example of Val-des-Bois he took the idea of partnership in industry, while rejecting Harmel's argument in favour of trade unions of employees, since they could too easily become instruments of class warfare. In their place he proposed local combinations of owners and workers within a single industry, federating together finally into a great national corporation. Disputes between management and labour would be settled by a "committee of honour" drawn from *la classe dirigeante*. These proposals were a blend of the practice of the Catholic factory owners of the Nord and of the aristocrats of the Œuvre des Cercles. By the time of Albert de Mun's "Counter-Centenary of the Revolution" the idea had broadened into a comprehensive political theory. Corporations would become the modern equivalent of the Orders of the *ancien régime,* and would reflect the true interests of the people as against the distorted image produced by the meretricious democratic process. True, such a corporate State would represent the basic economic interests of each group at the expense of depriving them of a say in broad issues of national politics; in the eyes of Legitimists this was no disadvantage. In practice, de Mun's "Estates General" of corporations meeting at

Paris in 1889 was a fiasco; at least, the workers showed no interest. But in the following year the corporative regime was accepted by the Fribourg group as the only arrangement "in which the representation of all interests can be ensured", and in various forms, respectable and sinister, it was to play a part in the political theory of the future.

Reports of the Fribourg discussions were followed attentively at the Vatican. Leo XIII had seen the evils of the new industrialism as nuncio in Belgium, and the poverty of the old peasant society as a diocesan bishop in Italy; a reader of foreign newspapers, he was aware of economic depression creeping over western Europe in the late 1880s, bringing a new harshness into the lot of the industrial worker. From the writings of French and German Social Catholics he had followed the rise of new currents of thought and idealism within the Church, and he was aware, too, of the divergencies of opinion they had caused in ecclesiastical circles. More especially he was concerned about the division of the French clergy on the issue of State intervention, and about the resentment some of them harboured against the dominating influence of the laymen of the headquarters of the Œuvre des Cercles. For both humanitarian and institutional reasons some pronouncement was required. The final decision to issue an encyclical owed much to Léon Harmel. With the naive directness of the honest business man, he organized mass pilgrimages to the Vatican; no fewer than 10,000 workers poured into Rome from their special trains in October 1889. The Pope was impressed and moved by these massive demonstrations. *Rerum novarum,* he was to say, was "the recompense for the workers' pilgrimages".

In this great encyclical, *Rerum novarum* (1891), Leo XIII condemned both economic liberalism and Socialism. Unprotected, the workers have been left to fall into an "undeserved misery" very close to slavery. As a remedy Socialism is as deadly as the disease, for it thrives on hatreds and denies the beneficial, civilizing influence of private property. In a well-organized society the classes are not "born enemies", for owners and employees ought to recognize reciprocal duties. One remedy for the ills of the age lay in the formation of Christian associations, whether of owners and workers in combination, or of workers by themselves. This reference to the possibility of independent organization by the workers was of the utmost importance, and the crucial phrase, "whether composed of workers alone, or mixed", absent from the earlier drafts, had been added by the Pope himself. Another remedy, of more immediate importance, lay in intervention by the State. The secular power had a duty, not only to keep order (for example, during strikes) but also to ensure distributive justice and to protect the weak. Thus the conditions of labour ought to be supervised by public authority, and the payment of a just wage—just meaning commensurate with the workers' needs—ought to be enforced.

Pronouncements on the social order which have to be accepted by all shades of opinion and social groups within the Church and are vested with the aura of infallibility must, necessarily, be balanced and counter-balanced, colourless. *Rerum novarum,* a towering landmark in Catholic thought, is no exception—it is a cautious document. From the conservative side, Leroy-Beaulieu in the *Revue des Deux Mondes* blandly maintained that the Pope was essentially championing private property and the principle that "social inequalities are a law of Providence", while the accompanying condemnations of opulence were but "commonplaces of ecclesiastical eloquence". Georges Goyau, under the pseudonym "Léon Grégoire", wrote a stinging reply in his *Le Pape, les Catholiques et la question sociale* (1893). The Pope, he said, was inviting the oppressed to protest and was calling on the State to exercise compulsion; he was no longer recommending the established principle of almsgiving, but was demanding justice. Both interpretations were one-sided, Leroy-Beaulieu's unreasonably so. The leaders of the Œuvre des Cercles, reading the carefully chosen phraseology of *Rerum novarum* with the insight of complicity, were delighted to hear Rome speaking for their side of the debate and uncompromisingly taking the interventionist point of view. On the other hand, some regretted the limitations of the encyclical. As La Tour du Pin noted, nothing was said about profit sharing; he also asked for clarification about the family needs of the worker, and was displeased when Cardinal Zigliara ruled the basic wage itself to be a matter of justice, the extra to support a family being a matter of charity. Perhaps there is significance in the bias of the over-free translation of a phrase in the French version of *Rerum novarum* issued by the Œuvre: instead of the State "surrounding" the workers "with care and solicitude", it becomes no less than their mortal "providence".

Cautious document as it is, *Rerum novarum* looks out towards vast horizons and forward to a distant future. At one blow it ended the secret assumption of so many propertied Christians that almsgiving was a sufficient ransom to pay for personal comfort. Properly read from the point of view of personal obligation, it implied a duty of participation in organized action to improve social conditions and to use political means to ensure State action on behalf of the underprivileged classes. In the long run it contributed to a transformation of the idea of Christian duty that still has far to go, and to a change of emphasis in the strategy of Christian evangelism. In the short run, so far as political tactics were concerned there was no gain and, perhaps, none was expected. The proclamation of the Ralliement had not persuaded a majority of French Catholics to abandon their Royalist hopes; *Rerum novarum* did not persuade a majority to abandon the comfortable paths of economic liberalism. Those who deplored the decision of the Pope on the political issue were, often enough, inclined to take the opportunity to encourage dissatisfaction against his ruling in social affairs; those who were glad to note the limitations of the encyclical lay in wait for the opportunity to enforce them against Social Catholics who welcomed it too enthusiastically. There was some defiance of Leo XIII's views, and a great deal of non-cooperative acceptance.

From this point the Œuvre des Cercles declined. The inclusion of the basic principles of de Mun's programme in *Rerum novarum* left less to fight for, and disputes about its meaning involved battles about less useful and less inspiring issues. The Ralliement had dealt the whole enterprise a deadly blow. La Tour du Pin and many others refused to relinquish their monarchist convictions, while de Mun and Harmel rallied. But even before this there had been signs of division. Harmel and the Christian industrialists rejected La Tour du Pin's proposal for a "family salary" as impractical. Some supplement as given at Val-des-Bois was possible, but the full application of the principle of need to wages would bankrupt the firms which failed to give priority in employment to bachelors and spinsters. There were difficulties too about the idea of profit sharing: no satisfactory answer was forthcoming about sharing the losses. "We are dying of theory," Albert de Mun complained, "we have become too learned; the influence of La Tour du Pin has ruined the Œuvre, his philosophical speculations have made it lose sight of its true line of action. We are fading away into smoke." To counteract the plague of theory, in 1890 de Mun deprived the journal of his organization, *L'Association Catholique*, of its official standing; henceforward La Tour du Pin's articles in its pages would simply be the expression of the opinions of a private individual. While disputes over theory and politics racked the headquarters of the Œuvre, the mass of the working class remained aloof. De Mun had become a leader before he had a programme, and when his programme was produced it turned out to be reactionary. The celebration of the counter-centenary of the Revolution in 1889 made him appear a quixotic distant figure, a "knight of the Syllabus", a *grand seigneur* who loved the poor rather than the workers' alternative to socialism.

As a political force, the French Catholics were divided by the policies of Leo XIII; as a spiritual force, they were strengthened by the rich diversity of initiatives, often ephemeral, but sincere and original, which *Rerum novarum* evoked. *"Catholicisme social"*, "Social Catholicism" now became the respectable title of a respectable movement. Before the encyclical the usual designation had been *"socialisme chrétien"*, which contained a censure in the noun and some evasion of Catholic responsibility in the adjective. The papal declaration was, above all, a challenge to the clergy, for it could be cited against those who stuck to parochial and diocesan routine and denounced innovations. An association of *prêtres ouvriers* was founded and won 400 adherents, though the priests concerned did not actually take up employment in the factories like the worker priests of the twentieth century. The Association Catholique des Patrons du Nord pressed on with the formation of the *syndicats mixtes*—by 1895 there were 177 such trade unions in France, with a total of nearly 30,000 members. A group of Christian industrialists founded the Union fraternelle du Commerce et de l'Industrie to reform commercial morality by buying only from firms recommended in an annual report. Owing to his son's death Harmel now had to spend most of his time at his factory, but he reappeared occasionally at these fraternal union meetings, looking into the hats of members to see if they had been bought from a recommended shop. Before the encyclical the Capuchin Ludovic de Besse had started banks of "popular credit". His example (though his own banks eventually failed) and that of the Catholic lending societies of the Rhineland and Westphalia encouraged the formation of mutual credit societies among the Catholic peasantry of France.

As the Œuvre des Cercles declined, Albert de Mun sought new fields of endeavour. In the course of 1885 he lectured to Belgian students at Louvain, and to Swiss youth at Fribourg, and was inspired by the enthusiasm and receptivity of his audiences; when in November the Vatican ordered him to wind up his short-lived attempt to found a political party, he turned his heroic creativity to winning young men in the colleges and universities into a new movement allied to the waning Œuvre des Cercles. Early in 1886 he founded the Association Catholique de la Jeunesse Française (ACJF), the first number of its *Bulletin* appearing in May, with the motto, "piety, study, action". Study was the operative word: in its first years the movement consisted essentially of students, who fortified their religious beliefs in annual retreats and monthly corporate communions, and organized study groups on the Christian's duty to society. But in 1896 the Federal Council of the ACJF decided to widen membership; the Association, it declared, "is open in principle to all young Catholics who are capable of exercising a degree of influence on those around them". Strictly speaking, the words implied a certain restriction to "notables", and two years later the president of the Association admitted that it was, as yet, impossible to have workers and students sharing the same congresses. Yet in practice, over the next few years, recruits flowed in from the peasantry and, to a smaller degree, from the urban working classes. In sincere, though quaintly patronizing terms, the *Revue de l'ACJF* in 1900 welcomed

> our friends . . .[who] handle tools or the plough, and come to our congresses in the picturesque costumes of peasants or miners; . . . composed as we are of thinkers, writers, orators, peasants— workers all—the Association is a force, because it is broadly based, and embraces all professions and all social conditions; deep-rooted too, since it reaches the workers in the countryside, the very foundation of our race.

By then the movement was in rapid expansion; within the next five years membership increased to 60,000—organized into 1,400 federated groups, most of them "popular" in composition.

Any movement founded by de Mun would necessarily be "social" in character. The study groups and news-sheets of the ACJF were filled with problems of wages and arbitration, strikes and industrial legislation. These discussions, disparate and platonic, became co-ordinated and vigorous when Henri Bazire (inventor of the famous phrase, *"Sociaux parceque Catholiques"*) became president in 1899. In 1903 the annual congress was held at Chalon-sur-Saône, a centre of industrial unrest, the subject for study being trades unions, and the final resolutions supporting the right of the workers to form their own independent professional organizations. The Arras congress of the following year was devoted to the study of mutual assistance societies, and the Albi congress of 1905 gathered grim information about the vicious over-working of young people in shops and bakeries. Naive and direct, the social propaganda of the Catholic youth movement was manifestly sincere; even so, its peculiar intensity owed something to the political situation as the final crisis of Church and State drew nearer. "This coincidence between the present persecutions and our social labours has not been sought by us," said the *Revue de l'ACJF* in 1903, "but we accept it as a symbol and welcome it with enthusiasm".

It was in the Association Catholique de la Jeunesse Française rather than in the Œuvre des Cercles that de Mun's social ideas became widely influential. The young men of the Federal Council of the ACJF had minds of their own. They revered their founder and consulted him, they accepted Jesuits in the office of their "chaplain-director", and they were deferential to the ecclesiastical hierarchy. Yet they insisted on making their own decisions. The chaplain-director gave direction in the sense of spiritual guidance, not orders; the bishops did not devise policy, they merely gave permission for the existence of ACJF groups in their diocese: Albert de Mun was a friend, not a master. Under the energetic presidency of Bazire, Jean Lerolle (1904–9), and Pierre Gerlier (1909–13), they broke through diocesan particularism and built "the first organization of national dimensions in the history of French Catholicism" (Latreille). It was first in another respect too, for the Federal Council's quiet assumption of lay control eventually, in 1907, won from Rome a significant letter of authorization—"the first pontifical document", says Molette, "that can be considered as a 'charter of the laity' ". The independent discussion of social problems sponsored by the leaders of the ACJF caught up Albert de Mun himself in their enthusiasms and swept him leftwards; at congresses he would be heard interjecting such remarks as "the Church is not a policeman in the service of *bourgeois* society". And the adoption of social ideas by a growing, self-governing youth movement constituted a revolution in the history of Social Catholicism. In the pioneering days of the Œuvre des Cercles, people had spoken commonly of "the ideas of M. de Mun", as if they constituted an individual idiosyncracy independent of the Church; but in the ACJF, the personal connection faded out, and de Mun's ideas became, in

Goyau's phrase, "an anonymous consequence of the Christian *credo*".

This was the psychological breakthrough needed to bring the ideals of *Rerum novarum* into wide acceptance among the Catholic laity, up to now, so generally unresponsive. In August 1903 La Tour du Pin, in the pages of the *Association Catholique*, complained of "the great ignorance and invincible antipathy" of French Catholics to the social problem; of ninety episcopal pastoral letters each year, only one would touch on it; apart from de Mun, Catholic deputies and senators "avoid it like sin itself"; only two Catholic professors of law and political economy and only four or five Catholic publicists show interest; while preachers and lecturers "find a thousand more agreeable or more interesting subjects than this immediate question of life or death for society". In his dedicated pessimism, La Tour du Pin was overlooking the ACJF congress at Chalon three months earlier; he was not to know that it was the beginning of a long process of study and propaganda within the Church by its younger members, infinitely more effective than the pamphlets of socially-minded priests or the much misunderstood devotion of "*la classe dirigeante*" to the workers.

De Mun's apostolate to youth was aided by the rise of a new phenomenon in literature, the Social Catholic novel. To the descriptions of the sordid conditions in industry common in the realistic novelists, René Bazin brought something of the insight and pathos of Christian involvement. In *De toute son âme* (1897), the story of the illegitimate daughter of an industrialist brought up in the household of a crippled worker, there is a grim account of a *veillée* that equals de Mun's. A new ideal of the parish priest, immersed in social works and mediating hazardously between capital and labour, is given in Fonsegrive's novels, *Lettres d'un curé de campagne* (1893) and *Lettres d'un curé de canton* (1895), volumes approved by Leo XIII and crowned by the French Academy. Other writers produced less subtle novels of this kind, didactic exposures of iniquities in society and of the obligation of Christian intervention. To Léon Bloy almost everything others wrote on the social question smacked of condescension. With the blinding, distorting lucidity only mental disequilibrium can achieve, he stripped his fellow-Catholics of every rag of self-respect, until in the end he spoke as if he had forgotten God's forgiveness. Like Baudelaire he was obsessed with the sordid and unbalanced by compassion. The poor belong to God in a special way: like the dying thief, they enter Paradise *today*. To serve them is so much a duty that it ceases to be praiseworthy, for "poverty is the very face of Christ, the Face that was spit upon, that put to flight the Prince of this World". Bloy expected God to strike the rich, even when comparatively virtuously engaged. "The small number of victims limited my joy", he wrote of those who perished in the Charity Bazaar fire of 1897. "At last, I thought, AT LAST, here are the beginnings of justice." No one has pilloried the hypocrisy of respectable Christians more harshly. The realism of Harmel, the soldierly directness of de Mun, the logic of La Tour du Pin, Leo XIII's politic initiatives, and the charity of all of them are far removed from the world of Léon Bloy. In him we see the confrontation of hatred that Socialism found in the class struggle, a new kind of hatred, elevated into the sphere of spirituality.

Bloy brought to an extreme, intolerable conclusion the central theme of the Social Catholic movement—justice. In 1877 La Tour du Pin, at that time military attaché in Vienna, had still thought the central theme was charity; he had said so in the presence of two princes, illustrious adornments of the German Social Catholic movement, and they had turned their backs on him. With all its caution, *Rerum novarum* gave priority to justice, and at a congress in Lyon in 1896 Harmel rose to confute Louis Durand:

> DURAND It is in the name of charity that we go to the people.
> HARMEL It must be in the name of justice.

The encyclical also validated Harmel's other favourite doctrine, one closely allied to the first: the necessity for the workers to run their own affairs and fight their own battles. These two themes, justice and autonomy, were to form the basis of a new movement, fissiparous yet united forcefully in intention, full of life yet doomed to be short-lived, *La Démocratie Chrétienne,* Christian Democracy.

11 "La Démocratie Chrétienne" and "Le Sillon"

The new venture began in Reims, after a visit from Harmel to explain *Rerum novarum* to the workers. Robert, a locksmith who had become disillusioned with Socialism, was the leader of a deputation which called on the *curé* of Saint-Rémy to ask him for help in founding an organization free from the patronage of the upper classes and independent of the professional politicians who "use the workers as an electoral spring-board". A group was established, similar groups sprang up over northern, eastern, and western France, and congresses of the movement were held at Reims in 1893, 1894, and 1896. The first two called themselves congresses of "Christian workers", while the third adopted the new title, *"Congrès démocratie chrétienne"*, and decided to form a party of this name, restricting membership to "those who are, or who have been wage-earners". Further congresses were held at Lyon in this same year 1896 and in the two following years. At the Lyon meeting of 1897 the party, "Christian Democracy", was formally constituted under the control of a Grand National Council. The original intention, to restrict membership to wage earners, was dropped in deference to the catholicity of Catholicism, and the Grand Council was divided into three sections—one of intellectuals (in which Harmel was included), one of workers, and one of ecclesiastics. The only way for the old *classe dirigeante* to raise its head would be to qualify, with Harmel, among the intellectuals.

The tripartite division of the Council reflected the change that had come over the movement in the short time since its inception. Christian Democracy had become a meeting ground for diverse groups and personalities inspired by the Ralliement and *Rerum novarum,* and obscurely conscious of their role as a new "left" within Catholicism. There were arresting, original figures among its clergy—the *abbé* Garnier, editor of *Le Peuple Français,* a huge Norman priest who had once been a papal *zouave,* the only man of his time, it was said, who could walk into the Vatican for an audience without an appointment; the *abbé* Naudet, editor of *La*

Justice Sociale and author of the famous saying: "Paradise! I want to give it to people now while they are waiting for the other one"; the *abbé* Lemire, a member of the Chamber of Deputies, where he pressed for social reform with masterly skill, restricting himself to non-religious arguments. Lemire, who was to be the most effective of the leaders of Christian Democracy, in his own person united the various progressive tendencies in Catholicism. Once a Legitimist, he now wished to reconcile the Church to the Republic; he would even have his fellow-Catholics accept the lay school and collaborate with the State schoolmasters. His social Catholicism was inspired by an idyllic dream derived from the myth of the Garden of Eden and his peasant ancestry: he wished to humanize industrial society by promoting "workers' gardens" and by encouraging family solidarity. His election in 1893 to the Chamber of Deputies by the Flanders constituency of Hazebrouck (an area of fervent religious practice), in the teeth of his Archbishop's disapproval and the competition of a distinguished candidate of the Ralliement, was a symbol of the revolt of the lower clergy against the ecclesiastical hierarchy and the great Catholic notables. Goyau rejoiced at his success: "You are going to represent in our Legislative assemblies an element which for long has been banished from them, the democratic clergy."

The first Lyon Congress of 1896 reflects the confusing diversity of elements coming together to form Christian Democracy. There were three congresses entangled with each other. One was the *abbé* Garnier's personal following, another was the social congress proper, presided over by Harmel and inspired by the *abbé* Lemire, and another was organized by Mouthon, the young editor of a local newspaper called *La France Libre*. This paper, "Popular, Republican, Catholic", advocated an advanced social policy, but also imitated Drumont's *La Libre Parole* in antisemitism, its title page bearing the legend "France for the French" alongside "Christ and Liberty". Mgr Couillé, Archbishop of Lyon, refused to take part in the congress because of its connection with *La France Libre,* but the Pope, unaware of these complexities, sent Harmel his blessing. For his part, Harmel attended all branches of the meetings and spoke at one of them about the war "against the Triple Alliance of the interior, the Masonic, Jewish, and Protestant coalition". Fortunately, the specialists in antisemitism were absent from the next Lyon gathering of 1897, Mgr (now Cardinal) Couillé and a number of bishops gave their approval, and Fonsegrive and

Georges Goyau were present, enabling Christian Democracy to be finally constituted under respectable auspices. Antisemitism, however, had become embedded in its programme, so that the next Lyon congress was disowned by the *abbé* Lemire and Cardinal Couillé.

"Programme" is too formal a word to use in connection with Christian Democracy. There were too many little newspapers and too many big personalities in the movement for a single statement of aims to win general acceptance. The congresses all declared their political allegiance as Republican, but they looked forward to changes in the spirit of government. "Long live the French and Catholic Republic", said the Catholic Workers Committee of Brest in 1894. "Down with the Jewish and Masonic Republic!" At the Lyon gathering of 1897, Goyau's report, "In Search of the National Will", met with much approval; it contained La Tour du Pin's corporations and proposals for proportional representation and the referendum, devices calculated to protect minorities against the tyranny of parliamentary majorities. On one point above all, there was universal agreement in the movement: the objective of social policy, directly pursued by the government, was to be the achievement of true equality. "Though natural inequality is a fact," said Naudet, "social equality is just as much a right". Private property is consecrated by the rulings of the Church, but small property only is meant, and its owners have heavy responsibilities. At Lyon in 1896 the *abbé* Tartelin condemned capitalism altogether, on the ground that financial resources are not property in the Church's sense, and in the following year, supported by Naudet, he called for the condemnation of all lending at interest. The workers, in search of economic equality, must refuse to accept inferior status; they must form their own unions and run their own affairs. The Reims congress of 1894 went so far as to accept mutual distrust between owners and workers as inevitable: "however generous the one or resigned the other, they are rivals", and the third congress of Reims two years later categorically condemned the "mixed" trades unions of the northern factory owners. *La classe dirigeante* was finished. In *La Justice Sociale* (5 August 1893) Harmel wrote its epitaph. "There are now only two social forces: the clergy and the working people; by uniting them we are preparing the way for the society of the future.... As for the well-off classes, paganism and self-indulgence have reduced them to impotence." Yet nobody recommended violence. The committee of Brest wanted "pacific reforms. We'll never obtain anything except by clearly formulated demands on the part of the workers whose justice good employers will be able to recognize." The demands formulated at congresses were of this kind—the ten-hour day, no night work, Sunday rest, insurance against accident, equally balanced committees of management and men to settle disputes.

Social Catholicism spoke of the Church's duty to transform society; Christian Democracy was original in so far as some of its members—in a hesitant fashion—suggested a transformation beginning with the Church. Here and there in its prolific journalism come suggestions for modifying the hierarchical ecclesiastical structure, simplifying the liturgy, making sermons homely, encouraging priests to earn their own living by working at secular trades, or to go out to give leadership to the world as journalists, economists, scientists, and politicians. A local newspaper of the movement proposed close co-operation with all other Christians in a "non-confessional Christian party", and in 1899 the *abbé* Garnier invented the phrase "non-confessional Catholics", by which he meant those who had no intention of seeking predominance or favour for their own religion and welcomed working with men of good will of other persuasions. These attempts to break down exclusivity were related to the optimistic attitude to the modern world prevailing among supporters of Christian Democracy. Where other Catholics saw the forces of free thought and anticlericalism massing to attack the beleagured Church, they saw all around them people "less supernaturally Christian", maybe, but "more naturally so".

The world has never been more naturally Christian, [said one of their newspapers, *L'Indépendant de la Somme* (19 July 1894)]. Those who live without the Church, oblivious to it yet following its morality, upright souls who strive, outside the boundaries of formal dogma, to remake a sort of sentimental Christianity—all these, without knowing it, are wrapped like a new-born child in the swaddling clothes of the Gospels.

This generous attitude to other faiths and virtuous humanists, and the proposals occasionally put forward for change within the Church itself, were unwelcome to many clergy. The pulpits had so long resounded with condemnations of class warfare that it was not easy for preachers to think in terms of a single class being entitled to organize to defend its rights. Providence was still invoked as an excuse for reaction. According to a Jesuit chaplain of the northern industrialists (in a sermon in 1893) men ought to pray to God for their daily bread rather than tampering with the contracts between employers and employees. Some of the bishops were hostile, and sometimes for good reasons; after his second skirmish with the antisemites, Cardinal Couillé forbade his priests to join Christian Democracy. The successive newspapers of the movement in the diocese of Nancy—*La Croix de l'Est, Le Bulletin de l'Union Catholique de Meurthe-et-Moselle,* and *La Croix de Nancy* were suppressed by Mgr Turinaz. Irresponsibly vigorous, hydra-headed, with no official spokesmen among the ecclesiastical dignitaries, Christian Democracy was calculated to arouse apprehensions among conservative churchmen everywhere. Its central command was incapable either of allaying fears or of organizing to fight. Paris was the home of its chief journalists, but workers could not come up from the provinces for frequent committee meetings. The rank-and-file membership fell into peculiar ideological groups according to which of the numerous newspapers they followed. In theory, most members were factory workers; in practice, there were numerous artisans—the bureau of the Reims congress of 1894 had five artisans out of a total of seven members. When conservatives manifested disapproval, the artisan element responded to the magnetism of the establishment and drew back from extreme courses. The older groups of Social Catholicism remained incurably suspicious of a movement so literal in its acceptance of the concept of equality. In 1897 Albert de Mun, on behalf of the Œuvre des Cercles, complained about the left of the Social Catholic movement moving away from the "upper classes". The Catholic industrialists stuck to their policy of mixed trade unions and did not co-operate with those composed entirely of workers. Outside the circle of its own uncoordinated enthusiasms, Christian Democracy had few real friends.

This became evident in the parliamentary elections of 1898, when the Grand Council joined the cartel of Catholic organizations to put up joint candidates. Within the cartel there was little mutual trust, and the voters showed little enthusiasm. Once the avenues of political influence were seen to be closed, disillusionment set in. Antisemitism had been rife among the propagandists of the party, and few of the leaders had had the courage to denounce it. This failure to rise to the highest principle proved disastrous when the storm over the Dreyfus case broke. The hurricane cut a swathe down the centre of Christian Democracy; many activists were blown clean off the course of social endeavour and ended up in new waters, dangerously, with the nationalist buccaneering fleet. There had been too many congresses, too much effort spent in reconciling conflicting views and settling points of theory. At the congress of 1900 only forty provincial delegates appeared. The movement was declining and disintegrating even before Leo XIII intervened to curb its reckless fervour.

There is no need to suppose the aged Pope had changed his opinions, or to invoke the so-called "rule" about liberal pontificates ending in reaction. *Rerum novarum* had been published with long-term ends in view. Already it had begun processes of change for later generations to bring to fruition. The clergy had been awakened to the social problem—witness the *abbé* Fontana's Missionnaires du Travail in the Tarbes area, the *abbé* Dehon's conferences of priests from thirty dioceses at Saint-Quentin, the Bishop of Soissons' committee on social affairs, and other initiatives in other dioceses. Christian Democracy had played its part in goading churchmen to take *Rerum novarum* seriously, but it was now endangering the balance of principles upon which the great encyclical was based. The new encyclical, *Graves de communi* (18 January 1901), directed as much against Italian exaggerations in left-wing Social Catholicism as against French ones, was concerned chiefly to emphasize the wickedness of class warfare and to draw a sharp boundary line between legitimate Christian enthusiasm and socialism proper. As many had found in the term "an equivocal and dangerous significance", the Pope ruled that "Christian Democracy" must mean no more than "a benevolent Christian action towards the people". This definition discouraged, if it did not actually prohibit autonomous action by the working class, and constituted a warning against an excessive preoccupation with justice as against charity. "A supreme honour!" cried *La Justice Sociale* bravely. "Christian Democracy has been taken into the official language of the Church." So it had, but the occasion was its epitaph.

Significantly for the future of the Church in France, as the Œuvre des Cercles and Christian Democracy declined, their inspiration was inherited by powerful independent youth organizations, in the one case by Albert de Mun's Association Catholique de la Jeunesse Française, and in the other by Marc Sangnier's "Sillon". From meetings of Sangnier and other young intellectuals in the crypt of the Collège Stanislas, in 1894 a journal, *Le Sillon,* was born, its first number dedicated to "our brothers of twenty years of age". This new publication proclaimed a cult of youth and friendship in place of dilettantism, art for arts sake, and pessimism, and as a remedy for the loneliness which an urban industrial society inflicts upon the individual, lost in the anonymous crowd. The call was not only to form Christians, but to build "a Christian society", democratic, socially just. From the beginning of 1899 "Cercles d'Études" were set up, bringing together students and young workers, and soon congresses of these Circles were being held. In September 1901 "La Jeune Garde" was formed "to ensure liberty of speech and discussion", that is, to protect religious meetings from hecklers and wreckers. A youth who joined was trained in boxing and fencing, spent a whole night in vigil before taking the oath, wore a uniform of black beret with embroidered cross, white shirt, and black tie. By 1904 the movement had five main regional groups, in the East, South, Centre, Brittany, and the North, each with its own local journal printed in the same format as *Le Sillon*—their picturesque titles, *Vive Labeur, L'Ami des Jeunes, Au large, L'Ajonc,* and *A la voile* redolent of the spirit of their endeavours: the workers and young people, the open sea and windy heath, the ship surging forward towards new horizons.

Though the movement was unified, there was no true administrative structure. Headquarters was just a small committee of friends of Sangnier meeting in premises he paid for himself; apart from subscriptions to the journals there were no levies, just gifts from well-wishers. Everything turned on personalities. Marc Sangnier himself had been inspired by the *abbé* Leber, one of the Marianists who ran the Collège Stanislas, by Soulange-Bodin, a *curé* of Paris famous for his pastoral experiments, by Blondel the Catholic philosopher, Léon Harmel, the *abbé* Klein, and by friends of his own age, the young students of the crypt. The history of the regional Sillons is the story of enthusiastic individuals, such as the lawyer Henri Bruchon in the East, the *abbé* Desgranges in the Centre, the editorial staff of a Catholic newspaper, *L'Ouest-Éclair* in Brittany. There was no chain of command, only the magic influence of Sangnier on his continual tours and visitations, and until 1904 there was no code of rules. The Sillon, said its founder, was simply *"une amitié"*, a friendship.

The committed membership of the Sillon groups was never very large. The delegates to the 1905 Congress represented 640 Circles with, possibly, a total of 10,000 members; except in Paris, the

Jeunes Gardes were few—only 200 or so altogether in the flourishing eastern region. Even so, the leavening influence of the movement was enormous. The Circles trained an *élite* of young people of all classes, and in "Instituts Populaires" a wider audience was reached through lectures, music, and theatrical productions. Sangnier himself specialized in what might be termed "confrontations", vast and sometimes tumultuous public meetings at which he disputed with prominent unbelievers, members of the "Féderation des Jeunesses Laïques", delegates of free thinkers' congresses, socialist politicians. Deliberately and proudly he concentrated his efforts outside the boundaries of the insitutional Church. His was a lay movement, owing obedience to the ecclesiastical hierarchy only in matters strictly religious; his followers were to penetrate the world of socialism and secular trades unions, using their inner Christian inspiration to serve the whole unredeemed community. Sillonists regarded themselves as scouts moving ahead of the main army; the ACJF they described as working within the existing ecclesiastical organization, defensively, while they themselves adventured forth converting individuals and setting an example in a dechristianized society. As one of them superciliously observed in advice to Catholic youth (in *L'Ouest-Éclair,* 14 July 1903): "If the Sillon scares you or scares your parents, you can safely enrol under the banner of the ACJF."

Friendship is a nobler bond of unity than administrative regulations, but to Catholics outside the radiant circle, the "friendship" came to look like exclusiveness, and the "union of soul" on which Sillon prided itself as an inclination to absorb and dominate, a threat to the independence of collaborators and potential allies. The ACJF and the Sillon went their separate ways. Each feared the other's expansive dynanism. Sangnier was inclined to regard the ACJF Congress of 1903, wholly devoted to trades union matters, as an encroachment on his private battlefield, and he suspected that the ecclesiastical authorities were looking for an opportunity to disperse his reckless shock troops into the ranks of the more docile legions of Albert de Mun's youth movement. Marius Gonin's Christian Democratic group in Lyon, centred around the journal, *La Chronique sociale,* held joint congresses with Sillon from 1902 to 1905, but broke off relations when the Sillonists insisted that the next congress bear the name of their own organization. In May 1903, Mgr Turinaz, Bishop of Nancy, forbade meetings of Sillon groups in his diocese. Sangnier hastened to Rome in September to seek reassurance from the new Pope; probably, he received instructions to be charitable to the ACJF and co-operative towards the ecclesiastical hierarchy. By the *Motu proprio* of 18 December 1903 the Vatican took action to discipline La Démocratie Chrétienne; it was a sort of practical instruction for the enforcement of *Graves de communi*—the Christian Democrats were to obey the ecclesiastical authorities, and their writers were to obtain the permission of the ordinary for their publications. *Le Sillon* did not publish this *Motu proprio* until 10 May 1904, and from henceforward Sangnier made it clear that he did not regard his movement as included in its scope. According to him Christian Democrats had tried to impose a particular conception of the meaning of the Ralliement upon the Church, while the Sillonists were exercising their freedom of political choice outside the ecclesiastical structure. On 20 May, in a public disputation at Épinal, Sangnier limited the necessary obedience of Catholics to articles of faith: the Pope and the bishops, for example, were not infallible when they imposed an excommunication—"*les hommes passent, la religion reste*". It was a courageous declaration of the independent, lay character of the Sillon, which was denounced by Mgr Turinaz and caused alarm at Rome and among the more conservative members of the French episcopate.

In the course of the next two years, as he fought for his right to formulate a political and social philosophy free from ecclesiastical control, Marc Sangnier brought his highly original theories to a sharper definition. Democracy, he argued, was the best of governments, because it demanded the exercise of the greatest virtues; it was "the social organization which tends to maximize the conscience and civic responsibility of each individual". Christianity had made democracy conceivable, for Christianity alone treats men as truly equal, and inspires true fraternity. But parliamentary democracy was a second best; the ideal State was not a multitude ruled by "sterile parliamentarianism", but the "harmonious and organic expression of free social groupings", especially trades unions and co-operatives. In the reformed society there would be complete economic equality (the new Sillonist journal, *L'Éveil démocratique,* created in October 1905, was run by a co-operative, in which each worker received payment solely according to his needs). On the other hand, society needs leadership, so the authentic superiority of an *élite* would have to be recognized. The affairs of the Sillon were managed, not by "election", but by "selection", and its chief operated the selective process to bring picked members of the working class from the Circles into the central organization of the movement. Albert de Mun's Œuvre des Cercles had relied on the *classes dirigeantes,* described by Sangnier in 1906 as "fallen now from their elder brother status and for long in the position of directing nothing at all"; the Sillon was to rely on an aristocracy of intelligence and character, drawn chiefly from the workers. So it would be in the democratic State of the future. A dedicated, unrewarded leadership would operate through "the organic expression of free social groupings"; it would be a combination of Plato's Republic with anarcho-syndicalism. But the way to the goal was not through violence; change would come from the moral education of the working class, chiefly through the inspiration of Christianity.

In practice, was this romantic vision a doctrine of the Right or of the Left? Through the complex and broken terrain of the confused debate on social issues, a clearly posted frontier line twisted its way, and in a controversy with Guesde and the Socialists in a public meeting at Roubaix in March 1905 Sangnier crossed it.

We are convinced [he said, in words bringing the Social Catholic movement in France to a crisis in its fortunes] that the different systems of property holding are called to succeed one another, and in our view only narrow and limited minds see contemporary capitalism as endowed with a strange and evil immortality. . . . The wage-earning system will last only for a time, and one day humanity will see a worthier, freer, more human social organization, one corresponding better to the needs of a regenerated society.

12 Intellectual Defeat and Spiritual Renewal

Rerum novarum turned the Church towards the highroad of social reform. By contrast, two years later, in the encyclical *Providentissimus* (November 1893) Leo XIII gave a clear indication that Catholic biblical scholarship must remain within the confines of the doctrines of plenary inspiration and total inerrancy. This liberal pontiff, with his gift for foreseeing the political and social issues of the future, proved as blind as most of his contemporaries concerning the intellectual dilemmas of Christianity. Though his encyclical nobly encouraged the study of the Scriptures, the whole Bible was stated to have been "written under the inspiration of the Holy Ghost. The divine inspiration, far from admitting the existence of error, by itself excludes all error". This, of course, was merely a reaffirmation of what had been often said before, and in making such a declaration the Pope was acting in conformity with the wishes of the vast majority of believers. Anticlericals were celebrating the victory of science over the Scriptures; miracles, they claimed, were now known to be impossible, and historical criticism had shown the Bible to be a mosaic of disparate writings, often dating from long after the events they described, and full of interpretive glosses and contradictions. With everything condemned and no effective reply available, it was tempting for churchmen, in desperation, to reaffirm everything indiscriminately. Even the *abbé* Frémont, that judicious opponent of the excesses of illiberal theology, thought so. He read the encyclical in a ravine on the Franco-Italian border overlooking the Mediterranean, and it seemed to him to glitter like the ocean in the sunshine, "vast, golden, harmonious".

"Do you know a company for insuring against the *Index*?" Louis Duchesne, professor of history at the Institut Catholique, asked. Even before *Providentissimus* there had been no question of allowing Catholic scholars to commit themselves freely to the task of historical criticism. Lenormant's *Les Origines de l'histoire* (1880), which accepted the composite structure of the Pentateuch and treated Genesis as a sacred legend, had been put on the *Index* in

1887. In private correspondence to Alfred Loisy, a fellow-professor at the Institut Catholique, Duchesne admitted the confusions of the Gospel story and concluded we must be satisfied with the general impression produced by Jesus; but he took no risks, and his published history kept just outside the boundaries of the New Testament period. His advice to Loisy was to follow this example of caution and to limit himself to Semitic philology. But here was a scholar of a finer temper, cherishing the hope of "defeating Renan with his own weapons" and unwilling to draw back or dissimulate. The crisis of 1893 and the encyclical *Providentissimus* were precipitated by Loisy's publication of a study of the Chaldean myths of the Flood and by the attempts of Mgr d'Hulst, Rector of the Institut Catholique, to defend him; "there are serious difficulties", said d'Hulst courageously, "in maintaining that absolute inerrancy is a necessary aspect of inspiration". A great outcry arose, and in a farewell lecture from his chair of Sacred Scripture (16 June 1893) Loisy frankly proclaimed the relativity of the biblical documents—a book can no more be absolutely true for all times than a triangle can be square.

Providentissimus replied to these attempts to separate inspiration from inerrancy by restating the doctrine of the Bible already enunciated in the Syllabus and by the First Vatican Council. Catholic scholars struggled, as they had struggled before, to meet the demands of historical criticism while keeping within the boundaries of papal pronouncements and stretching those boundaries as far as they dared. A few supporters of the old Jesuit doctrine of "content inspiration" tried to gain comfort from ascribing the ideas of Scripture to God and the words to men, using the principle of economy to limit God's intervention to the strictly necessary. More signficantly, a new school of exegetes, led by Marie-Joseph Lagrange arose, proclaiming a more subtle form of verbal inspiration. Leo XIII was encouraging the revival of Thomist philosophy, and St Thomas' doctrine of "instrumental causality" was adopted; the biblical writers were preserved from error, but the crudeness of their work as instruments in God's hand was still evident. But to most Catholics and, indeed, most Catholic scholars, these refinements and distinctions were unacceptable, and after *Providentissimus* the Church blundered on with the *abbé* Dessailly's proof that Jonah could have lived inside the big fish because toads have lived for thousands of years inside stones, with the *abbé* Vigouroux's "days" of Genesis as geological epochs, and with historical accounts of the life of Christ consisting of texts fitted together at face value, barring a few concessions on matters of chronology. In 1897, with Leo XIII's approval, the congregation of the Index solemnly affirmed the authenticity of the trinitarian reference in 1 John 5.5–7, in the face of complete scholarly evidence against it.

The whole sad story of the Church's blindness was related by the *abbé* Houtin in 1902 in *La Question biblique chez les catholiques de France au XIXe siecle*. Though his narrative was full of "perfidious irony and covert bitterness", said the *abbé* Wehrlé, it should still be applauded; since the ecclesiastical authorities refuse to make concessions to "prayerful candid souls", nothing was left but to unleash "the *franc tireurs* and desperadoes" against them. Two years later, when Leo XIII, tolerant even in his severe traditionalism was dead, and the Vatican was pursuing actively reactionary measures against historical criticism, Mgr Mignot, Archbishop of Albi, summed up the disastrous position of believers. Because of the Church, he said, we believe the Bible, but it must be conceded that the Scriptures contain "accounts which, humanly speaking, are impossible and would, indeed, suffice to make us regard as legendary a profane book that related them".

The one decisive voice in the French Church challenging the doctrine of biblical inerrancy was Loisy's. Yet he accepted *Providentissimus*. His faith in Catholic dogma waned, but he tried to go on fulfilling his vows as a priest and continuing to serve "a great spiritual force, the only one capable of imposing itself on the world". As long as they could, he and his sympathizers carried on within the Church. In the pages of *La Quinzaine*, the *Annales de philosophie chrétienne* and Loisy's own *Revue d'histoire et de littérature religieuses* articles, signed and unsigned, treated the biblical writers as men of their own time, fallible as men must be. There were sensations. Marcel Hébert's *Souvenirs d'Assise* (1899), published without his consent, explained the resurrection appearances as visions. In 1902 Loisy's *L'Évangile et l'Église* brilliantly replied to Harnack and the Liberal Protestant theologians, showing how the mysterious Messiahship and the Coming of the Kingdom were at the heart of the Gospel story, and how the life of Jesus, the tradition, and the Church are inseparable. But it soon became impossible for free historical criticism to exist within the boundaries of the Roman Catholic Church. In December 1903, five months after the death of Leo XIII, Loisy's five chief books were put on the Index. In 1905 Lagrange was called to Rome and ordered to keep silent, though unlike Loisy and his friends he did not incur a direct condemnation. The encyclical *Pascendi gregis* in 1907 fixed the name of "Modernism" on to the new movement of thought which was being ousted from the Church, giving it a doctrinal unity it had never really possessed. Loisy himself was excommunicated in 1908, and two years later an anti-Modernist oath was imposed on all clergy. Never has the Roman Church passed through such a period of self-imposed blindness, never has it been so helpless in the face of intellectual criticism.

With the mass of the faithful behind him and demonstrating as much moderation as the case allowed, Leo XIII had re-committed the Church to the defence of an indefensible teaching about the Bible. With the faithful equally behind him and with equal moderation he cut short the beginnings of a new ecumenical spirit among French Catholics when he condemned "Americanism". The 12,000,000 Catholics of the U.S.A., assumed to be living in peace with their neighbours of other faiths and deeply immersed in all the processes of democracy, were something of an ideal to would-be reformers of the French Church. Mgr Ireland, an American bishop, lectured in Paris in 1892, and the *abbé* Klein published Ireland's collected speeches two years later under the title of *L'Église et le siècle*, the general theme being the necessity for Catholicism to ally with democracy. Meanwhile, in 1893 a "Parliament of Religions" had been held in Chicago, where Protestants and Catholics, Brahmins and Buddhists, had joined in reciting the Lord's Prayer. Why not hold another such Parliament in Paris in 1900 to coincide with the Great Exhibition? The idea caught on; the *abbé* Naudet and the *abbé* Klein, Goyau and Fonsegrive and other influential laymen supported it. The project was soon knocked on the head by the Archbishop of Paris, but not before many clergy had rejoiced the anticlericals by their intolerant declamations. "There's only one God," said a bishop, "and we are the ones who have him.'

Next came the publication by the *abbé* Klein (with a preface by Mgr Ireland) of the biography of an American priest, Father Hecker (1897). Since Hecker's mission had been the conversion of Protestants, he had evolved techniques of minimizing prickly Catholic dogmas and giving generous interpretations to others. This being so, the *Vie du Père Hecker* brought out all the reactionaries in the French Church, led by Canon Delassus with his *L'Américanisme et la conjuration anti-chrétienne*. Leo XIII intervened with a letter to Cardinal Gibbons condemning "Americanism", more especially the view that the Holy Spirit can work without intermediaries, proposals for more liberty for the individual within the Church, and the tendency to prefer the active virtues to the passive. Cardinal Gibbons, Mgr Ireland, and their French admirers denied all knowledge of Catholics who held such doctrines, leaving Americanism as a phantom heresy, execrated by all but held by nobody. It had been a delicate exercise in ecclesiastical gamesmanship; no one got hurt too much and new hopes were stifled painlessly.

The ideal of ecumenical co-operation went underground in the Roman Catholic Church. The memory lingered on among deserters from Catholicism, as, for example, the *abbé* Charbonnel and *Père* Hyacinthe Loyson, sad ambiguous figures who met with so much contempt and deserved only pity. These men, and the *abbé* Houtin, some of the Modernists and a few others abandoned their priesthood, and whatever their motives it ought to be remembered that they were leaving a Church which had refused to face the intellectual challenges of the age. How many others were there who stayed at their posts with despair and frustration in their hearts? It was just such a priest Zola depicted in the *abbé* Pierre Froment who carried on his priesthood long after the intellectual foundations of his faith had disappeared. "And he felt that assuredly he was not alone; he felt he had brothers, fellow-priests ravaged by doubts, but staying on at the altar like soldiers without a fatherland, summoning up all their courage to maintain the divine illusion gleaming bright above the kneeling multitudes." Just the novelist's imagination? Perhaps, though this may be the price in human terms that had to be paid for such ringing proclamations as the Syllabus and for the great encyclical *Providentissimus,* glittering like the ocean in the sunshine, "vast, golden, harmonious".

In a brochure, *Le Clergé français en 1890,* the *abbé* Latty sadly described his brethren as useless at argument. "Their conclusion invariably is, take it or leave it, which throws Christians of good will into despair and repels the lukewarm and indifferent." But what else could they say? They belonged to an army pinned down by heavy fire, while its commanders were engaged in pulling back or dismissing the adventurous advance guards and reconnaissance units capable of locating the enemy guns and destroying them. Yet the clergy of France were resilient. Deprived of the intellectual leadership they deserved, many of them attempted to modernize pastoral methods, to change the role of the priest in the parish and the image of that role in the minds of their secular contemporaries. Some inspiration came from the Ralliement and *Rerum novarum* and some leadership from the Social Catholic movement and Christian Democracy. But the ferment was widespread in the parochial ministry, among priests of conservative opinions both in politics and social matters. Under the Concordat the parish priests had no opportunities to come together or create a sense of common purpose, they were very much under the power of the bishops, and there were legal difficulties about clergy meeting together outside their own dioceses. The new reforming movement was a sort of indirect protest against such limitations, and a spirit of exultation filled the parish clergy when at last they got together to share common problems, hopes, and fears, uninhibited by bishops or the rulings of the State.

In August 1896 a clerical congress was held at Reims, ostensibly to celebrate the fourteenth centenary of the baptism of Clovis, which brought in Cardinal Langénieux to bless the closing session. There were 700 participants, the vast majority being parish priests. The congress recommended the drawing up of a uniform Catechism for all dioceses, called for simpler and more direct sermons, the study of new methods of evangelization outside the church buildings and the circle of the faithful, and for measures to improve the training of the clergy. Among projects put up by individuals were: the relaxation of the rule about fasting Communion, the instruction of seminarists in the principles of architecture and in playing the harmonium, the consolidation and more efficient use of ecclesiastical revenues. The underlying theme of all the speeches was the alienation of the Church from the mass of the population, one speaker going so far as to regret the existence of the confessional schools which kept Catholic children in a compartment separate from the rest of the nation, and another declaring he would welcome the conscription of seminarists as a chance to gain access, through the barrack room, to social classes which never came near the *curé*.

This blameless congress was bitterly denounced by the press of the extreme left and of the extreme right. The government issued instructions forbidding the use of seminaries and other ecclesiastical buildings for future assemblies of clergy. Many bishops expressed hostility, including Isoard and Fuzet, two pillars of the Ralliement. "These meetings of priests which are not under the presidency of the natural leaders of the hierarchy, the Bishops, seem dangerous to me", said the Archbishop of Paris. Rome sent no reply to the customary telegram of fidelity despatched from Reims, and subsequently laid severe limitations on the subjects for debate at any future meetings. In spite of these difficulties a second congress was held at Bourges in 1900, under the patronage of the diocesan archbishop. About the same number of priests attended, but half were from the diocese of Bourges itself. Speakers called France *"un pays de mission"* and suggested new outlooks, new methods of evangelization. "If St Paul lived today he'd be a journalist", it was said; "today good Catholics themselves abhor clerical domination"; "we must love our country just as it is". Once more the reactionaries cried scandal. Mgr Turinaz, Bishop of Nancy, published *Les Périls de la foi et de la discipline de l'Église de France.* Soon, he said, we'll have congresses of conscripts to advise the generals, and of sacristans and the housekeepers of *curés* to run the parishes. The Vatican made its disapproval clear, and henceforward no bishop dared to offer his sponsorship. Like Christian Democracy, the congress movement ended.

The reforming movement among the parish clergy left a notable legacy to the future: the idea of the "worker priest". There was a profound dissatisfaction with the way in which priests were being reduced to overworked officials in charge of an endless procession of baptisms, marriages, and funerals. Soulange-Bodin, a *curé* of Paris famous for his experiments in new pastoral methods, published some *Lettres à un séminariste* in 1897 appealing to the laity to make it possible for the clergy to follow their vocation as "apostles". "The day of the sacerdotal official is over", said the *vicomte* de Montmorand two years later. "The future lies with the missionary, the seeker of souls, who has neither staff nor purse ... who travels the roads of France as if they were the roads of China, preaching the gospel." But in an industrial society the priest, maybe, was called to a different kind of sacrifice in less romantic circumstances. In 1893 a pamphlet, *Le Curé de cam-pagne*, told the story of a parish priest who heard a missionary, newly returned from Africa, saying how useless it was to approach pagans directly about religion: "We begin by rendering them material services." Acting on this analogy, the *abbé* Bernard makes himself an expert on viticulture, organizes his parishioners into a winegrowers' co-operative, and proudly sets up a crucifix in the tavern where they meet. He is working within the confines of the parish, of course; the idea of treating the factory itself as the unit for evangelization was not yet known. This limitation also applies to a more widely read plea for the ideal of the "worker priest" published by the *abbé* Calippe in 1902, an argument cast in the form of a serial story, *Moine d'après demain: journal intime*. The scene was set in the future, in the 1920s, with France ruled by the Socialists, and the monk of the title, a parish priest, works in a factory to win his way to the hearts of the people. If only there were others, he reflects, "a few volunteers, . . . a few snipers to push out an advance guard along the road which will eventually be the meeting place of Church and People".

The role of the congress movement was taken over and diversified by the *Semaines sociales,* an idea imported from Germany. The first of these "Social Weeks" was held at Lyon in 1904, a sort of "teach-in", a study retreat under lay direction. Harmel, German Social Catholics, French theologians and intellectuals came in force to lead the study groups. In the following year Henri Lorin, a dynamic business man, took over the leadership, and for the next eight years an itinerant Catholic "university" (including Brunetière, Blondel, Madelin, Goyau, and *Père* Sertillanges) toured the country. Attendance at these study sessions would be 1,000 or so, and usually half of those present were clergy, finding an opportunity to meet together again in a movement under lay control, less vulnerable to the disapproval of the hierarchy.

Meanwhile, Albert de Mun's Association Catholique de la Jeunesse Française and Marc Sangnier's Sillon were becoming forces in Catholicism. It may seem strange that they should have taken their rise among young university men at the very moment when the intellectual defences of Catholicism lay in ruins and the appointed guardians had abandoned their task. On the other hand, the insufficiency of the authorities may have helped to evoke a new spirit among the youth of the Church, anxious to do what could be done in their own independent sphere. And, surprisingly enough, the failure of the Church to defend the Gospels had less effect upon intelligent contemporaries than might have been imagined. The deadly, widespread effect lay in the future, part of the long, slow discrediting of belief which is so difficult to reverse because the findings of scholarship seem to be disseminated a generation *en retard*. What marked the end of the nineteenth century, indeed, was the advent of a brilliant Catholic literary revival, inspiring the new youth movements with the sort of writings youth loves to read. Two years before the first number of

Le Sillon was printed, the *abbé* Klein published an article in the *Correspondant* (10 February 1892) on "The neo-Christian movement in contemporary literature", and we can see in retrospect how from about 1886 onwards the phenomenon had been developing. In the nature of the case a religious revival in literature is well documented, and in this documentation lies something of the secret of the spiritual aspirations of this generation; here too may lie the explanation of the paradoxical coincident patterns of intellectual defeat and spiritual revival characteristic of the age.

The neo-Christian movement among the writers can be explained at different levels. At one level it fits into the course of literary history. A reaction against "brutal literature" had been rising since the early 1860s, and in 1887, as a protest against Zola's *La Terre,* five young writers abjured naturalism and appealed for other inspirations. The emotional legacy of Baudelaire and Verlaine was one of the bitterness of sin, the necessity of suffering, and of nostalgia for the divine. Writers were drawn to vertiginous subjects and left the pavement paths of scientific logic. Some fell into occultism or decadentism. Others rediscovered pity, and here the English novelists helped, for Dickens was popular and from 1885 translations of George Eliot became available. And from Russia came new and darker inspirations. In 1886 Melchior de Vogüé published a best-seller, *Le Roman russe,* a study of the Russian novel which was also a denunciation of pessimism, naturalism, and art for art's sake, and a call to soul-searching. Man was to co-operate with the divine work of redemption, exemplified by the Slavonic Christ in a window of the cathedral of St Petersburg who trembles with human anguish—a God for whom the task of redemption is unfinished, who has not yet said his final word.

Yet the revival, while being a literary phenomenon, is also a religious one, and the two interlock. The resurgence of belief fitted the literary mood of the generation while, paradoxically, it cut across the natural patterns of the history of ideas like tidal waters sweeping crosswise through the skeleton of a wreck. Catholics were helpless before the ravages of historical criticism, but the new literary converts scoffed at "scientific" history. Bloy, Claudel, Péguy, and Huysmans ridiculed its card-indexes and files, its endless probing into problems that kept no one awake at night. "Christ did not have time for guessing games", said Péguy. "He had no time to lose." A few thoughtful churchmen were in despair at the illiberal showing of their religious leaders; this, to some of

the converts, was a downright virtue. They spurned those "whose
only care is not to make M. Anatole France smile". Léon Bloy's
attack on the memory of Leo XIII (who had just died) is unparalleled for sanctimonious viciousness. The dying Pope asks what he
can say to God—he had sacrificed the sheep to reconcile the
wolves, he had destroyed the faith of the multitude to win Brunetière: "Have I paid too high a price for him, O Lord?"

But if the new literary *élite* of Catholicism were sometimes in
love with the follies of their Church like young soldiers displaying
picturesque medals won by service in Ruritania, essentially they
were drawn to, they clung to the deepest and most difficult inspirations behind the Christian hope. Conversion is mysterious and
personal. Yet for once we have detailed records of what happened
from brilliant pens and original, self-critical minds, and these
records, in their diversity, are worthy of study. Claudel went to the
cathedral of Notre-Dame on Christmas Day 1886, he tells us,
for a sort of decadent thrill.

> Then came the event which dominates my whole life. In an
> instant, my heart was stricken, and I believed. I believed with
> such dedicated force, with such an uprising of my whole being
> ... that ever since, all books, reasonings and the chances of a
> troubled lifetime have not been able to shake my faith, or indeed,
> to touch it at all. I suddenly had the agonizing feeling of the
> innocence, of the eternal infancy of God, in an ineffable revela-
> tion. How happy are those who believe! If only it were true!
> It is true—God is here. He is a Being as personal as I am—
> He loves me. He calls me. I was crying and sobbing by now,
> and the tender singing of the *Adeste* intensified my emotion.

He was, in fact, to take four more years to escape from "the hideous world of Taine and Renan", but this was the moment of
revelation.

Paul Bourget's conversion was a slower, more intellectual process. He had broken with the Church at the age of sixteen, the
Church which, in the person of the Archbishop of Lyon, had
demoted his father, a schoolmaster, because he was a Republican.
Thereafter, Bourget plunged deep, and with professional skill and
intent, into pessimism and scepticism. Taine taught the fragility
of reason, and the Commune demonstrated man's essentially animal
nature. In psychological essays and in a sensational novel *Cruelle
Énigme* (1884), Bourget showed how fallible we are, and how we

corrupt one another. Then, goaded by tensions within his own life, he came to recognize a duty to find a remedy for the maladies he had diagnosed. *Crime d'Amour* ends with a faint ray of hope: the wicked man can be touched by the sight of suffering, and though evil makes it impossible to believe in God, "why should not the secret of the mystery of life be a secret of salvation?" By 1887 conversion had come, the conviction that there is a Personality, the embodiment of goodness, at the heart of the universe. Two years later Bourget threw down his challenge to the age in *Le Disciple,* a novel caricaturing Taine and philosophers of his kind in the person of Adrian Sixte, who destroys youth by scepticism and scientism. Bourget went on writing novels analysing the corruptions of high society, but he left Paris, married a girl of no fortune, and lived out quietly his motto of simple duty and concern for "God, nature, work, love, children".

With Huysmans, conversion was an ascent from hell itself. He had chosen to go down into the gutter, into the clutches of prostitutes, into the underworld of black magic. Yet the vicious hero of *A Rebours* (1884) ends with a prayer: "Lord, have pity on the Christian who doubts, on the unbeliever who wishes to believe, on the prisoner of life who embarks alone, at night, under a sky no longer illuminated by the fixed stars of the old hopes." In *Là-Bas* (1891) Durtal is haunted by Grünewald's "Crucifixion": "not the Christ of the rich, the Adonis of Galilee" but "the Christ of the poor", abandoned by the Father, "the God of the morgue". When in *En Route* (1895) Durtal is converted, "disgust at existence" bringing him into the Church, "the hospital of souls", everyone asked whether the author himself had changed, or whether this was just another decadent gambit. In fact, Huysmans got out of the grip of the brothels and confessed and communicated in June 1892. In *La Cathédrale* (1898) Durtal prays to "labour and not ask for reward", to have "grace to obey and to be silent". This was what his creator was doing. Huysmans became an oblate in a monastery, wanting to suffer, praying to "Our Lady of Fear" and, when suffering came, refusing alleviation.

The common factor in these conversions, and in others, was disillusionment with existence, in the face of which men had chosen cynicism, scepticism or—with Huysmans—evil itself. Then came a breakthrough to certainty, to the vision, behind the sordid or pointless details of life, and the indifferent or hostile vastness of the universe, of a loving Personality. The necessity to find the divine secret of love once the possibility had been glimpsed gave conviction about the Gospels, not the historian's assessment of doubtful documentation. Suffering, the greatest stumbling block to intellectual belief, came to be accepted as the way to emotional certainty. The writers of the Catholic revival were concerned, often to a morbid degree, with the necessity to accept pain as the gift of God, with the beauty and value of vicarious suffering, with the holiness of total poverty, with the duty of self-abnegation and even of self-degradation. Georges Dumesnil, founder of one of the leading journals of the Catholic revival, *L'Amitié de France,* came to his crisis of faith when he realized the educative role of suffering: "*Qui ne sait souffrir, ne sait rien.*" Huysmans and Bloy went further, and gave suffering an objective, as well as a subjective value; they even condemned the "cowardice" and "sentimentality" of so much of the devotion at Lourdes—when would a Christian go there, Bloy asked, to pray for the gift of pain? To them St Paul's desire to make up what was lacking in the Passion of Christ was taken literally, to the point of becoming a heresy; a belief, not so much in mystical participation in Christ's self-offering, but in a doctrine of "mystical substitution". "God watches over the equilibrium of the world", wrote Huysmans in 1899, "when the side of the balance laden with offences sinks too low. He throws on to the other the tears of the saints." And these men were willing to seek the burden of pain deliberately to enable their lives to become part of the process of expiation. Huysmans gave up the world and died of cancer of the mouth, refusing drugs to ease his agony; Bloy made his own life a continual Calvary—"there is nothing supernatural here on earth except suffering". Others made the mystique of suffering the heart of their writing, as did Claudel, whose lovers are doomed to separation by a sort of divine necessity. Catholicism's apologetics had never been weaker and its "proofs" never so shopsoiled. But men still suffered, loved and died, and Christianity is a gospel concerned with suffering, love, and death, before which philosophy, science, and progress are ultimately irrelevant.

The Catholic literary revival had its demi-converts, and there were others who did not cross the line, although their hearts were touched. Romain Rolland at the École Normale had idolized Renan, whose message he summed up as "Life is excellent, though it's not much after all". Then came the crises of 1887 and 1888, the pantheistic vision of a *Pater Seraphicus* with whom we can be at one. In December 1891 André Gide was praying, "Lord, I return

to thee, because I believe that apart from thee, all is vanity",
though the mood ebbed and flowed. Some demi-converts became
what Goyau called "auxiliaries of the Church, auxiliaries more
useful than many believers". Ernest Psichari, grandson of Renan,
identified himself with Christianity years before he joined the
Church, like the Roman centurion in his novel, affirming Christ
without believing in him. Barrès accepted Catholicism as part of
the patriotic heritage of Frenchmen and as the vital channel of self-
realization: "Each of us finds in the Church the fullest expression
of his own soul." "Why ask me why I believe?" he said. "I am sure
that I belong to the civilization of Christ." Péguy, converted in
1905 through disgust at the world of Combes "where ingratitude is
a ritual", remained an anticlerical, refusing to go to mass and
accusing the Church of propagating "the formal religion of the
rich". Barrès accepted the Church as an institution but rejected its
dogmas; Péguy rejected the institution but believed.

The logic of Barrès' adherence to the "civilization of Christ" lay
in the absence of an alternative, for the dream of a religion of
science and of a humanistic morality had collapsed. Jaurès boldly
affirmed in the Chamber of Deputies the proud old doctrine of
humanism: if God himself appeared it would be man's duty to
argue, not to accept a master. This was the essence of Renouvier's
philosophy of "Personalism", the following of the intelligence
wherever it leads. But in attempting to fulfil its most urgent duty,
the production of a rational and workable morality, the intelligence
had failed. Goyau's *Esquisse d'une morale sans obligation ni sanc-
tion* (1885) and Desjardins' *Le Devoir présent* (1892) rang hollow
as soon as they were published. Was it sympathy or self-interest
properly understood that we rely on? Where is the objective
standard? How can a code be respected if no aura of mystery
surrounds it? Who will enjoy the enormous power of teaching the
new code? The family, said orthodox Positivists, afraid of the
tyranny of a State religion, of an "obligatory deism". Yet, if the
State is excluded, there will be no uniformity and, indeed, very
little teaching at all.

This was the situation of the argument when, like a thunder-
clap, came Brunetière's article, "after a visit to the Vatican" (1
January 1895)—Brunetière the great critic, sardonic, yellow-waist-
coated, successor to Renan and Taine, declaring "a morality is
nothing if not religious"! The teacher, the argument went, has a
moral responsibility, "a cure of souls", and since life consists of

action, not of discussion, he must give his moral instruction *now*, without delay. And where can he find the "first ring" on which to hang the chain of moral duties? Nowhere but in the Catholic tradition, which reckless theorists are urging us to abandon because of frivolous doubts drawn from exegesis or geology. On 12 January Richet in the *Revue Scientifique* asked "Is Science bankrupt?", and denied the proposition. Brunetière had not actually made this accusation, but a great debate turned around it. Berthelot, Durkheim, and Léon Bourgeois proclaimed the philosophy of "social solidarity", and Zola helped them with his gospel of "work". But no one could give a convincing reply to two questions Fonsegrive asked in *La Quinzaine*: "Life is mysterious and death is certain, surely this has some relevance to our duty?"; "Science may demonstrate the advantages of solidarity, but how does it demonstrate an obligation?"

A mood of pessimism settled on the devotees of Science and Positivism. From the standpoint of a new interpretation of Darwin (who had once been the source of so much optimism) Clemenceau and others saw life as a vast gladiatorial combat, and from Schopenhauer, now hugely influential, many took the idea of intelligence as necessarily linked with pain, sadness, and awareness of the inevitability of defeat. "Why are we sad?" asked Anatole France in 1889. "Who will bring us a new faith, hope and charity?" He it was who invented the novel of the sceptical intelligence: the doctors know what is wrong, but they cannot cure; ideals serve only to close the souls of men to pity. In *Le Procurateur de Judée,* Pontius Pilate, in comfortable, learned retirement talks over the old days in Jerusalem. The name of Jesus of Nazareth comes up; it eludes him. This is a tale for agnostics but it has a terrible double edge to it. The passionate new life is bursting forth, destined to outlive the Empire and flame on in diverse forms down the centuries; the fine intelligence, the trained political insight cannot see it. "Jesus, Jesus of Nazareth. I don't remember him."

13 From the Dreyfus Case to Waldeck-Rousseau

J'accuse! Clemenceau chose the title, Zola wrote the text, denouncing the leaders of the French army for concealing evidence proving Captain Dreyfus innocent of the charges of treason that had consigned him to a living death on Devil's Island four years earlier. From Zola's manifesto (January 1898) France was riven by a moral cataclysm. In this great cleavage so many of the tolerant decencies moderating the warfare between social and ideological groups within the Republic were destroyed—the subconscious affinities between enemies, the undefined acceptance of limitations, the recoil from the ultimate insult, the unwillingness to press for total victory. Commitment became a duty. The literary *salons* had to abandon art for art's sake and *fin de siècle* introspection. The writers of the age split into two hostile camps: on one side were Anatole France, Rostand, Maeterlinck, Proust, and Péguy, on the other Jules Lemaître, Bourget, Barrès, François Coppée, Valéry, Maurras, and Léautaud.The historians left their neutral and would-be scientific analysis of the past to join the propaganda mêlée, and the conservative politicians abandoned their schemes of a centre party above religious strife. Here was a moral issue making moral men accept the immoral assumption that they could not possibly be mistaken, and enabling corrupt and discredited politicians to don shining armour—old Boulangists pretending theirs was the purest patriotism, tainted men of Panama confuting them with cries of justice for an individual.

For a generation, the "Affair" dominated the political life of France. At a time when the ideals of the Republic were obscured by corruption and intrigue, the issues of principle aroused by the Dreyfus case served to recall the faithful supporters of the regime to their ideological origins. The intensity of their campaign for justice was not inspired by moral fervour alone; bitter passions surged and high stakes were being played for. The Boulangists had struck back at the Republican politicians who had defeated them by publishing sensational revelations about the "Panama affair" in the pages of the *Libre Parole* and the *Cocarde*, denouncing the deputies who had taken bribes and the paymasters (as it happened, Jewish) who had distributed them. Two years later, in 1894, it was the *Libre Parole*, still searching for scandals and scenting treason, which announced "the arrest of the Jewish officer A. Dreyfus". Then, when it was whispered that Dreyfus might be innocent, the hope of a counter-scandal, of a Republican revenge for Panama was born. Thus, obscurely, the fight for justice to an individual was also a war of revenge. It was also a war of political self-preservation. Helped by the revulsion in the electorate against the corruptions of the regime, the Socialists were gaining in strength (at the legislative elections of 1893 they increased their seats from a dozen to nearly fifty); meanwhile, the Ralliement had made Catholicism politically "respectable". *Bourgeois* and anticlerical, the rank-and-file Republican politicians were afraid of being forced into a dependence on the Left which would commit them to social reform and the income tax, or of finding themselves excluded when moderate Republicans drifted off into an alliance with moderate Catholics, perpetuating the *entente* formed under Méline. The Dreyfus Affair rescued them. It made possible a coalition of all defenders of the Republic on the basis of anticlericalism; the Catholic *ralliés* were no longer necessary and the Socialists no longer dangerous. Even after Dreyfus was vindicated, the Affair continued to divide the nation. The political strategem of the Dreyfusards remained in operation after the spiritual illumination of their cause had faded; their opponents transmuted their own defeated strategem to serve a nationalist enthusiasm which was a spiritual experience of the useless and dangerous sort.

Before the Affair, beneath the angry surface debates of the Third Republic, humdrum processes of tolerance and compromise had been developing. The viable part of the programme of anticlericalism was virtually exhausted. For most Republicans the task of undermining the Church had become a matter of routine tactics or vague principle. Then, suddenly, they were inspired (no doubt it suited many to be inspired) with a mystical hatred of the *Infâme* such as Voltaire had drawn from the whole history of Christian intolerance and from the grim details of the Calas case. Dreyfus, the argument went, had been a victim of those who supported the Army right or wrong. Perhaps, as Joseph Reinach had it, he had been destroyed by a Jesuit conspiracy; or, for those who could not swallow such lurid theories, the Catholics were guilty by association, for in their faith lay the ideological bond of unity of the whole unofficial right-wing "establishment" which was rallying to the Army's defence. Since it was anticlericals, not churchmen, who rescued an innocent man from Devil's Island, the inference was drawn that Catholics, in the last resort, put expediency before truth and order above justice.

The charge was unjust, though it had its peculiar justification all the same. Unjust, because the issue was controversial and the evidence was not publicly available, and because some churchmen at least were dedicated supporters of the revisionists. Colonel Picquart, a Catholic and no lover of the Jews, risked career, friendships, and his very liberty by refusing to remain silent about the confusions he had detected in the secret military files; without him the defence lawyers could never have obtained a leverage upon the monolithic weight of pseudo-evidence so damning to the prisoner of Devil's Island. The *abbé* Pichot and the *abbé* Brugerette wrote Dreyfusard pamphlets, the Catholic historian, Paul Viollet, founded a Comité Catholique pour la défense du droit. In March 1899 the Pope himself made his position clear to a visiting journalist in words which caused alarm among rigorist theologians: "Happy the victim whom God recognizes as just enough to join with His own Son in sacrifice." These examples, and others, did not receive great publicity. As Léon Chaine complained, the right-wing press kept silent about them to conceal the existence of Catholic supporters of Dreyfus, and the left-wing press to veil the activities of Dreyfusards who were Catholics. Comparatively speaking, the Catholic Dreyfusards were few in number; by contrast, the anticlericals were able to present themselves as a dedicated brotherhood and, as is the nature of the case when scandal is exposed, massive press support gathered behind them. And they mercilessly pointed to every example of prejudice on the Catholic side, as the 300 priests who subscribed to a memorial for Commandant Henry the forger, the Jesuit journal in Rome which spoke of the Jews as eternal and predestinate traitors, the observation of the Assumptionist newspaper *La Croix* that it was not a question of whether Dreyfus was innocent, but "who will win, the enemies of the army or its friends?" and other outpourings of the right-wing and clericalist press. Yet, as was evident, then as now, in a dispute of this complexity examples either way prove nothing; the justification for the anticlerical attack lay, not in what was said, but in what remained unspoken. Christians, on their own showing, must be judged by

Christian standards, and the consciences of the mass of French Catholics remained unmoved by the Dreyfusard campaign, blind to the possibility that an injustice had been committed.

As early as the end of 1897, a group of Catholic intellectuals had called on the Archbishop of Paris to warn him that the outcome of a scandal about Dreyfus would be an attack on the Church, probably on its religious congregations. "It is not the Church's business to intervene", replied Cardinal Richard. "The matter must be referred to the Courts of the land." Formally, his attitude was correct. In October 1899 the *Univers*, which had been impartial throughout, defended the episcopate on these narrow grounds of propriety.

> Can anyone cite a bishop who threw himself into the controversy or, indeed, came in on either side? True, they love the army, our bishops, and they have faith in its justice, but considering they had nothing to say, they said nothing. It was the same with the secular and regular clergy.

In times of sanity this demonstration of reticence and neutrality would have been a commendation; in a France shaken to its moral foundations it was an admission, a censored version of the charge levelled by the anticlericals. When the shadow of injustice lay heavy across the land, the Catholics had had nothing to say and had remained silent. Only 300 priests out of 55,000 subscribed to the monument to Henry, but fewer still had done battle on the other side and the vast majority had stood aloof. In 1901, when the great attack on the Church was under weigh, Léon Chaine, one of the religious Dreyfusards, sadly admitted "the Catholics are paying the penalty for leaving the defence of justice to others".

These are harsh words—too harsh, for only after the event was it easy to recognize the innocence of Dreyfus. As late as February 1899, the Radical newspaper, the *Dépêche de Toulouse*, declared the facts too obscure for certain judgement. And for years afterwards, intelligent men could still be honestly mistaken. Lecanuet, a clerical historian whose probity is beyond question, believed in the guilt of Dreyfus until April 1914; only then, as he wrote his chapter on the Affair, did he realize, to his horror, that the Protestants and Jews, Zola, Clemenceau, and Jaurès must have been right.

From the first, the fact that Dreyfus was a Jew made his treason more believable. With the publication of Drumont's *La France juive* in 1886, two massive volumes running through 127 editions in two years, antisemitism suddenly became a force in French life. Brilliantly, yet without ever establishing logical connections, Drumont produced a mythical history of France in which the generous days of the Middle Ages faded as the Jews moved into positions of influence—"when the Jew rises, France declines". An alien race, they had inspired the forces of anticlericalism and formed the advance guard of the money-mad revolutionary *bourgeoisie*. Would that "a Christian prince" might arise and confiscate their property and use it to experiment with the collective ownership of factories by the workers! With a subconscious instinct rather than with calculation, Drumont had woven the Catholic dream of a Christian Middle Ages, the Catholic hatred of the French Revolution, and the Social Catholic passion for a new order into the texture of his antisemitism. His newspaper, *La Libre Parole* (from 1888) carried on the propaganda, appealing to emotions of hatred for capitalists, speculators, foreigners, and anticlericals. Among the Catholic *bourgeoisie* and working class he had many readers, whose memories were continually refreshed with tales of the Jewish financiers behind the Panama scandal and the Jewish bankers who had brought down the Union Général in 1882 and ruined its Catholic directors and shareholders. Though he believed he was doing God service ("after all I have done for him", he complained in later life, when his eyesight failed), Drumont was no theologian, and no one could mistake his tirades for overflowings of Christian charity. But there were others, including theologians and charitable Christians, who used more refined versions of his themes and saw no incongruity. Almost a third of the antisemitic books noted by R. F. Byrnes as published in France between 1870 and 1894 were written by Catholic priests. A few of these writings were the works of perverted fanatics, such as *Père* Henri Desportes, who purveyed medieval tales of ritual murder (and for his pains was turned out of his post in a seminary by the Archbishop of Rouen); a few revived the old argument from the betrayal and crucifixion of Jesus, as, for example, the Assumptionist editors of *La Croix*, who in September 1890 proclaimed their publication as "the most anti-Jewish newspaper in France, the one that bears the [symbol of] Christ, a sign of horror to the Jews"; but most of them based their antisemitism, as Drumont to some extent did, upon the cry for social justice. The Jews, they said, are responsible for the unnatural harshness of capitalistic society, a society in which religion is scorned and the family imperilled. Social Catholics attacking big department stores and the anonymous power of high finance, or clerical editors denouncing gold and mammon, tended to end up by adducing Jewish examples, as if there were no Gentile bankers or financiers.

Without the Dreyfus Affair, this sort of writing would have rapidly passed into oblivion. For Catholics—as indeed for Socialists—antisemitism was a "sick" demogogic phenomenon on the margins of social idealism, flatly contrary to central principles, and therefore essentially ephemeral. By July 1894 Drumont had lost most of his supporters and the circulation of *La Libre Parole* had sunk to a few thousand. Then Dreyfus was accused of treason, and the antisemites found themselves publicly acclaimed. And when the Jews tried to overturn the verdict, this is what was to be expected. Just as, in anticlerical circles the shifty manoeuvres of military men against Dreyfus were unreasonably summed up as "clerical" machinations, so too, among Catholics, from the very beginning the whole revisionist movement was denounced as a "Jewish plot", an invention of the *"syndicat juif"*.

The irrationality, hysteria almost, of this accusation is a pointer to an aspect of the popular Catholic mentality anticlericals have preferred to ridicule rather than explain and Catholics have preferred to forget. The long-sustained Republican attack on religion had created a persecution mania among the defeated. Churchmen, belonging to a tightly-knit organization themselves, imagined their foes as linked together in a conscious continuous design. The Jews were such an enemy group, bound up by mysterious ties of race and history; so too were the freemasons, whose lodges provided meeting places for the leading Republican politicians and secular humanist thinkers of France. It is astonishing today to reflect that credence was once given, by many religious people, to the saga of Diana Vaughan as revealed between 1895 and 1897 in the pages of a monthly journal, *Mémoires d'une Ex-Palladiste*. From the security of a convent in Charlestown, U.S.A., this notable convert described how she had been corrupted by the inner group of Satanists behind the masonic movement, how she had slept at the foot of a statue of Lucifer and seen the devil on a throne of diamonds; "always listen to the voice of reason" had been his irreligious advice. Miss Vaughan was due to appear in person at a mass meeting in Paris in 1897, but in her place turned up a grinning, whitebearded old sinner, Léo Taxil, who had originally made a living by anticlerical pornography, then had turned to piety, masonic revelations, and the invention of Diana Vaughan to obtain a new clientele of readers. Another incident in 1897 of a very different kind, not a hoax but a tragedy, in its peculiar way is equally revealing. On 4 May, in Notre-Dame, the obsequies took place of the 117 victims, mostly women, of the great Charity Bazaar fire. For the first time for twenty-five years the President of the Republic and leading ministers were present at a religious ceremony. The preacher, a Dominican, took the opportunity to castigate the crimes of France against religion. Relying on science, men had defied God; in reply, God had turned the resources of science against them (the marquee had been set on fire by an electrical short-circuit). The Church had been betrayed; to avenge it, God had sent his Angel of Death, and so much life and beauty had been trampled into the bloodstained mud and destroyed in the searing heat. "By the dead bodies strewn along the way, ye shall know that I am the Lord." Amid the outcry against this diatribe of vengeance, no one paused to ask questions about the subconscious fears and hatreds persecution had created in the minds of French Catholics, of which this sermon was a startling and pathological manifestation.

To those who believed France had betrayed its mission as "the eldest daughter of the Church" and saw the Republic falling a prey to freemasons and Jews, the army stood as the one uncontaminated institution. The officer corps of the Second Empire had been continued intact into the Republic, and as a conservative group had been strengthened by the influx of young men of Catholic and Royalist families, finding there the one career in which they could still serve the nation. It was too, Lyautey taught them, a career conferring a unique social responsibility, to be the moral educators of the new conscript generation. As Psichari was to say, the army was "the age-old institution binding us to the past—not mingled with the nation, but above it, . . . bearing the role, the lofty mission of the protector of society, once belonging to the Church, but which the Church can fulfil no longer". How then could Dreyfus be innocent seeing the honour of the army was involved in his condemnation?

After the suicide of the forger Henry, the government of the day declared the Dreyfus case reopened. This was on 14 September 1898; a fortnight later, the English ambassador asked for the immediate recall of Marchand from Fashoda, and France was on the brink of war. It was hard, just then, to listen to discreditable rumours about the higher command of the armed forces. By the following February the Republic was facing its most dangerous internal crisis since Boulanger. President Faure died on the 6th "in a state of mortal sin" (with another man's wife) in the *salon d'argent* of the Élysée. Loubet succeeded him as President, Loubet the "Panama Premier" who had hushed up the great financial scandal. Déroulède and the nationalists planned a *coup* for the 23rd, the day of Faure's funeral; it was a fiasco, but when Déroulède was put on trial, a jury acquitted him. With the hated Republic tottering, the army seemed more than ever sacrosanct, and the men of the Left were proclaiming the innocence of Dreyfus with a zeal proportionate to their need to distract attention from the corruptions of the regime. It is not entirely surprising to find the Catholics of France leaving the defence of justice to others.

On 7 August 1899, a new court martial was convened at Rennes to review the Dreyfus Case. The Commandant de Bréon, a pious Catholic, was one of the two judges (out of seven) who had the courage to dissent from the absurd verdict that Dreyfus was still guilty, though "with extenuating circumstances". The dangerous period of ministerial instability that had followed the fall of Méline was ended by a ministry of Republican concentration, and from 22 June Waldeck-Rousseau was in command, with a government composed of moderates backed by the Radicals and the Left generally. The Senate acting as a High Court condemned Déroulède for the attempted *coup d'état*. Millerand, the first Socialist to become a minister, initiated some social reforms to placate the working classes. A bristling Republican general, the *marquis* de Gallifet, notorious for his role in crushing the Commune, became Minister of War. In a few months he purged the army of the generals who had protested against the revision of the Dreyfus verdict, and established ministerial control of the promotion of officers. He then resigned and returned to his mistress in the country, being seventy years of age and having no time to waste (though to his wife, who wanted him back, he replied that "being both good Christians we have all eternity to meet again"). Now the Republic was secure there was no need to attempt to conciliate the Catholics. Triumphant in the Dreyfus business, the anticlericals were in the mood for vengeance. As always when diverse factions of Republicans had been obliged to unite themselves, their policy necessarily had to be the only policy on which they could all agree—as Albert de Mun had said, "religious war" was "the cement of their union".

If there was to be an anticlerical revenge, the religious congregations were predestined victims. Their teaching functions had for long been the object of Republican complaint. More significantly,

new grievances against them had accumulated, for in the furore of
the Dreyfus Affair attention had been drawn to what Waldeck-
Rousseau called "the parasitic, turbulent and political intervention
of the militant orders". Myths about power-mad Jesuits revived;
they were supposed to have packed the military General Staff
with their pupils (in fact, in 1898 only a dozen General Staff
officers out of 180 had attended their schools). The Assumptionist
newspaper *La Croix* had been rabid in its antisemitism, and in
January 1899 had openly appealed for a *coup* against the regime—
"Ah! who will rid us of this gang of brigands?" *Père* Ollivier's grim
sermon over the bodies of the Charity Bazaar victims was matched,
for vicious theology and sheer folly, by the discourse of *Père* Didon,
another Dominican, at a prize-giving at the *collège* of Arceuil on
15 July 1898. He called for the arrest of those who denigrate the
army—"we must brandish the sword, terrorize, cut off heads. . . ."
These and other verbal excesses were gleefully reported in the
Dreyfusard press. In strict logic, if someone had to be punished for
the perversion of justice, the army higher command ought to have
suffered. But once General Gallifet had carried out his limited purge
at the top, he recommended caution. 'We'll need the army,' he told
Waldeck-Rousseau, "it must be won over by honest procedures."
Since these honest procedures would enrage left-wing supporters of
the government, it was important to find a scapegoat. The Jesuits
with their connections with high military circles, and the Assumptionists and Dominicans who had defended the army too vocifer-
ously were conveniently available.

It is easy to see why the attack was concentrated on the congregations, though not so easy to see why so moderate a Republican
as Waldeck-Rousseau should have led the onslaught. He was not a
freemason, and there was no ebullience about his anticlericalism.
Contemporaries were puzzled. According to one theory, he anticipated a "Jacobin" oppression of the Church and, under the guise
of disciplining the congregations, was hoping to give many of them
secure legal status. Another view saw him as caring only for office.
On this interpretation, to conciliate his left-wing supporters he had
to make an anticlerical gesture, both to head them off from pursuing
the army and to prevent them bringing forward that most deadly
time-bomb for *bourgeois* France, a scheme for a progressive income
tax.

There may be truth in both these suppositions; even so, for
Waldeck-Rousseau the law on the congregations was more than a

manoeuvre or a gesture—it was a logical step, necessary even if unenthusiastically taken. Devoid of passion, his anticlericalism was essentially political in motivation. His gradual abandonment of the pious tradition of his family had nothing to do with reading Renan, the spell of Science, or the influence of the *quartier latin*. Silent, stooping, myopic, with the glazed look of a dead fish in his eyes (both Léon Daudet and Barrès hit upon this comparison; a bishop was more complimentary and said his appearance had "the frigid and distant impartiality of an English statesman"), he had no enthusiasms, except for his art collection and, of course, as a successful company lawyer, for making money. But he did have convictions. Like his father, who had been a proscript of 2 December, he believed in the Republic. He had heard the clergy of Nantes declaiming in favour of the temporal power of the Pope and praising the Second Empire, and the clergy of Rennes applauding the *seize mai*; he had been called an enemy of the Church solely because he supported obligatory education. A sincere Republican, by 1899 Waldeck-Rousseau had made a political decision against the Church because he had seen how the clergy played politics against the Republic. This conviction was intensified when, during the Dreyfus Affair, he had asked for clarification of the evidence and had been branded by the conservative press as a revisionist. Unlike most Republicans he was not prepared to believe the danger to the regime ended when Déroulède was arrested. "The physical conspiracy has vanished," he said, "but the moral conspiracy remains." The ministry he formed in July 1899 was described as one of "Republican defence", and his attempt to restrict the influence of the Church was, to him, part of an essentially defensive political strategy.

The new Prime Minister brought a sense of conviction and a lawyer's seriousness to his "defensive" sortie against the congregations. Cut off by his own psychological make-up from the intense emotions accompanying sexual experience and parenthood, he had a resentment of an intense theoretical kind against a system which encouraged a man to renounce his natural right to self-fulfilment. The country was expecting new legislation to permit greater freedom of association and, as a lawyer, Waldeck-Rousseau was unwilling to put forward a decree which did not mention the congregations in case it was taken as tacitly authorizing them. As the adviser of big business, he saw by analogy how, over the years, ecclesiastical corporations might accumulate vast fortunes and the power that goes with them. His arguments against the monks had the flavour of those of Gallican canonists of the *ancien régime*—citations of precedents from the capitularies of Charlemagne onwards and contrasting appeals to the natural rights of man, references to the menace of mortmain and to the way in which the regulars steal the most distinguished penitents and richest legacies from under the noses of the secular clergy. Like the *avocats* of the eighteenth century he believed Church and State ought to remain united by a Concordat, leaving the State with power to discipline the clergy. Monks and nuns, outside the Concordat, with no roots in secular society and looking towards Rome for leadership, he saw as a menace to the Republic, as they had been to the old monarchy.

The draft legislation put forward by the government in November 1899 was extensively amended in the Chamber and the Senate and finally became the law of 1 July 1901. Religious corporations were to apply to Parliament for authorization. If this was refused, their corporate property would be auctioned and the members dispersed, being given pensions from the proceeds of the sale. Modifications were introduced into the original draft, all on the side of harshness; they transformed "a law of Republican defence", says Sorlin, into "a beginning of a Republican offensive". Like other moderates, Méline, Poincaré, Ribot, and Rambaud, the author of the law disapproved of what was happening, yet like other Prime Ministers before him, he accepted the amendments and, indeed, overdid his tactical anticlerical protestations to the point of betraying the cause of moderation. Waldeck-Rousseau's speech at Toulouse on 28 October 1900 contained two memorable, disastrous phrases, about the "*milliard*" he supposed the property of the congregations to be worth, and about "*les deux jeunesses*", the two sets of youth within the nation, brought up in separate, hostile compartments. Still, the elections of 1902 were coming up, so the country had a chance to pronounce its verdict on the new anticlerical policy before the Deputies and Senators began their task of deciding which congregations should be authorized. It was to be a dour electoral battle, with fully 80% of the voters going to the polls, and a straight fight, uncomplicated by other issues. "There will only be two candidates," said a Jesuit preacher in a printed sermon, "Barrabas and Jesus Christ."

14 The Government of M. Combes

In the election of 1902 the right-wing groups—conservatives, monarchists, nationalists, the old *ralliés*, and, under the name of "Progressists", Méline and some other moderate Republicans who were disillusioned with the war against the Church—were better organized and co-ordinated than ever before. So too was the Left. Bound together by Freemasonry and the Dreyfusard Ligue des droits de l'homme, the Radicals had come into a tight nexus, the first real "party" to emerge in French politics. The inaugural congress of this "Radical and Radical-Socialist Party" met in June 1901 and drew up a firm programme—anticlerical, in favour of a progressive income tax but conservative about private property. Once the *enfants terribles* of the regime, the Radicals were now its rank and file, its indispensible infantry. On the right flank they were allied with Waldeck-Rousseau's Alliance républicaine démocratique, a group of moderates who remained anticlerical, and on the left with the Parti socialiste français, the main body of socialists from which Guesde's Marxist group had separated.

On the first ballot (25 April) the conservatives came within 200,000 votes of their opponents' total and won more seats outright. On the second ballot, Republican solidarity routed them. Something like 350 seats went to the Republican bloc (210 Radicals and Radical-Socialists about equally divided between these two nuances, ninety-five Alliance démocratique, and forty-five Socialists), as against 230 to the Right. Paul-Boncour took the news to Waldeck-Rousseau who waited, impassive behind the smoke of his eternal cigarette, for the final figures. "*Ils sont trops*", was all he said. The majority was excessive and excessively weighted towards the left. His hope of a moderate enforcement of the law against the congregations was fading.

At this point the leader of the Republican bloc made two decisions, one unprecedented, the other almost inexplicable. Before the Chamber met he resigned, the first time in the history of the Republic that a ministry had given up before it was actually defeated. No doubt he was unwilling to rule in complete dependence upon the Left, and was disposed to get out of the mêlée to conserve his failing health and to build up his image as an impartial elder statesman worthy to become President of the Republic. Then, having resigned, he made the astonishing recommendation to Loubet of Émile Combes to be his successor as Prime Minister. Henceforward, Waldeck-Rousseau's role in politics was limited to protesting against the unjust enforcement of his own legislation by the man he had deliberately nominated to govern in his place. One can only assume he had hoped for left-wing support for his candidature for the Presidency because of the laws against the congregations, with the Right turning to him as a moderate once they had experienced the abrasive rule of an extreme anticlerical.

The new Prime Minister was sixty-seven years of age, short of stature, with a large nose, a white goatee beard, and a venerable frock coat, an ensemble forming an irresistable combination for cartoonists, an old-world Balzacian figure, a mediocre politician who had at last arrived. He came from a lower middle class family of the Department of the Tarn. This being the land of the Albigensian Crusade, contemporaries were quick to point out a geographical explanation for an anticlerical career: here was a descendant of heretics inspired by folk memories of orthodox cruelty, "the last victim of Simon de Montfort". A more realistic explanation, though this too could easily be oversimplified, saw Combes wreaking a revenge upon the Church which had turned him down for ordination. After proceeding to a doctorate with a thesis on Aquinas (hinting that the great schoolman was too liberal) and winning a fair report at his seminary ("Piety ordinary, conduct good"), he had finally been censured as "Proud" and encouraged to leave. Thereafter this disappointed theologian made his way as a medical practitioner (a profession in those days full of sceptics and atheists), as a freemason, and as a local politician in the Department of the Charente-Inférieure. Eventually, in 1885, at the age of fifty, he was elected to the Senate. Thus, tardily, from a provincial milieu Combes emerged, Flaubert's M. Homais risen into national affairs with no aim beyond breaking the "will to domination" inherent in Catholicism. His anticlericalism was not of the sort common among the experienced politicians of Paris, shrewd and supple, but rather that of the electors of small provincial towns, voting ostentatiously against the Church and too proud and pig-headed to give open approval to the compromises their representatives eventually had to make in the interests of public peace. Combes oversimplified French politics and ignored its unwritten laws. He assumed, because the electors had sent up a majority of anticlericals to the Chamber, that they wanted an anticlerical policy ruthlessly enforced, ignoring the possibility of their willingness to be deceived; he assumed his duty as Prime Minister extended to the use of his parliamentary majority to act punitively against minority opposition in the country, even if, as the first ballot showed, the minority was only a quarter of a million votes behind.

"*J'ai été toute ma vie un spiritualiste fervent*", said Combes in his memoirs, that is, he had always been a devotee of the "spiritualistic philosophy", he believed life had a religious meaning. Religion was one of the great moral forces in human history, and Positivism and materialism were dangerous, he told the Chamber in January 1903, and was naively astonished at the outcry in the ranks of his own supporters. On his family tomb the curious could read the legend engraved by order of this most anticlerical of Prime Ministers: "In death as in life, our hearts tell us there is no eternal separation". Here was one of those opponents of Catholicism whose hatred was rooted neither in unbelief nor scepticism, but in a fervent deism. From this conviction, with the aid of readings from Michelet and memories of his early Catholic training, Combes inferred the existence of a guiding providence. His own call to form a government was an operation of "the unknown law that presides over the progressive development of human societies", and in his old age he went further and claimed mystical experiences. So the analogy with Flaubert's M. Homais is not entirely just. In spite of the meanness of his policies, the new Prime Minister was more than a dreary provincial anticlerical. The foreign diplomat who described him as "possessed by the Devil", the *vicomte* Melchior de Vögué who talked of "the national antipope", and Ribot who complained of this "theologian who had strayed into politics" had seized on another aspect of a peculiar character. Combes was a religious fanatic persecuting Catholicism in the interests of the true religion; as Chastenet says, "Homais, Torquemada and the Savoyard *vicaire* rolled into one".

The first task of the new ministry was to put into effect Waldeck-Rousseau's law on the religious congregations. Already the news of its passage was having an impact. Educational activities which had quietly been resumed after Ferry's purge now ceased. Some 138 non-authorized congregations (out of the total of 753) had decided it was useless to apply for recognition; Jesuits, Assumptionists, Carmelites, and others had gone into exile or dispersed. Young Teilhard de Chardin, who at twenty-one years of age had just completed his noviciate with the Jesuits of Laval, went off with the rest of the house to Jersey; he remembered how the good fathers disguised themselves in lay attire provided by local sympathizers and, not knowing the fashions of the world, wore top hats with sporting flannels and motoring caps with morning coats. Combes, who had tightened up parliamentary procedures and party liaisons to ensure the effective use of his majority, subjected the wording of the law to a close analysis to ensure no accident of mercy or nonsense about merit intruded into its application. The Conseil d'État ruled that all projects must be put to Parliament as proposals for positive authorization which either house, acting alone, could definitively reject. This enabled the government to put before the Senate the half-dozen cases it was willing to let through (the Trappists, the White Fathers of North Africa, and so on), leaving the rest to face certain abolition by the Chamber. Here discussion was discouraged by bringing forward the projects in bunches, as someone observed, in tumbril loads for the guillotine. The anticlerical majority sank to sixteen when eighty-one congregations of nuns were destroyed in a single vote; otherwise all went smoothly.

Having bent the law itself, the government also resorted to chicanery on its borders. In spite of protests by the moderates and riots in Brittany, it closed some 3,000 schools founded by the authorized congregations since the date of their authorization. A new law ordering these congregations to abandon all teaching functions within the next ten years was forced through. Deputies who voted for it knew they had passed the point where individual liberty was betrayed. With his usual insensitivity (or lack of hypocrisy?) the Prime minister blandly reassured them: "Liberty of education is not one of those essential rights which are inseparable from the person of the citizen ... [it is] a concern of the social power, which has the right to regulate its usage." For him, of course, "the social power" meant the government of the day, however ephemeral, and "regulate" meant "annihilate", as the whole affair of the congregations demonstrated. Had the Senate not stood firm, the Chamber would have forbidden former members of religious congregations to teach for five years after their secularization, and Combes did, in fact, trespass so far upon individual freedom as to forbid the ex-monks to preach. "Preaching is their only trade," said *La République Française.* "Everyone cannot be like M. Combes and, after leaving the cassock, make a living out of politics."

Combes did not mean anyone to starve, but he wasted no time in officious striving to keep monks and nuns alive. The law offered them pensions from the proceeds of the sale of their corporate property. In fact, the disposal of this property was another of the great financial scandals of the Third Republic, and though Waldeck-Rousseau's *"milliard"* had been a myth from the start, what money there was melted away as it passed through the hands of lawyers and liquidators. A high administrative official, Louis Méjan, a Protestant and a supporter of measures to control clerical influence, described how his department could give only "derisory" help to a frail and starving ex-abbess whose teaching community had once possessed "a considerable fortune". "The vow of poverty", he observed, "does not include suffering from hunger and cold, and it is not for the State or the law to impose it." But for the fact that numbers of ex-monks and nuns managed to carry on as teachers in schools opened under a façade of lay control, there would have been more individual tragedies of this kind. If Combes and his majority in the Chamber had had their way, members of the dispersed congregations would not have enjoyed even the elementary freedom to earn their living.

Waldeck-Rousseau had hoped to conciliate the secular clergy and the laity while the attack on the congregations proceeded. This was not the way of the Combes administration, which preferred to be deliberately provocative. Three bishops had their salaries stopped for petitioning on behalf of the regulars, soldiers were forbidden to spend their leisure in confessional circles, ecclesiastics were excluded from certain State examinations, crucifixes were removed from the law courts. The navy, traditionally religious, was the object of special measures. Nuns were turned out of its hospitals, a battleship was named after Ernest Renan, the prince of sceptics, the Good Friday fast on shipboard was abolished, so too was the mass of the Holy Spirit at the beginning of term at the naval academy. "A few more measures of this kind," observed the *Débats,* "and it's all up with the English naval supremacy."

As for the old anticlerical tactic of plausible conciliatory talk at the Vatican while the Church in France was being undermined, Combes would have none of it. As early as December 1902 he deliberately invited a head-on collision on the most important issue in the whole field of Church–State relationships, the right of the French government to nominate the bishops. Without any of the usual preliminary soundings, without any unofficial understanding, he sent three names off to Rome. The Pope refused to provide the bulls of canonical institution, and the whole matter was put to the French Chamber as involving the possibility of a cancellation of the Concordat and the separation of Church and State.

In July 1903, shortly after the beginning of the quarrel over episcopal nominations, Leo XIII died. The new Pope, Cardinal Sarto, Patriarch of Venice, who took the name of Pius X, was a saint, spoken of as such in his lifetime and formally canonized within forty years of his death. Although he was from a poor family (the only pope of the two centuries before 1958 who had known true penury), and in spite of his experience of pastoral administration, he had none of his predecessor's knowledge of the ways of the world—he did not share Leo XIII's overriding concern for the social question, had little sympathy with the intellectual ferment stirring within Catholicism, and no conception of the importance of diplomatic expertise to spiritual men who have to seek spiritual objectives within an uncomprehending materialistic society. His reforming tendencies manifested themselves strictly within the institutional boundaries of the Church, in the encouragement of pastoral care, in liturgical practice and sacred music, canon law and central administration. To his role of leader in the external battle against anticlericalism and scepticism, he brought no capacity for manoeuvre, no sense of timing. All he could offer was courage and honesty, though after all, these were supreme virtues, and in the harsh struggle that lay ahead even a good man might have faltered in the practice of either.

With *"Combisme"* rampant in France and a vigorous, unyielding Pope newly elected, an open rupture between Church and State became a real possibility. If peace was to be preserved, a delicate web of conciliation would have to be woven by professional negotiators on either side, more especially by the new papal Secretary of State. But the choice of Pius X was unfortunate. Merry del Val, a Spanish aristocrat and son of a diplomat, intelligent and master of many languages, seemed technically well-qualified; in fact, he was young, brash, and incisive in a post and at a time when experience, caution, and studied evasiveness were the qualities needed. As for Combes' attitude, the death of the aged pontiff of the

Ralliement and rumours from Rome of his successor's inclination
to favour old Royalists and nationalists of the new Action française
was a signal to be even more ruthless, and Pius X was soon confronted with further unilateral episcopal nominations.

Subjected to cold psephological analysis, any method of appoint-
ing a bishop is potentially scandalous. Popes and Patriarchs, synods
and committees, the clergy and laity in hierarchy or *en masse* can be
ill-informed, misled, or partisan about politics or religion, unenter-
prising or reckless. When Church and State are in alliance, the
argument in defence of appointment by the secular authority rests
largely upon the safeguard that the reputation of a monarch or a
ministry can be adversely affected by unsuitable choices, while the
way is left open for those eccentric candidates—scholars, reformers,
visionaries—which ecclesiastical authority might wish to avoid and
mass voting or committee decisions would be inclined to pass over
in favour of straightforward pastoral zeal or safe mediocrity. On the
other hand, the dangers of secular choice had always been recognized. When, under the Civil Constitution of the Clergy of 1790 a
system of election by the ordinary political electors of the Department had been laid down, the clergy had protested this would
subject them to the whims of local notables and allow Protestants
and unbelievers to cast a vote. Even so, Mirabeau had replied that
the practice of the *ancien régime* under the Concordat of 1516 had
been no better, for royal mistresses and aristocratic courtiers had
pushed their nominees into the Gallican hierarchy. The Concordat
of 1801 as operated under the Third Republic lent itself, *mutatis
mutandis,* to similar abuses. In *L'Orme du Mail* (1897) and its
sequel *L'Anneau d'Améthyste* Anatole France ironically rehearsed
the processes elevating the *abbé* Guitrel to the bishopric of
Tourcoing. Mme Worms-Clavelin, the Jewish prefect's wife, for
whom he buys antique ecclesiastical vestments to cover stools for
her drawing room, sacrifices her virtue on his behalf, in a cab, to
the nephew of the Minister of Religious Affairs. Another chain of
connections leads Mme de Gramance to promise to her lover that
she will appeal to the Minister—she is not exactly overdressed at
the time she agrees to put through this delicate ecclesiastical
negotiation. Loyer, the Minister himself, "a *philosophe* grown
white-haired in clandestine love affairs and bar-room gossip"
welcomes the appointment of Guitrel when he hears him declaim
against the spirit of revolt among the religious orders, and the story
ends with the new bishop, safely installed, publishing a manifesto

calling on the monks to refuse to pay taxation. This scandalous tale
has its verisimilitude. It was common for governments to complain
of ecclesiastics concealing awkward opinions until their bishopric
was secure. There was *curé* Marpot, for example, a protégé of
Grévy and a "Republican", who was appointed Bishop of Saint-
Claude in 1880; then, said the prefect, "He threw off his mask very
cynically once he was consecrated." The *abbé* Bougaud had a
"liberal" reputation until he became Bishop of Laval (Mayenne) in
1888, but his first pastoral letter was full of devotion to the Sacred
Heart, eulogies of the Jesuits, and condemnation of the regicides
who had executed Louis XVI. "*Je ne reconnais plus mon homme*",
the prefect lamented. As Briand said, "a Minister of Religious
Affairs is like a hen sitting on ducks' eggs".

Even so, the episcopal appointments of the Third Republic were,
for the most part, unexceptionable. Governments were anxious to
avoid right-wing firebrands, but they still had to find someone
capable of leading the clergy of the diocese, otherwise the most
exemplary loyalty to the regime was useless. Sceptics might wish to
avoid obscurantist churchmen (or seek them out to discredit
religion?) but even fervent anticlericals had their local pride, and
were not willing to accept an inferior bishop. In some departments,
the Catholic Republican vote was significant, and Catholics, however tenuous their religious allegiance, would be insulted by a jobbed
appointment. So the nominations generally fell on men of dignity
and intelligence, good pastors and sound administrators. Though the
government did not concede that Rome had a *right* to be consulted,
it was customary to reach an understanding with the nuncio (the
"*entente préalable*") before a particular name was officially proposed. Negotiations rarely fell into a deadlock. Of the forty-eight
episcopal vacancies from 1891 to 1902, nearly half were settled
within three months and only one see remained vacant for more
than a year; of the eighteen translations of this period, in all cases
except four, Government and nuncio had reached agreement before
the translated prelate had left his diocese. Combes, who ignored the
unwritten laws of French politics, also ignored the unwritten code
for dealing with the Vatican which made the Concordat workable.
Once the nomination of bishops by the anticlerical Republic
became a take-it-or-leave-it matter conducted in the glare of
publicity, the system inevitably broke down.

Pius X began by showing a will to conciliation. He accepted the
demand of the French government for the amendment of the

phrase *nobis nominavit* in the bulls of canonical institution— *nominavit* would stand alone. Of the two new names for bishoprics, one was accepted, one refused. But the government took notice only of the refusal, and in January 1904 declared no future vacancies would be filled until the earlier nominations were accepted, a demonstration of pique that even anticlericals thought illogical.

Unluckily, at this point another problem arose concerning, not the appointment of new bishops, but the removal of established ones. Bishop Géay of Laval was accused of immorality, and Bishop Le Nordez of Dijon of consorting with freemasons. The former was supposed to have carried on a sentimental correspondence with the Mother Superior of a nunnery, the latter to have worn a masonic apron in a masonic procession—and once this story got out, rumour added the ordination of his natural son and misappropriation of money collected for a statue of Bossuet to the crime sheet. Everything becomes easier to understand when we realize they were both Republican prelates ruling over ultra-Royalist dioceses. In June 1904 they were summoned to Rome. Eventually they went, were ordered to resign, and attempted to do so. According to the Organic Articles, it was illegal to obey a Roman summons without the permission of the government. It was doubtful if the Pope had the right to demand a resignation without reference to the secular power, and the charges of immorality and masonic allegiance had not been cleared up—the essential charge levelled against the bishops at Rome was that they had revealed the contents of papal correspondence, they had "handed over to the secular arm the secrets of the Church". Combes, therefore, had some technical justification for refusing to accept the bishops' resignations, though with characteristic meanness, he also stopped their salaries on the ground that they had left France without permission.

Combes' ministry lasted for two years, seven months, and ten days. This period, brief in absolute terms, but long for a ministry of the Third Republic, saw the rapid interlocking of all the issues that had troubled Church–State relationships for a generation, as if circumstances were conspiring to prove Combes' providential theory of his own rise to power (or the opposition theory of diabolical inspiration). The dispute over education, the battle against the religious congregations, the expulsion of the clergy from official ceremonies, the deadlock over episcopal nominations under the Concordat, and the challenge, through the application of the

Organic Articles, to papal control of the bishops—each theme came in turn to play its part in the orchestration of a thunderous finale. And at the very end came the Roman question. Here was a motif from the earlier movements of the symphony, by now almost forgotten. The Pope remained a "prisoner" in the Vatican, refusing to recognize the Italian seizure of Rome. Yet a *modus vivendi* had been reached. Italian governments were respectful and the papacy maintained its position in theory rather than in practice. The royal march had been played in the Vatican and Pius X, so the story went, in private had said his advice to the king of Italy would be "Stay where you are". Foreign nations had lost interest and, as Binchy says, "the Roman question had virtually disappeared from the agenda of international politics". That this mine, so deeply buried, suddenly exploded was the unnecessary outcome of what ought to have been a purely formal disagreement about the ceremonial details of a developing Franco–Italian entente.

In October 1903 the King of Italy made a state visit to France. Obviously, President Loubet had to return the compliment by visiting Rome, whatever displeasure this gesture might cause in the Vatican. The European situation became full of menace for France; on 8 February 1904 the Japanese navy sank the Russian squadron in Port Arthur, and from henceforward the Russians were no longer available to hold Germany in check with a threat from the rear. With the Russian alliance useless, it was more than ever important to court Italy. In March 1904 the credits for the visit of the French President were voted, by 502 against 10 in the Chamber of Deputies and 258 against 2 in the Senate. In April Loubet saw the King of Italy in Rome and on the 28th of that month the fateful note of protest was despatched from the papal Curia to Paris.

When the visit to Rome had first been mooted, the Vatican had been inclined to show only moderate disapproval. Pius X told a journalist he appreciated the difficulties of France, and hoped the French would understand "that for reasons that are equally political I have to follow the lines of conduct adopted by my predecessors". Just possibly, the crudeness of the choice between Pope and King could have been offset by some conciliatory gesture. Two schemes were mooted: Loubet might be received in audience by His Holiness, or the French Foreign Minister, Delcassé, might meet Cardinal Merry del Val in the French embassy. Only the second proposal was feasible, and it was rendered impossible by a deliberate indiscretion of the *Figaro*. Merry del Val, it appears, regarded the cancellation of the meeting as an insult and, as often happens, the situation was worse after conciliation had been tried than it would have been in the first place. So the visit proceeded without camouflage or conciliatory gestures, and Merry del Val drafted the papal protest.

If this protest had been kept secret, no great harm would have resulted, but the Cardinal Secretary of State was preoccupied to the point of folly with the maintenance of papal prestige, and he circulated a copy to all governments. Not surprisingly, there was a leak; on 17 May Jaurès published the whole document in *L'Humanité*. Frenchman could now read how the Pope considered they ought to be grateful for being allowed the protectorate of Catholic interests in the Orient, and for their large representation in the College of Cardinals (they had seven, the Italians had forty), and how they ought to be willing to sacrifice their national security to share in a papal feud against the kingdom of Italy which had fallen out of fashion even in the Vatican. They could also read a sentence (found only in the copies, not in the original to the French government) which seemed to imply that the nuncio was only staying on in Paris because the fall of the Combes government could confidently be expected. It would have been difficult for an anticlerical forger (even the incomparable Léo Taxil himself) to have invented such a provocative and discreditable document.

There was universal outcry in France. The French ambassador was recalled from the Vatican. The Catholics, who had fought so hard with every argument for their schools and congregations, were reduced to despair and silence. Anticlericals could strike their next blow where they willed; the whole Church–State relationship was in jeopardy. The folly of Merry del Val had presented Combes with his last and greatest triumph.

15   Towards the Law of Separation

In theory, anticlericals looked forward to the abrogation of the Concordat and the separation of Church and State; in practice, up to the reign of Combes, ministries came and went and nothing was done. Gambetta had taught the Republicans how to combine the luxury of violent words with the security of moderate policies; like the *revanche*, the dream of a war of revenge against Germany, the Separation was a subject for hope, not for action.

One reason for delay was the lack of consensus of opinion about ways and means, and in an affair of this magnitude these were of the essence of the operation. Conflicting precedents were cited—Ireland, Mexico, the United States, and France itself during the Revolution after the law of 3 *Ventôse* year III. French jurists, too preoccupied with the rights of man as an individual, had struggled throughout the century to reconcile the authority of the State with the freedom of independent associations within society; the Church, complex in its internal ramifications and inextricably linked to an external authority, presented the extreme case which challenged all their principles and precedents. Few anticlericals defended the *budget des cultes* as necessary compensation for ecclesiastical property sold during the great Revolution, but there were some who agreed with Yves Guyot's proposal (December 1886) to allow the taxpayers of each commune to decide for themselves if they wished to pay the clergy. A great deal of property, of distant or recent origin and entangled through bequests and legacies with the interests of many families was at stake. The country was not likely to accept brutal schemes of confiscation like those put forward by Jules Roche in 1882 and by the Socialists Allard, Dejeante, and Vaillant in January 1901, nor was it likely to abandon to an independent corporation buildings and lands that were, in some sense, a national heritage. When problems were so complex and majorities so fluctuating, it had seemed best to successive governments to avoid the issue of the Separation until the time became ripe and some consensus of opinion began to appear.

Though anticlericals spoke of the Concordat as a traditional arrangement which they were tolerating until the march of progress swept it away, this was not the whole story. Sometimes they were frank and admitted Bonaparte's old agreement was useful to them, indispensible almost. "We see in the Concordat", said Paul Bert in 1881, "the surest guarantee we possess against the encroachments of the Catholic Church"—the famous old argument that a treaty which bridled the Church could not lightly be abandoned. If the Vatican appointed the bishops and issued irresponsible orders, if Royalist nobles and reactionary industrialists provided the bulk of ecclesiastical funds, if the clergy could not be kept out of electioneering by the suppression of their salaries, and if pious Catholics became accustomed to regard the State as completely alien to religion and morals—what would happen to the Republic if years of crisis or scandal came again? An official of the Department of Religious Affairs told Méjan in 1902 that to separate Church and State would be as foolish an act as to release wild beasts from their cages in the Place de la Concorde to pounce on pedestrians. This, no doubt, was the exaggerated analogy of a civil servant who felt his job was in danger, but it reflected the real concern of Republican politicians. The famous phrase invented by a French Protestant in 1842 and adopted by Cavour, "a free Church in a free State", was regarded by them with the utmost suspicion. It conjured up a picture of the two powers treating on a basis of equality. "The French doctrine, on the contrary," said Ferdinand Buisson, "is that of national Sovereignty. The State is not free, it is sovereign, and the only sovereign." Raoul Allier, a Protestant professor of philosophy, writing in *Le Siècle* (6 November 1904) adjusted the formula to read, "the Church religiously free in the State politically secure from its menaces"; Louis Méjan's simpler version was "the free Church within the sovereign State". Whatever its faults, the Concordat preserved the sovereignty of the State. If there was no treaty between France and the Vatican, and Church and State were separated, how could this sovereignty be secured without open breach of all the principles of liberty?

These cautionary arguments could not retain their force for ever. From time to time, originally as a sort of anticlerical ritual, proposals for the separation of Church and State were put forward in the Chamber. In 1894 only 149 votes were in favour, less than in 1886. Then the rise begins; 183 votes in 1896, followed by a slight drop three years later, then 194 on 20 November 1900, and as many as 237 on 19 May 1903 during the ministry of Combes. By then the question was under permanent examination, for on 20 October 1902, by 290 votes against 254, a Commission had been set up to examine "all propositions relating to the separation of the Churches and the State, and for the denunciation of the Concordat". True, the matter was not treated as urgent, for the thirty-three members of the Commission were not named by the Chamber until 11 June 1903, after a delay of eight months. From then onwards, however, with Buisson as chairman and Briand as *rapporteur* work proceeded steadily.

"*Ils sont trops*", Waldeck-Rousseau had said after the victory of the Republican bloc in the elections of 1902. This was the decisive point—all the bitterness of the years after Dreyfus had been distilled into the creation of a solid anticlerical majority in the Chamber of Deputies. The once distant prospect of a separation of Church and State suddenly became a real and early possibility. Combes, with all his inquisitorial mentality, was in principle a man of Gambetta's school, seeking to limit the Church within the boundaries of a narrowly interpreted Concordat, not to set it adrift from the State. But he was to be pushed along by his left-wing supporters. The 1901 Congress of the Radical party had included the Separation in its official prospectus for the voters. Clemenceau, who hated the Church for reasons most of which Combes would have considered as recommendations—for its teaching of immortality, its belief in the possibility of individual altruism, for its useless foreign missions, and its turning of high society into charitable activities which camouflage the struggle for existence—was there to goad the Radicals towards the extreme courses their manifesto had vaguely proclaimed.

Further to the left, the Socialists were now committed to ending the Concordat. This decision might have gone the other way, for it did not arise from basic ideology nor, so far as the politicians were concerned, from irreconcilable hatreds. Jaurès praised those "great religious aspirations which, under a diversity of myths, symbols and dogmas have uplifted the human mind"; he did not deny the usefulness of the Church in the long years while men were groping towards the true religion of justice, and in particular he applauded the sincerity of Albert de Mun and his antediluvian Social Catholicism. True, Jaurès was unique in the breadth of his interests and tolerance. But other Socialist leaders, harsher and more doctrinaire, such as Paul Lafargue, Marx's son-in-law, and Guesde himself, followed Jaurès in regarding the religious question as secondary and consequential—the whole furore against the Church was a device of the capitalists to divert the workers from warfare against their true enemies. In strict logic then, it was not necessary for the Socialist deputies in the Chamber to join the *bourgeois* politicians in their attack on Catholicism.

That they did so was partly a result of pressure from the anticlerical rank and file of the working class. In his maiden speech in the Chamber (December 1891) Lafargue had contemptuously dismissed anticlerical agitation as a capitalist "toy" to divert the workers, and had praised Albert de Mun. Immediately he was assailed with protests from his followers in the country at large, and he hastily covered himself by producing a project for the separation of Church and State and by making an onslaught on the "confessional police" and the "religio-capitalist" teachings of Social Catholicism. In the Nord and the Aube the working classes were bitterly anticlerical, and these two departments set the tone for the whole Socialist movement. In the Aube we hear of Socialist groups holding "civic first communions" with a diploma presented in the shade of a red flag, of "civic baptisms", and meat teas on Good Friday; in the Nord, of burial clubs to keep priests away from funerals, and of a Socialist prefect who anticipated the Clochemerle epic by replacing a Calvary with a urinal. But the deputies in the Chamber also had more rational and directly political motives for their decision to embrace the anticlerical programme. One obvious response to the capitalists' diversionary "toy" was to refuse to collaborate with the *bourgeoisie*, but a more subtle one was to join them wholeheartedly, force through their programme, and exhaust it. From the end of 1901 this became a conscious policy. As the final crisis drew near, Jaurès proclaimed the objective openly. "It is time", he said on 15 August 1904, "for this great but obsessive problem of the relations of Church and State to be finally settled, so that democracy can devote all its attention to the immense and difficult task of social reform . . . which the proletariat is demanding."

With the Socialists on the warpath behind them, even moderate Radicals found it hard to stop short of the full implementation of their official policy. Those behind cried forward, even when those before cried back. Perhaps anticlericals would have hesitated more if churchmen had shown awareness of the possible advantages of freedom from State control. Few did so. The official policy of the Vatican was the maintenance of the Concordat. An inquiry by the journalist, Julien de Narfon, at the end of 1903 showed that only one bishop (Le Camus of La Rochelle) was clearly in favour of Separation. Christian Democrats and Catholic Republicans wanted to keep things as they were, lest the Church in rural areas became an apanage of the château and in towns of the rich. The *abbé* Lemire increasingly felt the weight of this argument. In 1889 he had been in favour of ending the Concordat, and in the *Univers* he told how Cardinal Manning had said to him, "So long as you receive money you will not be free"; but in his parliamentary speeches on the Law of Separation six years later he was expressing his fear "that capitalists would infiltrate the Church of France". For all his complaints of servitude to the State, the *abbé* Frémont had little faith in the ability of the clergy to make effective use of their freedom, and he preferred to have them continuing to receive official salaries rather than "unleashed all over France, brandishing crucifixes in their rage". As Catholics clung to the Church–State connection, anticlericals were more inclined to deprive them of it. In place of the old view of the Concordat as a barrier to clerical encroachment a new analogy became fashionable—it was a framework which kept a potentially fissiparous Catholicism together as an institution. Allard described his plan for a separation as calculated to dissolve the "Roman bloc" into "little chapels without property or cohesion". "Break the bonds by which you attach the Church to the State," wrote Anatole France in 1904, "break the forms by which you give it the appearance and the standing of a great political corporation, and soon you will see it disintegrating in its [new found] liberty."

On the Commission to examine "all propositions relating to the separation of the Churches and the State", the anticlericals had a majority. Seventeen of its members (eighteen if we include one who wanted his opinion verified by popular referendum) were in favour of the abolition of the Concordat. Allard (who described the Christian religion as "a scourge whose ravages on the human mind can only be compared to those of alcoholism") early forced a vote establishing the aim of future sessions as the working out of a coherent plan for the Separation. From June 1903 when the Commission began its sittings, various proposals sent up by individual deputies or senators since April were discussed. Two proposals, one from Gustave Hubbard and another from Boissy d'Anglas (a direct descendant of the author of the law of 3 *Ventôse* year III) favoured the *simultaneum*, the leasing, for limited periods, of church buildings to various religious bodies with arrangements for their "simultaneous" use. From Flourens came a liberal scheme which would have left the Church free to do as it wished under the common law, including bringing back the expelled congregations. By contrast, Grosjean's proposal was designed to forbid monks of non-authorized congregations to perform religious functions during a long cooling-off period, after which a new Concordat was to be negotiated with Rome. While these discussions proceeded, the crisis of relations with the Vatican came. On 17 May 1904, *L'Humanité* published Merry del Val's letter of protest against President Loubet's visit; on the 21st, the French ambassador left Rome. On 29 July the continuing deadlock over Bishops Géay and Le Nordez decided Combes to break off entirely all relations with the Papal Curia since, "in view of the stand the Holy See has taken, there is no further point in them". The anticlerical determination to force a final reckoning was intensified. France had been insulted and public opinion would now support extreme measures of retaliation against the Vatican.

For as long as he could, consistently with his determination to remain in office, Combes resisted pressure to put forward an official governmental proposal for the Separation. In August 1904 he was saying that income tax and workers' retirement pensions would be given priority, which meant the Concordat would survive at least to the elections of 1906. But on 29 October, with a scandal, the affair of the *fiches*, threatening to disintegrate the Republican bloc, he put up a scheme to the Commission. On 10 November, in reply to a derisive challenge from a nationalist deputy, the Prime Minister finally handed over his text as the formal project of a law. This whole document was a startling revelation of the persistence of the old theory that a Church freed from State control would be a menace to society. Combes proposed to allow the Church to retain the use of its property provisionally by renewable decennial grants to associations in each diocese. These associations were forbidden to league together on a national scale, and their reserve funds would be limited to the ridiculous maximum of one third of annual income. Priests who performed acts or made speeches compromising "the honour of citizens" or implying "accusations against individuals" would be liable to fine or imprisonment. A group of Protestants led the way in pointing out the injustice of these regulations. "Are there special police measures for societies of freethinkers?" they asked. "And for socialist groups and masonic lodges?" The whole project was a Civil Constitution of the Clergy for a limited, weakened State Church, rather than a law of Separation; as Clemenceau said, it was *"le règne concordataire sans le Concordat"*.

Ten weeks after the deposition of his draft design, Combes' administration came to its inglorious end. From the start his government had made clear its intention to reserve official posts for its own supporters. This was not surprising, but on 28 October 1904 the Chamber learned that the promotion of army officers was being influenced by secret dossiers compiled within the masonic movement. "Very cold and very reserved: was present at his son's first communion"—these were the sort of reports, the *fiches* from the files of the Grand Orient read out by Guyot de Villeneuve to the scandalized Assembly. Within a week, General André, the Minister of War was driven to resignation. Syveton, the nationalist deputy who slapped the general's face in the Chamber, was found dead, murdered, it was said, by the masons or the police. More evidence of government by espionage accumulated; even deputies had been the subject of confidential investigations. It was "an inverted form of Jesuitism", said Clemenceau. On 14 January 1905, the government majority sank to six, and four days later Combes resigned.

"Who will bring us a new faith, hope and charity?" Anatole France had asked sixteen years ago. For a brief moment he and the idealists among the anticlericals had found what they were seeking in the form of passionate allegiance to the cause of justice for the individual, the cause of Captain Dreyfus. The impetus for the final assault on the Church had come from their victory. But their moral exhilaration was to be shortlived, and under Combes the lofty principles of the Dreyfusards ended up as ideological props for the corrupt domination of a Republican "establishment" virtually untouched by the pale gleams of the new religion of secular humanism and justice. Joseph Lotte, Péguy's friend (they made their mutual admission of conversion to Christian belief in a famous conversation in September 1907), was still an anticlerical in 1903, but was bitterly disillusioned by the conduct of the anticlerical politicians. The oppression of the congregations by Combes was, he thought, a manoeuvre as cynical as those used against Dreyfus, and the intolerant and dishonourable pressures used to affirm the domination of anticlericalism in the provinces revolted him. "Here", he wrote (from Loudon), "no official is entitled to go to mass. That's why I sometimes feel I'd like to go myself." Yet they were all under orders to go to an anticlerical banquet: "All the poor devils of schoolmasters . . . have to pay their subscriptions . . . to come and digest the unpalatable food and the unpalatable discourses of the *Combistes* of the *arrondissement*. Needless to say, I didn't go." Lotte's hatred of the "tyranny" of the ruling group was shared by Péguy, who, in the same year, described their policies as nothing more than a trick to stay in office: "A government which does nothing and does not attack the Church falls; a government which does nothing and attacks the Church stays." There were many Frenchman who thought, obscurely, like Lotte and Péguy, and it was not long before men of all parties were to agree in rejecting the "abject" system of Combes. His administration had destroyed the new mystique which the battles over the Dreyfus case had given to the anticlerical cause, and its shoddy and divisive policies mark the beginning of the end of the idealism and religiosity which had formed such an important driving force within the anticlericalism of the century which had just ended.

Yet the decisive reaction against *"Combisme"* was delayed, and his fall and discredit made no difference to the progress of the attack on the Church. A new ministry, formed on 24 January under Rouvier, had little in the way of a programme beyond the promise to legislate for the separation of Church and State. This was now regarded as inevitable.

History was repeating its patterns. Rouvier, a moderate of the school of Gambetta, who had accepted the help of the Right against Boulanger, was reluctant to alienate conservative forces from the Republic, and his preference, shared by Delcassé and two other ministers, was for the maintenance of the Concordat. But the price of left-wing support, as usual, had to be paid. In February Bienvenu Martin, the Minister of Education and Religious Affairs, produced a new project for a law of Separation, which was sent up to the Commission. After this all went smoothly. Briand (who did much to make the new legislation more liberal and conciliatory than had been expected) reported the Commission's proposals to the Chamber from March onwards, and the law was voted there on 3 July, by 314 votes against 233. By its provisions church buildings and property (with the exception of certain limited categories acquired since the Concordat) were taken over by the State. *Associations cultuelles*, religious associations, "conforming to the rules of the general organization of the religion whose exercise they propose to ensure" (an important qualifying clause, whose history will be considered later) were to be formed, and would be put in charge of the church buildings and, for a limited time of two to five years, of the presbyteries and seminaries also. There was no attempt, as in Combes' scheme, to isolate and weaken the *associations cultuelles*; they could federate together, set up reserve funds, and, presumably, "conforming to the rules of the general organization" of Catholicism, give due attention to the rights of the clerical hierarchy in the manner in which their business was conducted. The State would cease paying the salaries of the clergy, though there would be a tapering-out period of four years to ease the transition, and existing pension rights were safeguarded. Some vestiges of old privileges would remain, in so far as seminarists would be free from military service, providing they really did proceed to ordination and a parish, and the State and communes would be allowed to pay chaplains "to ensure the liberty of religion in public establishments", for example, at an army camp or hospital far-removed from parish churches. Henceforward the bishops would be free to correspond with Rome, and to adjust diocesan and parish boundaries. Existing religious emblems would remain in place and religious ornaments were to be allowed in cemeteries, but a mayor could forbid other "exterior manifestations" and would have the decisive say in controlling the ringing of church bells, with appeal against him to the prefect.

In the interval between the vote of the Chamber and the vote of the Senate, sensational political events intervened—the Tangier crisis and the fall of Delcassé, followed in November by the disintegration of the Republican bloc over the question of the right of schoolmasters to strike. But the Law proceeded on its way. It was accepted by the Senate on 6 December by 181 votes against 102, and officially promulgated on 11 December. In a year's time the Separation was to come into effect. Like the National Assembly of 1790 which had devised the Civil Constitution of the Clergy, the French Parliament had legislated on ecclesiastical affairs without consulting the Church. It remained to be seen if the Church would accept what was proposed.

16 For and Against the Law

Is the road to Canossa beautiful?

I don't know: Briand takes us there in a closed carriage.

Clemenceau's reply to Pelletan's sardonic question is a testimony to Briand's greatness. Without his skilful steering the Law of Separation would have been the documentation of the bitter, definitive triumph of anticlericalism, a charter devised to weaken and subvert the Church. To many deputies of the Left the *associations cultuelles* were meant to be committees of laymen reflecting all the old Gallican and anticlerical tendencies latent in French Catholicism, backing parishioners against the *curé*, the *curé* against the bishop, the bishop against the pope. Indeed, there were those who looked forward to seeing discontented priests and groups of laity breaking with the hierarchy and insisting on having their own local church building, thus weakening the Church with schism and divisions—or, putting the case in more elevated terms, there would be scope for freedom of thought and the expression of lay opinion within the authoritarian shell of Catholicism. Certainly, the *associations cultuelles* were the stumbling block in the way of acceptance of the Law. Their "essential vice", wrote the bishops to the President of the Republic on 28 March 1905, "is to create and to impose upon the Catholic Church a purely lay institution".

While Briand was not indifferent to these hopes of weakening or transforming the ecclesiastical structure, he had the common sense and the sense of justice to see that the Law of Separation had to be kept a strictly honest document. Unlike so many deputies of the majority, he was not a convinced anticlerical; like Jaurès, his chief aim in supporting the Separation was, in his own words, "to exhaust the political programme of Radicalism so that we can compel an examination of our own conceptions". An upbringing among the seafaring population of Nantes, where the women at least were deeply pious, had left him with a residual respect for religion. And

in 1893 he had become disillusioned with professional anticlericalism by discovering that an article, "A monster in a cassock", in
the newspaper he was working for was a cynical inversion of the
true story of a priest who had dived into a river to save a child from
drowning. Like Jaurès again, and unlike most politicians, Briand
recognized women, voteless though they were, as half the population
of France, a consideration moderating the crude majoritarian
argument for anticlerical policies. Hence the intervention at a
Socialist meeting in 1901, when Jaurès was under attack for allowing his wife to send their daughter to make her first communion.

> *Jaurès*   What can you do with your wife?
> *A voice–* I would have strangled her!
> *Briand*   Perfect! That's the only way you could have won the
>   argument, and you'd have scored too by being able to
>   give her a lay funeral.

The remark was typical of the whole career of a statesman who had
no time for demonstrative violence or luxurious gestures of defiance,
whether in foreign policy against other powers or in priestless
funerals to spite the Deity. Briand was not of the *bourgeoisie* or of
the Université; he came up the hard way, and was suspicious of
grand objectives and extreme and logical attitudes. Though his
affinities were with the militant syndicalist Left, he was a realist
and a born conciliator. The world was to be improved for the
present generation, and politics was the art of getting useful things
done.

The law of Separation would not be useful or improving if it was
rejected by the Church and the country was left in a state of
undeclared civil war. The difficulty lay in the *associations cultuelles*,
and Briand worked to make them compatible with the current
Catholic view of ecclesiastical government, not instruments of
potential schism. Jaurès supported him. Maybe in time the laity
would come to dominate the clergy because they would be paying
their salaries; maybe, with lay support, democratic priests and
intellectuals would arise to defy the bishops. But, said Jaurès,
this was no affair of the legislator: "*La France n'est pas schis-
matique, elle est révolutionnaire.*" To give some guarantee of
episcopal control in the *associations cultuelles*, Briand added to
Article IV a sentence specifying that these committees would be
created "*en se conformant aux régles d'organization générale du*

culte dont elles se proposent d'assurer l'exercice". He frankly admitted his objective, to prevent a priest who defied his bishop and managed to set up a committee of laity from staking out a claim to church property. Extremists were furious. The Radical newspaper, *La Dépêche de Toulouse*, complained, "the Socialists do not wish to provoke schisms; they are going one better, they are setting to work to render schisms impossible". Even so, Article ɪᴠ passed the Chamber by a huge majority, 485 against 52, evidence of the basic good sense of so many anticlerical deputies once they were given a tolerant lead by men who had afforded proof of their sincerity. Nine irreducibles of the extreme Right joined with eighteen Socialists and twenty-five Radical-Socialists (mainly from the dechristianized departments of the Loir-et-Cher, the Isère, the Saône-et-Loire, the Var, the Allier, and the Yonne) in voting against. The Catholic press exulted. Albert de Mun in *La Croix* declared (inadvisedly, for this provoked anticlericals to tighten up in other articles) that Article ɪᴠ undermined the rest of the Law. According to *Le Pèlerin* (on 30 April) Catholics now had a duty to assist in making the Separation workable.

This view was taken by a varied spectrum of Catholic opinion ranging from one extreme to the other. Bishops used arguments of administrative convenience, civic concord, and national unity; leading laymen such as the *comte* d'Haussonville, Étienne Lamy, and Brunetière pointed out the advantages of freedom from erastian control and of increased lay participation; the Christian Democrats and the adherents of the Sillon reiterated the same considerations in revolutionary tones. Realists saw the Law as more generous than might have been expected and affording solid material advantages; idealists were anxious to accept what was offered quickly, so that the Church would be free to turn at once to measures of internal reform. This was the view of the *abbé* Hippolyte Hemmer, a *vicaire* of Paris, who published two articles in the *Quinzaine* (1 May, 1 June) proposing radical changes: the clergy to have a say in the appointment of bishops, the laity brought into mesh with church government by representative assemblies and the publication of full information about ecclesiastical business and finances, and the formation of communities of priests to run groups of rural parishes and evangelistic missions.

The opponents of the Law were a more homogeneous and vociferous group than its supporters. Most of the Catholic newspapers were hostile; numerous clergy, in particular members of the disbanded congregations, came out against acceptance, and they found leadership in the writings of Albert de Mun (in spite of his approving comment on Article IV), Mgr Turinaz, Bishop of Nancy, and Mgr Dubillard, Bishop of Quimper. Old Royalists and new nationalists were continuing the game of playing out the cards in the Church's hand when they had lost all other possible tricks; Drumont's *La Libre Parole* and Cassagnac's *L'Autorité* urged resistance. The Legitimist monk *Père* Ange le Doré published a pamphlet in November 1905 prophesying bloodshed, demanded by God in wrath and to purify Christians by suffering, and by the persecutors to satisfy their lusts. Mgr de Cabrières, the Royalist Bishop of Montpellier, opposed the law but welcomed the freedom it would bring, an unusual position to take, but strictly logical.

One of the complaints of the party against the Law of Separation was the way in which it was imposed, involving a unilateral breach of the country's engagements to the Holy See. The government claimed simply to be abrogating the Law of 18 *Germinal* year X which rendered the Concordat operative since Rome, by her actions, had already demonstrated that the treaty was no longer executive for her. In fact, there was no need to go to these lengths of legal definition; as the Concordat contained no stipulations about duration or termination, unilateral declaration could reasonably be assumed to be the way in which the treaty would necessarily, one day, come to its end; bearing in mind the folly of Merry del Val, it was not unreasonable to suppose that now was the time to do it. More serious, however, was the argument condemning the Law as an invasion of property rights. It took from the Church property legally acquired since 1801, and abolished the *budget des cultes,* which was understood to be compensation for the confiscation of ecclesiastical lands during the Revolution. Here was a precedent more welcome to Socialists than to the *bourgeois* anticlericals they were supporting. Indeed, any examination of the foundations of the Law was awkward for its supporters. Historically, all the precedents concerned the alliance between Church and State, and only six years, years of war and corruption when the ideals of the great Revolution had been betrayed, concerned their separation. The legislative preamble, with its comical historical errors, did not improve the argument—the Carolingian and Capetian dynasties were confounded, and bishops were frequenting the palace of the Tuileries a century before it was built. By the Law of Separation France was once again cutting herself off from her historic past, with the usual vague phrases in the preamble promising to respect "the sacred domain of conscience". In place of liberties firmly established by precedent, Charles Benoist told the Chamber, we have words—"The English by their traditions, the Americans by their precautions, have rights; we, for our part, have declarations of rights!'

Even if tradition was abandoned and the crude principle of majority rule prevailed, how could the Republic justify the decisive, irrevocable change it was making? Only 130 deputies had the separation of Church and State on their electoral manifestos, M. Denoix told the Senate, and many of these had merely been inserting old Republican clichés without thought of their meaning. In what sense then did the two chambers have a mandate for the Separation? It would be easy to find out, said Méline; let the Senate insist on putting the matter to the verdict of a referendum. The case for a popular vote was only superficially plausible, and there was never any chance of its acceptance. It was impossible to consult public opinion directly on the broad issue of the advisability of severing the links between Church and State, for everything depended on the actual terms which were proposed, and probably no combination of possible arrangements capable of satisfying a majority of Frenchmen could have been devised. The extremes of Right and Left were passionate; in matters like this they would be likely, for differing reasons, to unite to sabotage even the most reasonable solution. Méline's and Denoix's point, however, retained some force. To what extent is a government claiming to be founded on popular sovereignty entitled, admittedly in facing an unexpected crisis, to force through irreversible changes in the social structure which have not been subjected to the process of debate and criticism arising in a general election? There was, at least, an argument for delay.

Popular sovereignty was one pillar of Republican political theory, and individual liberty was the other. Since the Revolution, Frenchmen had been more adept at ensuring the liberty of the isolated citizen than of the individual as a member of free associations within the State. Something of Rousseau's distrust of independent groups distorting the expression of the General Will had lived on in the minds of the legislators, along with their *bourgeois* fear of combinations of the underprivileged. This prejudice was dangerous; as Tocqueville had shown, it favoured dictatorship, the machine of power moving forward easily over a dust of atomized uncompacted individuals. France now had more generous legislation on associations, but thinkers of the school of Tocqueville still drew attention to the threat to liberty embodied in the omnipotence of the governmental machine of the Third Republic. If the State severed its connection with the Church and withdrew its subsidies, what right had it to prevent the Catholics of France from doing as they pleased within the ordinary laws applying to everyone? Why should the mayor be able to control their processions, why should the Law of Separation include special sanctions against clergy guilty of defamation, and a regulation excluding them from membership of municipal councils for the next eight years, and why did it not abrogate the existing laws making the formalities of civil marriage a necessary prelude to the sacrament? True, the State could not treat the Church, even when disestablished and independent, as if it was an accidental gathering of individuals. On the other hand, any limitations which the State put upon the activities of the Church had to be jealously scrutinized, for there were those who wished the Law of Separation to be a law of erastian control—as the project of Combes had shown. And it was not enough to look suspiciously at the actual wording of the legislation. Sooner or later all the boundary lines of such a vast overall settlement would be tested by litigation. The Law as it stood was one thing; the interpretation the courts might put upon it was another. In this respect, Article VIII was the danger point. Here it seemed, in the regulation governing future litigation, was the device to retain for the State its ultimate control of the Church. According to Ribot, the men who invented it wished "to ensure the permanent grip of the administration upon the Churches; they vote for separation without actually believing in it, in fact, without wanting it at all".

Article VIII laid down that disputes arising over the *associations cultuelles* would be judged by the Conseil d'État, *"en tenant compte de toutes les circonstances de fait"*. The original form of the article (number VI in the earlier draft legislation) had been different; disputes were to have been brought before the ordinary courts and, in place of the vague reference to the obligation to take "circumstances" into account, there had been a proposal to use the phrase Briand had put into Article IV, "conforming to the rules of the general organization of the religion whose exercise they propose to ensure". The earlier and more acceptable form had been lost, partly because of muddled thinking among men of good will (a moderate had moved for the Conseil d'État and a Catholic had turned down

Briand's offer to restore the *"en se conformant"* clause), and partly because Clemenceau and the anticlerical extremists were hoping to twist the wording to create difficulties for Catholics over the formation of the *associations cultuelles.* These associations were unfortunately named—*cultuelles* suggested powers over divine service; *ecclésiales,* as proposed by Berger to the Senate, would have been better. But whatever their title, they would still not be acceptable to the Church unless in composition and procedures they complied with the principles of hierarchical government. The phrase about the *"règles d'organisation générale du culte"* in Article IV was a safeguard, but once Article VIII had been formulated, the last word was left with the Conseil d'État. According to Briand, there was no cause for anxiety, since Article VIII was necessarily subordinate to Article IV; in practice, he said, if two rival groups were competing to be recognized as the *association cultuelle,* the Conseil d'État. would simply have the task of deciding the practical question, which of the two is subject to the diocesan bishop? Catholics were dubious. The Conseil d'État was the inner sanctuary of the Republican legal establishment; its ruling interpreting Waldeck-Rousseau's legislation had enabled Combes to make good speed in destroying the congregations. Over the next few years it might make decisions bringing into jeopardy the whole parochial and diocesan hierarchy. The danger could be near, for anticlericals were already in touch with priests who had broken with the Church, encouraging them to form committees of lay supporters and come forward to claim the use of ecclesiastical buildings.

However the Law was interpreted, it could always be changed, and the debates in the Chamber of Deputies had revealed a widespread unsatisfied desire to impose further shackles upon the Church. In earlier drafts the Commission had revealed the sort of provisions it might have used to limit the powers of the episcopate: the imposition of a certain number of lay members on the *associations cultuelles* and safeguards to prevent bishops abolishing parishes, especially those with Republican municipal councils. Were these ideas really forgotten? Extremists among the anticlerical majority clearly regarded the Law of Separation as only a step towards more ruthless measures. Forty Radical Socialists voted for a motion declaring the present settlement "provisional", Clemenceau openly reserved the right to change it, and Vaillant said he accepted it reluctantly and with the hope that the people at large would ignore it and take over the churches by revolutionary assault.

If Catholics swallowed their pride and accepted the Law as it stood, there was no guarantee that this would be the end. New ministries would arise, amendments and new legislation might be devised, imposing a long, humiliating, and possibly divisive trial upon the Church. It might be better to refuse all compromise in the first place and stay united in defiance.

Defiance, if this was to be the decision, could have been undramatic and businesslike—formal pronouncements by the ecclesiastical authorities, followed by a general refusal to form the *associations cultuelles*, with no disturbances. But the legislators would not have been Frenchmen if they had formulated a law concerning the custody of so much property without thinking of accountability, and thus the unfortunate idea of comprehensive inventories arose. Obviously, for those who had eyes to see, the prying and publicity involved would provide a ready-made focus for hostile demonstrations. In matters of this kind anticlericals could be blind; their bias was towards strictness and legalism, as if they were subconsciously inspired with a longing for a sacrilegious confrontation. How else can one explain the item in the detailed instructions issued by the Direction générale de l'Enregistrement (2 January 1906) ordering its officials to ask priests to open the tabernacles for inspection?—a provocative detail which *La Vérité* and *La Croix* seized upon with morbid relish. On the first two days of February, when inventories were being taken at the Parisian parishes of Sainte-Clothilde and Saint-Pierre du Gros-Caillou, mobs attacked the police with stones and chair legs. Already there had been minor troubles in the countryside; the Parisian example led to more serious affrays. On 3 and 6 March two demonstrators were killed in riots in the West and North. The Rouvier government failed either to withdraw or to be firm, and was overthrown in the Chamber as a result of its mismanagement of the crisis. Sarrien took over on 14 March with Clemenceau at the Interior and Briand in charge of Education and Religious Affairs. Peace was restored when Clemenceau suspended the inventories. "The counting of candelabra is not worth a single human life", he said, an unexceptionable sentiment which, on 6 March, he had not been prepared to allow to Rouvier.

In all their official statements the French bishops had discouraged violence. So too had the papal encyclical *Vehementer* (11 February, published 18 February), though its uncompromising attitude to the Law of Separation had intensified Catholic discontent. The Parisian rioting was the work of Royalist and nationalist groups who sent in their bands of young men, the Camelots du Roi, the marchers of La Voie and Le Rayon. Apart from angry bystanders, the only truly Catholic element in the outbreak in the Parisian parishes was provided by some of Marc Sangnier's Sillon fighters (who went apparently, to prevent the extreme Right claiming a monopoly of muscular Christianity). Naturally, the clericalist areas of France were the scene of most of the disturbances. Except in Paris, Lille, and Roubaix, the riots were mostly in rural districts and were confined to twenty Departments of the West, Flanders, and the eastern fringe of the Massif Central. But the significant point to notice is how certain strongly Catholic areas were quiet. In some cases the explanation is found in the intervention of a conciliatory bishop (Arras, Rouen) or prefect (the Loire). More generally, the exceptions were areas Catholic in religious sentiment but Republican in politics, as, for example, the Hautes-Pyrénées, the Haute-Savoie and Savoie, and the Haute-Saône. In a final fling and with little hope of genuine political advantages, the malcontents of the Right were using the tribulations of the Church as a weapon against the Republic, and their initiative, for the most part, was taken up only in districts where religion and right-wing politics were indissoluably linked. And once again the anticlericals had foolishly presented the enemies of the regime with an opportunity to capitalize on religious grievances. The extreme priest-haters, indeed, resembled their opponents of the anti-Republican Right in being willing to sacrifice concrete interests to the gratification of hatreds. The politics of the Third Republic had once again been bedevilled by their competing brinkmanship.

17 The Law Rejected

On 11 February 1906, in the encyclical *Vehementer*, Pius X issued his condemnation of the Law of Separation. For some time this encyclical had been in preparation, so there was no truth in the boast of journalists of the Action française that the rioting at Sainte-Clothilde and Saint-Pierre du Gros-Caillou had made up the Pope's mind for him. But the tumults aroused by the inventories may have had some effect—they may have persuaded Pius X to publish his opinion earlier than he had originally intended, both to censure the violence and to prevent divisions among Catholics as the revulsion against disorder set in. *Vehementer* condemned in principle the idea of the separation of Church and State. This was a foregone conclusion. In proclaiming the duty of the State to pay public deference to the claims of God and to admit the Church to a role in the social order, the encyclical was only saying what Leo XIII had said in *Immortale Dei* and *Libertas praestantissimum*. The idea of Separation was wrong because (in the actual words of *Vehementer*) it limited "the action of the State to the sole pursuit of public prosperity in this life, which is but the proximate reason for [the existence] of political societies, and takes no heed, as something not regarded as relevant, of their ultimate end, which is eternal happiness". This was the thesis, and on Dupanloup's famous distinction between thesis and hypothesis, it might still have been possible to accept the new French legislation as a matter of practical necessity. But the encyclical went on to describe the Church as a hierarchical society in which the flock "has no other duty but to follow the lead given to it", an institution incompatible with a law which remained silent about the hierarchy of pastors. There was the reference to "the rules of the general organization of the religion" concerned, but since all disputes were to be brought before the Conseil d'État, the Church was being pushed into an unworthy dependence upon the civil power for the exercise of its traditional governance. On 26 February, in an allocution to fourteen newly consecrated French bishops (named now by the Pope alone independently of the government) Pius X reaffirmed the objections he had made in *Vehementer*. The Law of Separation favoured schism; it was unacceptable.

Inevitably, there was speculation about the motives of Pius X and his entourage, and the historian can do little more than follow up probabilities among the diverse opinions of contemporaries. Merry del Val was accused of being preoccupied with "prestige". No doubt he was, but it was not prestige for its own sake, but prestige to serve great objects of policy. The French government was ostentatiously ignoring the Vatican in all its proceedings; the attempt of Montagnini, the *chargé d'affaires* in Paris and *baron* Denys Cochin to open up an informal channel of negotiation was rebuffed. The Papacy, which claimed to rule the universal Church, was being placed in a strictly take-it-or-leave-it position, and there would automatically arise a temptation to demonstrate authority by refusing gifts offered on non-negotiable conditions. Mgr de Cabrières, Bishop of Montpellier, a Royalist and an intransigent, did the Pope a disservice in September 1906 by gloating over his rejection of the Law: "*on l'a laissé dehors, il y est resté,* they left him out: he stayed out", almost as if the papal policy was a tit-for-tat devised in a mood of authoritarian pique.

Méjan, a Protestant official of the Department of Religious Affairs, gave a harsher twist to this particular type of interpretation. From his confidential correspondence he knew most bishops wanted to come to some sort of agreement with the State, and in his view this was precisely why Rome refused to do so. "It is primarily because it wanted to abolish utterly and definitively all possibility of a revival of Gallicanism—which it fears and abhors—that the Holy See was implacably opposed to allowing the slightest contribution of the French episcopate towards any sort of application of the new legislation." The Papacy was affirming its authority over the French bishops and trampling on the proud independent traditions of the Gallican Church.

This sort of accusation was easy to make and impossible to refute. Another contemporary, the *abbé* Frémont (who, surprisingly, approved of the encyclical *Vehementer*) went to the opposite pole of interpretation. The Church was beset by Modernsim within and free-thought without; now was her chance to show herself united and unworldly, contemptuous of the material possessions dangled before her as a bribe. By rejecting the Law of Separation Pius X "had placed in position an enormous rock against which the vessel of free-thought would come to shipwreck". The French Church was called on to make sacrifices, not on behalf of the prestige of the Papacy, but to demonstrate the purity of the Church as a supernatural institution.

Between these two sharply contrasted explanations of papal policy—both, no doubt, having some relevance to the discussions that had proceeded in the Vatican—lies a broader and simpler highway of interpretation. The clues to finding it lie in two observations made to the *abbé* Birot when he visited Rome early in January 1906 as the representative of the Archbishops of Albi and Besançon to put their arguments in favour of accepting the Law of Separation. In an interview on 9 January, Pius X told Birot he was waiting to see what administrative regulations would be required to bring the Law into operation: "We do not want any new Organic Articles." The reference was to the police regulations Bonaparte had annexed to the Concordat of 1801, and the implication was clear—even a Concordat had not been proof against machinations of politicians, and the present Law passed by the French Parliament was much more open to abuse. It was not, in any sense, a treaty with the Church, at any time it could be amended, and the jurisprudence and administrative regulations of the Conseil d'État might interpret some of its clauses in surprising ways. There were no safeguards. At any time, new demands, new "Organic Articles", or, more dangerous still, creeping piecemeal impositions could be forced upon the Church. And the danger was not confined within the frontiers of France and threatening the French Church alone; the Law of Separation constituted an international precedent. As Merry del Val said to Birot, "We must ensure that the example of France does not extend to other powers." Perhaps he was thinking of his own country, Spain, where the possibility of a change in the relations of Church and State had become a live political issue, or perhaps he was thinking of growing tensions in Switzerland. It would be dangerous to allow the world to assume that Rome could be manoeuvred into abandoning the standard procedure of negotiating a Concordat and pushed into acceptance of unilateral legislation by the civil power. On these grounds, essentially, the Papacy had rejected the Civil Constitution of the Clergy of 1790, a refusal to compromise which had led eventually to a formal Concordat eleven years later. What was at stake was the right of the Vatican to be consulted, to share in negotiations, to be given a formal treaty lifted above the possibilities of infringement by administrative decree or vitiation by the amendments of a fluctuating parliamentary majority. The *abbé* Birot, very French and Gallican in his outlook, recognized the force of this argument, though in a letter to Frémont he said he was still dissatisfied: "Europe and all its numerous Concordats from which hang all the diplomatic prerogatives of the Holy See and the phantom of temporal power preoccupy [the Vatican] at least as much as the free and courageous reorganization of the Church of France."

So long as the Church is an institution in the world, the acts of its rulers are open to two contradictory interpretations: measures for the conversion of souls can be ascribed to a will to power, the humble acceptance of persecution can be made into a design to enjoy the political advantages of being victimized. The contradictory interpretations do not always correspond to the views of churchmen as against outsiders; they exist within the institution itself whenever alternative policies become a subject of dispute. Seen from Rome, the preservation of the property of the French Church might apear primarily as a material interest, and the maintenance of the international standing of the Papacy as primarily spiritual. Seen from Albi or Besançon, the roles might be reversed, property becoming the basis of the effective exercise of the Church's ministry, with the diplomacy of the Holy See (as the *abbé* Birot hinted) looking like a relic of the days when popes had pursued temporal ends and wordly greatness.

Certainly, the majority of French bishops had come to accept the first half of this proposition; to them property and financial arrangements were an essentially spiritual matter. They were preoccupied with the problem of maintaining the pastoral work of their dioceses and with the "free and courageous reorganization of the Church of France". They wished to keep buildings, property, and such transitional arrangements as would ease the strain on their clergy, and to avoid the wasted effort and ill-feeling involved in disputes. Practical men immersed in administrative tasks, they saw no insuperable difficulty in forming *associations cultuelles* or something like them; they spent half their days negotiating with prefects and anticlerical officials—this would just be another chore to add to their routine diocesan diplomacy. The shadowy menace of schismatic competitors or biased rulings of the Conseil d'État scared them less than the prospect of administrative chaos and financial disaster. On 28 December 1905, the five French cardinals (Richard of Paris, Labouré of Rennes, Couillé of Lyon, Lecot of

Bordeaux, and Perraud of Autun) had met and agreed that the Law of Separation could be made workable, given certain precautions. From 4 to 10 March a small committee of bishops (Richard, Lecot, and Couillé, together with Fulbert-Petit, Archbishop of Besançon and Mignot, Archbishop of Albi) held discussions and provisionally accepted a proposal for a revised version of the *associations cultuelles* devised by Mgr Fulbert-Petit; this proposal was to be put to a full conference of the episcopate as soon as it could be arranged. The case for the acceptance of the Law was fortified by an open letter signed by twenty-three leading Catholic Academicians and intellectuals, including Brunetière, d'Haussonville, Leroy-Beaulieu, Albert Vandal, Henri Lorin, Georges Goyau, Denys Cochin, and the *marquis* de Vogüé. The Church must take some form of organization which is legally recognized by the State, they said; if this form is rejected, what is the alternative? To conform to the "rules of the general organization' of Catholicism, the *associations cultuelles* must consist, at the very worst, of laity in communion with their *curés*, and *curés* in communion with their bishops, who necessarily would be in communion with the Pope. What further safeguards could be desired? If the Church refused to co-operate, the traditional religious heritage of France would be squandered, medieval churches would become "barns or dance-halls", and Catholicism would become a "private religion" without influence on society, controlled by the wealthy laymen who put most on the collection plate.

Albert de Mun replied to this manifesto of the Academicians— "the green cardinals"—in an article in *La Croix* on 28 March. The intellectuals have the clever arguments, he said, but the people know instinctively what is right, they have "the invincible power of simplicity". He meant the Catholic laity. The people of France generally, or at least the male voting population, had a chance to declare their attitude to the Law of Separation in the parliamentary general election of May, and voted overwhelmingly in favour of it. In spite of their careful co-ordination of effort in the constituencies, the Catholic and right-wing groups lost sixty seats and were reduced to a total of 175 deputies. Radicals and Socialists could govern alone without help from moderates. It was no longer possible to talk about lack of a mandate, about the necessity for a referendum. Challenged by the tumults raised against the inventories, the country had given a decisive answer. The *abbé* Frémont, who had greeted *Vehementer* with enthusiasm, now regretted that the Pope had issued his encyclical prematurely, for had his condemnation of the Law of Separation not been so categorical, in face of these election results he might have thought it wiser to "pass from thesis to hypothesis" and allow the *associations cultuelles*.

The declared will of a majority of voters was yet another argument to encourage the bishops to urge Pius X to move on to the hypothesis. The plenary assembly of the French episcopate finally met on 30 May 1906. Two documents were put before it. One was the report of the Archbishop of Besançon recommending the formation of committees to fulfil the purpose of the *associations cultuelles* under the more respectable title of *associations canoniques et légales*. The other was a report by Mgr Fuzet, Archbishop of Rouen, on the Prussian legislation of 1875 which had been accepted by the Catholics of Germany with the approval of the Vatican. By the Prussian law church property had been put into the charge of parish assemblies elected by all Roman Catholic inhabitants; if such an assembly disagreed with the bishop, the Minister of Religious Affairs settled the dispute. Fuzet grimly drew a comparison between the German law approved by Rome and the French law which Rome had rejected. "The law of 1905 does not mention the bishop, but it makes him omnipotent. The Prussian law mentions him formally but only to enslave him." The contrast was oversimplified; all the same, it formed a powerful argument.

The assembled bishops made four decisions. Firstly, they condemned the principle of the Law of Separation by 72 votes against 2; secondly, they approved the idea of finding some *modus vivendi* by 48 votes against 26. Thirdly, they approved the specific proposal of Mgr Fulbert-Petit for the formation of *associations canoniques et légales* by 56 votes against 18. Finally, a permanent commission of eighteen bishops was set up to carry on business between plenary assemblies (this commission met only once, as the Vatican was to disapprove of it). These decisions and proceedings were strictly confidential. Only Rome was allowed to know what had transpired, and everything now depended on the Pope's decision about the bishops' proposals.

The Roman decision came in the encyclical *Gravissimo* (10 August 1906, published four days later). "We decree that the *associations cultuelles* as the law imposes them can under no circumstances be formed without violation of the sacred rights that are indispensible to the very existence of the Church." Any other kind of association was also declared out of the question unless

there was a "certain and legal" guarantee "that the divine constitution of the Church, the immutable rights of the Roman Pontiff
and the bishops, such as their authority over the property necessary
to the Church, more especially over the sacred edifices, shall be
irrevocably and securely preserved within the said associations".
This was the death blow to episcopal manoeuvres for a compromise. The bishops, indeed, thanks to the dishonest draughtmanship
of the encyclical, were blandly cited as if they had never asked for
one. "We see that we ought to confirm and establish with our
apostolic authority the practically unanimous decision of your
assembly. . . ." Only the first episcopal vote was mentioned; since
the proceedings of the bishops had been secret no one was to
suspect that they had voted for the *associations canoniques et
légales*. (And so it would have remained, had not the Bishop of
Tarentaise's secretary—the *abbé* Houtin, who abandoned his
priesthood six years later to write learned works of anti-Roman
propaganda—handed over all the documents to *Le Siècle*). But
whatever the bishops had said was irrelevant now. Henceforward,
there was no hope of forming any sort of association to accept the
devolution of ecclesiastical property. Cardinal Lecot of Bordeaux
had craftily set up parish and diocesan committees which he
claimed were in accordance with the law of 1 July 1901 on associations and only fortuitously related to the Law of Separation, and
Mgr Fuzet of Rouen had planned a Société de Saint-Romain
to be accidentally available for the same purpose. There was no
further point in these ingenuities. The second plenary assembly
of bishops met on 4 September. It attempted to provide for immediate financial needs by imposing an obligatory levy on the
faithful, the *denier du culte*, and issued a statement in accordance
with the encyclical *Gravissimo*, forbidding the formation of all
manner of associations. Only Mgr Lacroix, Bishop of Tarentaise,
tried to evade this prohibition; in October he proposed to set up
diocesan societies composed entirely of priests, but his clergy
refused to follow him and he soon resigned his see. The period
of grace allowed for the formation of the *associations cultuelles*
was to expire in December. The State would then be in a
position to appropriate all ecclesiastical property, the cathedrals
and parish churches included.

Faced with the refusal of churchmen to co-operate, the government wavered between conciliation and harshness. On 9 November
Briand, representing the first tendency, extended the period of

grace for a year, to 11 December 1907. He also instructed the prefects not to make a strict application to the Church of the law of 1881 requiring a "previous declaration" for all public meetings; a single annual declaration would suffice. There was no response to these gestures, except a circular from the Archbishop of Paris forbidding the clergy to render any sort of declaration, annual or otherwise. Then in December Clemenceau intervened with the policy of harshness. Mgr Montagnini, the papal *chargé d'affaires* was expelled, his archives were seized and some of his confidential reports on French ecclesiastics were leaked to the press. These documents discredited the system which had encouraged them, and the way in which they had been confiscated dishonoured the rulers of the Republic. The government pressed on with evacuation of seminaries and episcopal palaces. In a law passed 2 January 1907, these edifices and the presbyteries of the *curés* were described as being taken over "definitively"—there would be no returning them. Yet the law of 2 January also contained a conciliatory possibility: the cathedrals and parish churches could be used, either by *associations cultuelles* according to the Law of Separation, or on a contractual basis by a common law association formed under the provisos of the law of 1901. In their third plenary assembly the French bishops drew up a specimen contract which the Vatican was willing to approve, but the scheme fell through because the government insisted on stringent terms and short leases. In its turn the Vatican vetoed an innocuous arrangement for the custody of the funds available for infirm and aged clergy by committees called *mutualités ecclésiastiques*. The deadlock was complete. The Pope had stood firm, and the Church of France—though many of its clergy thought his policy too rigid—stood united with him. A prelate who had little sympathy with the ultramontanism of so many of his clerical brethren was inclined to say that it served them right. "They wanted an infallible Pope: they have got one."

18 After the Separation

The Law of Separation had been rejected by the Church, but life must go on and working arrangements had to be invented. For Algeria and the colonial empire no detailed provisions had been made; here, the Law was to be applied by administrative regulations. As it turned out, for this rich diversity of territories a diversity of applications was needed. The less developed areas were left as they had been, and in Madagascar, Martinique, Guadeloupe, and Réunion, where the Separation was introduced, many religious congregations were left undisturbed and government money continued to support their hospitals. In Algeria, since Islam was still to be subsidized, it would have been absurd to miss out Christianity, so the formal Separation did not end payments to the Catholic clergy. The French churches in foreign capitals survived by oversight, tolerant officials in government departments refraining from drawing the attention of the legislators to their existence.

At home, religious services continued to be held in the churches. By the law of 28 March 1907 the insistence on an "annual declaration" was abandoned; only one vote was cast in the Chamber against this concession. True, having lost their proprietary rights in the religious edifices, Catholics felt (in the words of the Archbishop of Paris) like "visitors in a museum", and communes sometimes neglected repairs or connived at vandalism, with results described by Barrès in *La grande pitié des églises de France*.[1] But local authorities who tried to turn churches to secular use generally met with a refusal from the Conseil d'État; in four years only twenty out of 150 applications were granted. In spite of all the encouragements of C'emenceau and his friends, few schismatic *associations cultuelles* were formed and by 1909 there were only ten of them left. In some areas of the country public opinion still regarded the

---

[1] The law of 13 April 1908 allowed, but did not oblige, the State, departments, and communes to do repairs. The legal position is clearly analysed in Louis de Naurois, "La Mise en œuvre juridique de la Séparation", *Revue de droit canonique* XIII (1962), pp. 65–80.

clergy as the only authorities qualified to dispose of the sacred buildings. In 1907 the Bishop of Montpellier allowed the wine-growers of the province to sleep in the town churches when they came up for a political demonstration; the civic authorities, who had refused the use of public buildings, were angry, but the prefect advised the government to turn a blind eye to the Bishop's presumptuousness. The final jurisdiction over disputes concerning ecclesiastical edifices lay with the Conseil d'État, and, contrary to the expectations of many, its lawyers showed remarkable impartiality; indeed, they proved to be positively well-disposed towards the Church. Of the three principles they detected in the Law of Separation, precedence was given to liberty of religious practice, as against the potentially incompatible principles of liberty of conscience and the separation of Church and State. Their judgements emphasized the phraseology in the Law indicating "continuity", and this, together with Article IV, safeguarded the hierarchical organization of the Roman Church. By a ruling of 1911 a priest who was recommended by his bishop and who could prove he had regularly celebrated divine office in a particular church was entitled to be called the *"occupant sans titre juridique"*, which meant that he would have his own keys, decide the details of furnishings, and control seating arrangements. Mayors who tried to prevent traditional bell-ringing generally lost their cases, unless it was a question of nocturnal peals disturbing the sleep of citizens. The Conseil d'État even made it possible for a Commune to allow its parish priest to live rent-free in the presbytery and to pay him a salary for acting as its caretaker.

After the First World War had destroyed the bitter old anti-clericalism, the moderate and civilized rulings of the Conseil d'État during the ten pre-war years provided a basis for an understanding with the Vatican. They were a sort of guarantee that the State had no intention of challenging the hierarchical principle of Roman Catholicism. In 1924 Pius XI agreed to the formation of *diocésains*, committees not unlike the old *associations cultuelles*, to hold ecclesiastical property and control legacies offered to the Church. From then onwards a "quasi-concordatory" relationship could develop, a whole series (in Gabriel Le Bras' words) of "little concordats ... understandings with the government on particular points". Such arrangements and *rapprochements* over the span of a generation helped to create the new climate of opinion in which, after the Second World War, the State was to go so far as to give subsidies to Catholic schools, a denoument that would have been unbelievable to contemporaries of Clemenceau and Combes.

Looking back after the compromise of 1924 on the rejection of the Law of Separation eighteen years earlier, Briand praised the far-sightedness of Pius X. He had been "the only one to see clearly.... He did not wish [the Church] to die slowly, tragically. He wanted to live, and life means adventure. . . . His sacrifice was necessary: it brought its reward." Yet the French clergy paid a heavy price for the heroic gesture, and because an agreement was reached in the end, we cannot automatically conclude that Briand was right in saying the sacrifice was necessary. This is what we can never know. The conduct of the Conseil d'État in these intervening years suggests it may not have been, provided we are entitled to assume the jurists would have come to the same decisions if the Church had not been intransigent, a likely but not a certain proposition.

For the laity, apart from the new obligation to pay the *denier du culte*, the Separation did not bring startling changes in the routine of religious observances. But the clergy were hard hit; the presbyteries and seminaries had been taken over, the *budget des cultes* was finished and the gifts of the faithful fell short of replacing it. Penury gave new reality to the idea of "worker priests". The *abbé* Ballu published a pamphlet on "suitable employments for the priests of the future" (1906), in which he urged his brethren to support themselves by working with their hands, by the same token proving to their people that they were no longer "*bourgeois*". The *Univers* and various bishops denounced the proposal as contrary to canon law and tending to degrade the status of the clergy. This pathetic touchiness about status was understandable, for with the sustained anticlerical attack on the Church, the social standing of the parish priest had been declining for a generation. A writer in the *Revue des Deux Mondes* in 1892 had described the *curé* as

> banished from the school, excluded from the committee directing official charities, regarded with malicious distrust or jealous hatred by the mayor and the schoolmaster, kept at arms length as a compromising neighbour by all the minor officials employed by the commune or the State, spied on by the innkeeper, exposed to the anonymous denunciations of the local newspaper . . . he spends his mornings reciting prayers to empty pews and his afternoons planting cabbages and pruning roses.

The separation of Church and State completed the process; henceforward the parish clergy had no official standing, they celebrated mass at altars where they were allowed only on sufferance, they were miserably poor and dependent on the charity of their flocks. The number of ordinations fell; there had been 1,753 in 1901, and there were only 825 in 1913. The decline in church attendance continued. In 1903 Jean Vernant made the first technical statistical inquiry into churchgoing in France, and put only 2.4% of the population of the Department of the Seine-et-Marne into the category of practising Catholics. In the following year Jean de Bonnefon wrote, "the urban masses are becoming atheists, the rural masses pagan". In Limoges statistics suggest that the crisis around the Law of Separation marks the decisive collapse of traditional conformity, for between 1901 and 1907 the number of births without baptism rose from 8% to 25%, of lay funerals from 6.85% to 22.9%, and of civil marriages from 18.5% to 48.5%.[1] Anticlerical propaganda and legislation had stimulated churchmen to renew their loyalties and affirm their solidarity, but they had also weakened the position of the Church in the life of the nation and deprived the clergy of social standing and local leadership.

If a retreat is not to degenerate into a rout, a beaten army must close its ranks and obey orders implicitly. In the French Church the process was exemplified by the way in which the episcopate came under the domination of the Vatican. The Pope named new bishops, with only a show of considering the opinions of the occupants of neighbouring sees. Plenary meetings of the episcopate were forbidden (no more were held until 1951). When Pius X reduced the age for First Communion, the bishops were not consulted. Catholic France—the France of Loisy, Duchesne, Goyau, and La Gorce, of the philosophers Le Roy and Blondel, of Claudel and Maritain—could have produced a brilliant apologetic for the faith that was in it. But from Rome came an oath obligatory on all clergy, a twenty-six page-long document condemning Modernism, and insisting on the ability of the natural reason to prove the existence of God, and on miracles and prophecy as the external proofs of revelation. In 1912 the French episcopate, now largely renewed, showed its contempt for scholarship by joining Merry del Val in applauding Mgr Fuzet, Archbishop of Rouen, who

[1] In the diocese of Montpellier the trough of practice was reached before the Separation, but 1907 marks the collapse of sacerdotal vocations. Even so, the explanation is complex. (See Cholvy, op. cit., pp. 241–59.)

sustained the legend of Lazarus, Mary, and Martha bringing Christianity to Gaul, against Canon Vacandard's demonstration that the story went no further back than the eleventh century.

The reaction against adventures in the intellectual sphere extended also to those in the social and political. De Mun and the ACJF and the Semaines Sociales movement had come over to Harmel's belief in the right of the workers to organize their own trades unions independent of the owners; the intellectuals of Social Catholicism were developing the theory that a man's trade is as "natural" to him as his membership of a family or of the State, from which they deduced the moral obligation of Catholics to form and support their own trades unions, and the right of the unions to speak for all workers, even those who refused to join. But in 1909 P. Fontaine, a reactionary Jesuit, launched an attack on this "social modernism". In letters from Rome Merry del Val supported him, condemning (this in an open letter to de Mun) "the unreasonable enlargement of the domain of justice to the detriment of that of charity, and the subordination of the right of property to its use, usage being made into a function, not of charity, but of justice".[1]

If Albert de Mun came under censure, how could Marc Sangnier hope to escape? To Catholics of reactionary political views, old style Royalists and new style Action française, the Sillon was a dangerous left-wing rival. To moderate churchmen, the movement seemed too exclusive, too independent in its relations with groups within the Church, and too welcoming in its relations with those outside it. The local Sillonists of Limoges threw off their allegiance at the end of 1907 in protest against its excessive cult of unity, and those of Dijon cut themselves off two years later. In the Épinal disputation of 1904 Sangnier had proclaimed his independence of the hierarchy, incurring the wrath of the Bishop of Nancy; in 1906 the Bishop of Quimper forbade his priests to join the Sillon, and in the course of the next four years forty to fifty diocesan bishops followed his example. The coadjutor of the see of Cambrai, Mgr Delamaire, provided an argument to counter the theory of independence in matters political; opinion may be free, but all actions have something of a "moral" nature, and are therefore subject to rulings by the episcopate. Meanwhile, at the Roubaix confrontation with the Socialists Sangnier had taken the revolutionary side on the issue

[1] Independent Christian trades unions of workers were finally justified in a Roman directive to the Archbishop of Lille (5 June 1928, published 9 August 1929).

of property, and in 1907 he founded "le grand Sillon" for political activities in alliance with Protestants and unbelievers. Since this adventurous policy of *rapprochement* with the social Left was the inspirational work of a charismatic individual, without a clear theoretical basis or distinctive name, it was so much harder for the ecclesiastical authorities to marshal their deep suspicions into specific censures. Early in 1908 the reactionary *abbé* Barbier supplied the missing identification tag for the purposes of a condemnation: Christian Democracy and the Sillon, he said, were the social aspect of "modernism", that newly invented heresy.

The end came for the Sillon with Pius X's letter of 25 August 1910. The movement was condemned for acting independently of ecclesiastical authority and failing to make the defence of the Church an article in its programme, for collaborating with Protestants and free thinkers, making the doctrine of "humanity" the bond of unity to bring men into a new sort of "church", for teaching that the principle of authority is in the people, that democracy is more just than other forms of government, and for aiming at levelling the distinctions between classes. The mere enumeration of the reasons for the condemnation is sufficient to explain why the influence of Marc Sangnier lived on to inspire the spiritual life and social endeavours of French Catholics throughout the century, in youth movements, pacifist groups, the Resistance, in the formation of the MRP, in the discussions of the role of the laity at the Second Vatican Council. "They do not work for the Church, but for humanity"; within half a century, this papal summary of the aims of the Sillonists, written as a censure, came to sound like a testimonial of praise. But in 1910 Sangnier submitted, the Sillon ended, and, as Aulard said, a demonstration had been given of "the folly of wishing to reform the Church".

For forty years there had been disputes about the right of churchmen as such, to intervene in national politics on behalf of a particular opinion or party. The alliance of the Church with reactionary forces had been the essential justification for the attacks of anticlericalism, and Leo XIII had attempted to break the vicious circle of right-wing affiliations drawing down persecution and persecution strengthening right-wing allegiances. A Church forcibly given its independence by the State presumably can issue such political instructions to its faithful as it chooses; certainly, the Ministry of Religious affairs could no longer stop the salaries of priests accused of electioneering. On 11 May 1909 a speech by

Colonel Keller raised the issue of policy for the legislative elections of the following year; he called on Catholics to unite on "an exclusively Catholic and religious ground", by which he meant "battleground", for he pictured the new Crusaders, closing ranks around their bishops and marching together to "restore France to Christ". In the name of the Pope Merry del Val gave formal approval. The end was glorious; but what of the means? Two schools of thought arose, the one advocating "the Nancy project", the other "the Toulouse pact". Mgr Turinaz, supported by *La Croix*, wanted the formation of a vast opposition party, ostensibly lay in direction, with Catholics forming its central core; his fellow-prelate of Toulouse, Mgr Germain, supported by the *Univers*, advocated restricting Catholic votes to candidates who signed a declaration in favour of liberty of education and an understanding with the Pope, while the bishops would give more precise instructions in doubtful cases.

Both these proposals were rejected by the Sillonists, the first because it would throw the Church into alliance with the Right, the second because it would mean ecclesiastical interference in matters strictly political. On the contrary, Marc Sangnier argued, the phrase "exclusively Catholic and religious" left churchmen free to vote in national elections according to their individual consciences. Already the Sillon was acting on Sangnier's thesis. In February 1907 "le plus grand Sillon" had been created to include Protestants who had a social conscience and well-disposed trades unionists, whose "religion of solidarity" could be construed as part of the quest for St Paul's "Unknown God". In April 1908 the Seventh National Congress of the Sillon decided to put forward candidates for Parliament; Sangnier tried twice, unsuccessfully, with a strictly lay programme of income tax, a minimum wage, workers' retirement pensions, Sunday holidays, and the right of civil servants to form their own trades unions. Mgr Turinaz wished Catholics to be unanimous in politics; Sangnier said that they would necessarily be divided: the Nancy project was for an alliance with the Right; the Sillon intended to seek allies among the social Left.

Sangnier's burning temperament brought the confusions of enthusiasm into his theory of political action. In strict logic, however, he stood for the Republican *abbé* Dabry's formula: Catholics were to be "the leaven of political groups, and for this purpose . . . should enter all of them, except those which are opposed to the tradition and doctrine of the Church, for example" (a sardonic postscript) "the Royalists and the Socialists". After the papal condemnation of the Sillon, the chief exponent of Dabry's ideal was the *abbé* Lemire, who had represented the constituency of Hazebrouck in the Chamber of Deputies for seventeen years, self-consciously acting as a citizen, not as a representative of religious interests, working for the Church as an example, not as an agent. To promote the interests of the poor he had collaborated with Socialists, Radicals, anticlericals, and to promote civil concord he had even urged churchmen to accept the State educational system. To ecclesiastics who still dreamed of a united clerical interest in politics, the deputy for Hazebrouck was "the chaplain of the Republican bloc", "Catiline in a cassock". The Archbishop of Cambrai had attempted to prevent his candidature in the 1906 elections; Rome had ruled that the bishop's permission was necessary for a priest to enter politics, but had made an exception for existing commitments. In May 1913 the Roman ruling was renewed, this time without exceptions. "You have to choose", said Clemenceau in an open letter to Lemire, "between absolution and liberty." Mgr Charost, the newly appointed bishop of the new see of Lille, was determined to root out "social Protestantism, ... the doctrinal error of the independent civic conscience"; he therefore suspended Lemire from his priestly functions and attempted to engineer his defeat in the 1914 elections. Harmel and most of Lemire's Catholic friends urged him to submit. Courageously he refused to yield; it was not the hierarchical discipline of the Church that was at stake, he insisted, but the freedom of priests to live "as men among men", and the freedom of Catholics to act as citizens.

In spite of all the efforts of the clergy to encourage support for a rival candidate, the *abbé* Lemire was returned on the first ballot; according to the sub-prefect only 3,000 of his 8,000 voters were Republicans—the rest were churchgoers defying the hierarchy. What happened at Hazebrouck, a centre of religious practice, was typical of the electoral situation in most of France. The chief group supporting the Church, the old Action libérale of Piou, returned only twenty-three deputies. It had been demonstrated again that the mass of nominal Catholics could not be transformed into Catholic voters; they were not prepared to forgo their political convictions to serve the interests of the institutional Church. A few of the bishops, notably the Archbishop of Lyons, issued political directives for the 1914 elections in pastoral letters or "electoral catechisms". But most of them kept silent. As the

Bishop of Valence pointed out, if Catholics made specific demands on candidates for favour to their Church, they could not complain if others made specific demands against it.

The history of the French Church from 1870 to 1914 is para-doxical. The story ends with a great institution whose leaders had refused to face the intellectual challenges of their age and in fear had abandoned their duty to enlighten the minds of those who sought for truth, who had faltered and hesitated on the path of social reform and social justice belatedly indicated by *Rerum novarum*. Yet within, new life was stirring, a new social conscience had been aroused among Catholics of the upper and middle classes, and a new sense of man's need for God had swept into intellectual and literary milieux. The Separation of Church and State seemed to have encouraged this efflorescence of vitality in French Catholic-ism. The *abbé* Brugerette enumerated the multiplicity of new social ventures—consumers' leagues, clubs for soldiers, holiday camps, popular advice bureaux, rural lending banks, associations of women workers, and Christian trades unions (with Albert de Mun himself now repudiating paternalism) and reflected that they were, perhaps, "the Church's revenge for the Separation". Certainly, the ACJF, exulting in its rapidly growing membership (there were 150,000 adherents by 1913), proclaimed the social gospel with a fervour consciously intensified by the anticlerical onslaught. In a sense, the revenge for the Separation can also be seen in the growing influence of the Catholic revival in literature. In 1913 Robert Vallery-Radot (who, with other writers such as François Mauriac, Eusèbe de Bremond d'Ars, André Lafon, and Francis Jammes belonged to Claudel's "Co-operative of Prayer") dated the decisive change from 1905, the year at which the young intellectuals began to abandon their "obscure Nietzchean paganism" for the Christian philos-ophy. True, the Separation had also played its part in affirming and consolidating the hierarchical nature of the government of the Roman Church; even so, at this very time the lower clergy of France were finding their independent voice, and the spirit of lay initiative overflowed and abounded.

The story ends with a Church that has lost its status as a national institution, is losing its sheer numerical claim to respect, and has undergone a long-sustained, decisive political defeat. Yet Catholics remained fanatical patriots. In this respect one might almost say they forgot their true faith in the interests of another common to all Frenchmen. When the war came, Socialists, Radicals, Royalists, nationalists, clericals, and anticlericals—everyone—joined in the *union sacrée* against the invader. The heroism of the clergy and the Catholic soldiers, especially the officers of right-wing inclinations, and the sense of the overwhelming need for unity annihilated the vicious, routine Republican anticlericalism of the previous generation. No Commune, no recriminations between politicians and churchmen followed the war of 1914–18. The Radicals who tried to end the Concordat in Alsace-Lorraine and withdraw the new embassy from the Vatican were defied and ridiculed. The old hatreds had burnt themselves out, and the way was open for Pius XI's acceptance of the *diocésaines,* and the beginning of a quasi-concordatory relationship. Catholics had proved that they accepted the Republic by fighting for it and dying for it. In the trenches the slow-moving policies of Leo XIII came to fruition, and the Ralliement became a believable reality.

A Note on Further Reading

This limited bibliography was composed to list the basic indispensible works and give references to the books and articles which the writer found most stimulating for shaping the interpretations given in this essay. Whatever space was then left was devoted to titles which seemed most likely to be useful to a reader wishing to push further an inquiry into particular themes, some of which have received only cursory mention here. There can be no pretence at completeness; under certain headings (I, IV, and XB) only a fraction of available material is mentioned—for reasons of space, and because of the limitations of the writer's own knowledge. To construct a fuller bibliography, the best way to go to work is to study the files of the *Revue de l'histoire de l'Église de France,* which lists all relevant articles in local as well as in national periodicals.

It is worth noting that many actors in the drama left memoirs or historical accounts of the events in which they played a part (e.g. Albert de Mun (1911), Mgr Ferrata, the nuncio (1922), Andrieux, the Prefect of Police (1885), Loisy (1930–31), Houtin (n.d.), Combes (1956), M. de Gailhard-Bancel (1928)). Also, an extraordinarily varied and brilliant range of novels of this period deal with clerical and anticlerical themes and issues of belief and unbelief—by Barrès, Bourget, Bloy, Zola, Anatole France, and various lesser writers.

I GENERAL WORKS ON POLITICAL HISTORY

D. W. Brogan, *The Development of Modern France, 1870–1939.* 1940.

G. Chapman, *The Third Republic, 1872–94.* 1962.

J. Chastenet, *Histoire de la Troisième République.* 6 vols. Vols. I, 1952; II 1954; III, 1955.

J. M. Mayeur, F. Bedaria, A. Prost, and J.-L. Monneron, *Histoire du peuple français. Cent ans d'esprit républicain.* 1964.

F. Goguel, *La Politique des partis sous la Troisième République*. 3rd edn. 1958.

R. Rémond, *La Droite en France de 1815 à nos jours*. 1954.

S. Osgood, *French Royalism under the Third and Fourth Republics*. 1960.

Amid the vast literature on the Dreyfus Affair, particular light on the attitude of Catholics is thrown by:

R. F. Byrnes, *Antisemitism in Modern France*. Vol. I. 1950.

J. Jurt, *Les attitudes politiques de Georges Bernanos jusqu'en 1931*. 1968.

D. B. Ralston, *The Army of the Republic: the Place of the Military in the Political Evolution of Modern France, 1871–1914*. 1967.

P. Sorlin, *"La Croix" et les juifs (1880–1899): contribution à l'histoire de l'antisémitisme contemporaine*. 1967.

Among the biographies of politicians concerned with legislation on ecclesiastical affairs, the following are indispensible

P. Sorlin, *Waldeck-Rousseau*. 1966. A brilliant study.

G. Suarez, *Briand, sa vie, son oeuvre*. 5 vols. Vols. I and II. 1938.

II HISTORIES OF THE FRENCH CHURCH

(A) For the Second Empire

J. Maurain, *La Politique ecclésiastique du Second Empire*. 1930.

(B) 1870–1914

E. Lecanuet, *L'Église de France sous la Troisième République*. 4 vols. 1907–30.

J. Brugerette, *Le Prêtre français dans la société contemporaine*. 3 vols. 1933–37. Vol. II *Vers la Séparation, 1871–1908*. 1935.

Lecanuet and Brugerette were priests of liberal opinions—Brugerette was a defender of Dreyfus. Their histories are packed with full quotations from contemporary sources, especially newspapers.

A. Debidour, *L'Église catholique et l'État sous la Troisième République, 1870–1906*. 2 vols. 1960–9. Anticlerical.

C. S. Phillips, *The Church in France, 1789–1907*. 2 vols. 1929–36 A masterly interpretation.

A. Dansette, *Histoire religieuse de la France contemporaine*. 2 vols. 1948–51. E.T., abridged, 2 vols. 1961.

M. Darbon, *Le Conflit entre la droite et la gauche dans le Catholicisme français, 1830–1953.* 1953. Good interpretation of a central theme.

A. Latreille, R. Rémond, J.-L. Palanque and E. Delaruelle, *Histoire du Catholicisme en France.* 3 vols. Vol. III. 1962. Excellent selective bibliography. The best short account.

Daniel-Rops, *L'Église des Révolutions, II Un Combat pour Dieu.* 1963. Extensive bibliography. Treats aspects of church life (liturgical, architectural, etc.) which are often crowded out of general surveys.

L. Capéran, *Histoire contemporaine de la Laïcité française.* Vols. I *La Crise du seize mai et la revanche républicaine.* 1957; II *La Révolution scolaire.* 1960; *L'Anticléricalisme et l'affaire Dreyfus 1897–1899.* 1948; *L'Invasion laïque de l'avènement de Combes au vote de la Séparation.* 1935.

For legal points concerning legislation on church affairs, see A. Rivet, *Traité du culte catholique et des lois civiles d'ordre religieux, 1789–1947.* 2 vols. 1947.

(C) After 1914

(Works particularly important for interpretation of pre-1914 happenings)

A. Dansette, *Destin du Catholicisme français, 1926–1956.* 1957. Perceptive.

H. W. Paul, *The Second Ralliement: the Rapprochement between Church and State in France in the Twentieth Century.* 1968.

R. Rémond, ed., *Forces religieuses et attitudes politiques dans la France contemporaine.* Cahiers de la Fondation nationale des Sciences Politiques. 1956.

A. Coutrot and F. G. Dreyfus, *Les Forces religieuses dans la société française.* 1965. Excellent bibliography.

III RELIGIOUS PRACTICE AND METHODOLOGICAL PROBLEMS

Y.-M. Hilaire, "La Pratique religieuse en France de 1815 à 1878", in *Information historique* (March–April 1963), pp. 57–69.

F. Boulard, *An Introduction to Religious Sociology: Pioneer Work in France.* E.T. from the French of 1954 by M. J. Jackson. 1960.

Gabriel Le Bras, *Études de sociologie religieuse.* 2 vols. 1955–56. Incorporates most of the same author's *Introduction à l'histoire de la pratique religieuse en France.* 2 vols. 1942–45.

Y. M.-J. Congar, *Jalons pour une théologie du Laïcat*. 1952.

F. A. Isambert, *Christianisme et classe ouvrière*. 1961.

Y. Daniel, *L'Equipement paroissial d'une diocèse urbain: Paris, 1802–1956*. 1957.

F. L. Charpin, *Pratique religieuse et formation d'une grande ville, Marseille, 1800–1958*. 1962.

Christianne Marcilhacy, *Le diocèse d'Orléans sons l'épiscopat de Mgr Dupanloup, 1849–1878*. 1962; *Le diocèse d'Orléans au milieu du XIXᵉ Siècle*. 1964.

F. Boulard and J. Remy, *Pratique religieuse urbaine et régions culturelles*. 1968.

G. Cholvy, *Géographie religieuse de l'Hérault contemporain*. 1968.

In addition to the above, Chapter 2 draws on the following two works for certain details.

A. Dansette. *Destin du Catholicisme français, 1926–56*. 1957.

G. Dupeux, *Aspects de l'histoire sociale et politique du Loir-et-Cher, 1848–1914*. 1962.

IV ECCLESIASTICAL BIOGRAPHIES

There are innumerable biographies. The older lives of bishops, often by some admiring canon of the particular diocese, are uncritical but packed with information. There is space to mention only a few, chiefly modern works of solid scholarship.

F. Lagrange, *Vie de Mgr Dupanloup*. 3 vols. 3rd edn, 1883–84.
To be read in conjunction with Mlle Marcilhacy's distinguished studies of the prelate and his diocese (see section III above).

Agnès Siefried, *L'Abbé Frémont, 1852–1915*. 2 vols. 1932.
A superb source of primary materials. Frémont's diary and correspondence provide an intelligent commentary on events.

Ch. Cordonnier, *Mgr Fuzet, archevêque de Rouen*. 2 vols. 1946.
Important documentation.

M. Bruyère, *Le Cardinal de Cabrières, évêque de Montpellier 1830–1921*. 1956.

E. Catta, *La Doctrine politique et sociale du Cardinal Pie*. 1959.

J. Gadille, *La Pensée et l'action politiques des évêques français au début de la IIIᵉ République, 1870–1883*. 2 vols. 1967. A sophisticated modern analysis.

For the bishops at the Vatican Council:

J.-R. Palanque, *Catholiques Libéraux et Gallicans en France face au Concile du Vatican, 1867–1870*. 1962.

V THE VATICAN AND ITS POLICY

R. A. Graham, *Vatican Diplomacy: a Study of Church and State on the International Plane*. 1959.
S. W. Halperin, *Italy and the Vatican at War*. 1939.
E. E. Y. Hales, *Pio Nono*. 1954.
E. T. Gargan, and others, *Leo XIII and the Modern World*. 1961.
Ch. Ledré, *Pie X*. 1952.

VI THE BATTLE OVER EDUCATION

(A) Basic accounts

M. Ozouf, *L'École, l'Église et la République, 1871–1914*. 1963.
F. Ponteil, *Histoire de l'enseignement en France, 1789–1965*. 1966.
B. Mégrine, *La Question scolaire en France*. Que sais-je? series, 1960.
E. M. Acomb, *The French Laic Laws, 1879–1881*. 1941.

(B) Useful for certain aspects

A. Léaud and F. Glay, *L'École primaire en France*. 2 vols. 1934.
C. Duveau, *Les Instituteurs*. n.d.
L. Legrand, *L'Influence du Positivisme dans l'œuvre scolaire de Jules Ferry: les origines de la laïcité*. 1961.
M. Reclus, *Jules Ferry*. 1947.
L. Dubreuil, *Paul Bert*. 1934.
J.-B. Trotbas, *La Notion de laïcité dans le droit de l'Église catholique et de l'État républicain*. 1959.
A. Audibert, A. Bayet, A. Latreille, L. Trotbas, and others, *La Laïcité*. Université d'Aix-Marseille 1960.
See also L. Capéran under "Histories of the French Church", p. 179 above.

VII THE RALLIEMENT

A. Sedgwick, *The Ralliement in French Politics*. 1965. The essential introductory work.
Mgr Baunard, *Le Cardinal Lavigerie*. 2 vols. 1912 (first edn, 1896).
J. Tournier, *Le Cardinal Lavigerie et son action politique*. 1913.

Xavier de Montclos, *Lavigerie, le Saint-Siège et l'Église*. 1965. A
major work of research. See also the same author's excellent
brief introduction to the documentary collection, *Le Cardinal
Lavigerie: la Mission Universelle de l'Église*. 1968.

—— *Le Toast d'Alger: Documents 1890–91*. 1966.

D. Shapiro, "The Ralliement in the Politics of the 1890's", in *The
Right in France, 1890–1919*, ed. D. Shapiro. *St Anthony's Papers*
XIII. 1962.

J. E. Ward, "The French Cardinals and Leo XIII's Policy of
Ralliement", in *Church History* XXXIII (1964), pp. 60–73.

J. E. Ward, "The Algiers Toast: Lavigerie's Work or Leo XIII's?",
Catholic Historical Review LI (1965), pp. 173–91.

VIII   THE FINAL CRISIS AND THE LAW OF SEPARATION

M. J. H. Larkin, "Loubet's visit to Rome and the question of Papal
prestige", in *Historical Journal* IV. 1961.

—— "The Vatican, French Catholics and the Associations Cultuelles", in *Journal of Modern History* XXXV. 1964.

These two articles are indispensible. (See also the same historian's
"The Church and the French Concordat, 1891 to 1902", in *English
Historical Review* LXXXI. 1966.)

M. O. Partin, *Waldeck-Rousseau, Combes and the Church: the
Politics of anticlericalism, 1899–1905*. 1969.
Clears up some doubtful points by use of archival sources. But
the original thesis antedates Sorlin's great work on Waldeck-
Rousseau.

Axel Freiherr von Campenhausen, *L'Église et l'État en France*. 1964.

J.-M. Mayeur, *La Séparation de l'Église et de l'État, 1905*. 1966.

L. V. Méjan, *La Séparation des Églises et de l'État: l'œuvre de
Louis Méjan*. 1959. Contains many documents.

J.-M. Mayeur, "Géographie de la résistance aux inventaires,
février–mars, 1906", in *Annales* XXI. 1966.

A. Appolis, "En marge de la Séparation: les associations cultuelles
schismatiques", in *Revue de l'histoire de l'Église de France*. 1963.

M. Denis, *L'Église et la République en Mayenne, 1896–1906*. n.d.,
1967.

J. Ameye, *La Vie Politique à Tourcoing sous la Troisième République*. n.d., 1967. Chapter III.

IX REVIVALS AND NEW MOVEMENTS WITHIN THE FRENCH CHURCH

(A) Social Catholicism

A. Vidler, *A Century of Social Catholicism, 1820–1920*. 1964. Good introduction.

J. B. Duroselle, *Les débuts du Catholicisme social en France, 1822–70*. 1951. Definitive work on the earlier period.

G. Hoog, *Histoire du Catholicisme social en France*. 1942.

H. Rollet, *L'Action sociale des catholiques en France, 1871–1914*. 2 vols. 1947–58. Essential.

R. Talmy, *René de La Tour du Pin*. 1964.

—— *Albert de Mun*. 1964.

G. Guitton, *Léon Harmel, 1829–1915*. 2 vols. 1927.

Miriam Lynch (Sister), *The Organized Social Apostolate of Albert de Mun*. Lithographed, 1952.

(B) "Christian Democracy"

M. Montuclard, *Conscience religieuse et démocratie: la Deuxième Démocratie Chrétienne en France, 1891–1902*. 1965. The essential monograph; brings clarity into a confusing subject.

See also:

M. Montuclard, "Aux Origines de la Démocratie Chrétienne", in *Archives de Sociologie des Religions* VI. 1958.

J.-M. Mayeur, "Les Congrès nationaux de la Démocratie Chrétienne à Lyon, 1896, 1897, 1898", in *Revue d'histoire moderne et contemporaine*. July–September 1962.

J.-M. Mayeur, *Un Prêtre démocrate, l'abbé Lemire, 1853–1928*. 1969. A major work of research. Important bibliography.

M. Vaussard, *Histoire de la Démocatie Chrétienne*. 1956.

M. P. Fogarty, *Christian Democracy in Europe, 1820–1953*. 1957.

(C) Le Sillon

Jeanne Caron, *Le Sillon et la Démocratie Chrétienne, 1894–1910*. 1967. A work of detailed research.

Jean de Fabrèques, *Le Sillon de Marc Sangnier*. 1964.

(D) Other New Movements

R. Rémond, *Les deux Congrès ecclésiastiques de Reims et de Bourges, 1896–1900*. 1964.

E. Poulat, ed., *Journal d'un prêtre d'après-demain*, by the *abbé* Calippe. 1961. Poulat's introduction gives the early history of the "worker priest" idea.

P. Dabry (*abbé*), *Les Catholiques Républicains, histoire et souvenirs, 1890–1903*. 1905. Full of information on Christian Democracy and other topics.

R. Talmy, *Le Syndicalisme Chrétien en France, 1871–1930*. 1965.

Ch. Molette, *L'Association Catholique de la Jeunesse Française, 1886–1907*. 1968. Detailed research.

X   BELIEF AND UNBELIEF

(A) Intellectual Tensions within Catholicism

A. Vidler, *The Modernist Movement in the Roman Church*. 1934. Short introduction.

Philip Spencer, *Politics of Belief in Nineteenth-Century France: Lacordaire, Michon, Veuillot*. 1954.

G. Weill, *Histoire du Catholicisme libéral en France, 1828–1908*. 1909.

A. Houtin, *La Question biblique chez les catholiques de France au XIXᵉ siècle*. 1902.

J. T. Burtchaell, *Catholic Theories of Biblical Inspiration since 1810*. 1969.

E. Poulat, *Histoire, dogme et critique dans la crise moderniste*. 1962.

A. Marlé, s.j., ed., *Au cœur de la crise moderniste*. 1960. Correspondence.

(B) The Catholic Revival in Literature

R. Griffiths, *The Reactionary Revolution: the Catholic Revival in French Literature, 1870–1914*. 1966. Indispensible.

J. Calvet, *Le Renouveau Catholique dans la littérature contemporaine*. 1927.

L. Frazer, *Le Renouveau religieux dans le roman français, 1886–1914*. 1936.

M. Mansuy, *Un moderne: Paul Bourget*. 1960. Of wide-ranging interest beyond its title.

R. Baldick, *The Life of J.-K. Huysmans*. 1955.

M. M. Belval, *Des Ténèbres à la lumière: étapes de la pensée mystique de J.-K. Huysmans*. 1968.

P. Duployé, *La Religion de Péguy*. n.d., 1963.

Romain Rolland, *La Cloître de la Rue d'Ulm*. 1962.

L.-A. Maugendre, *La Renaissance Catholique au début du XXe siècle.* 2 vols. 1962–64. A study of two particular groups.

(C) **Intellectual Tendencies Hostile to Catholicism**

(A) BASIC SURVEYS

Alec Mellor, *Histoire de l'anticléricalisme français.* 1966.

G. Weill, *Histoire de l'idée laïque en France au XIXe siècle.* 1925.

(B) PARTICULAR TENDENCIES AND INDIVIDUALS

D. G. Charlton, *Positivist Thought in France during the Second Empire.* 1959.

—— *Secular Religions in France, 1815–70.* 1963.

H. W. Wardman, *Ernest Renan.* 1964.

H. W. Paul, "The Debate over the bankruptcy of Science in 1895", in *French Historical Studies* v (3). 1968.

J. Hemmings, *Émile Zola.* 2nd edn., 1966.

R. Ternois, *Zola et son temps: Lourdes–Rome–Paris.* 1961.

A. Sareil, *Anatole France et Voltaire.* 1961.

J. Levaillant, *Essai sur l'évolution intellectuelle d'Anatole France.* 1965. Like Ternois' volume on Zola, full of interesting information extending well beyond the range of the title.

E. Weath, *La morale kantienne de Ch. Renouvier en son influence sur la constitution de la morale laïque.* . . . 1947.

(C) THE ATTITUDE OF SOCIALISTS TO THE CHURCH

M. Launay, *Jean Jaurès: la question religieuse et le socialisme.* 1960.

M. Rebérioux, "Socialisme et religion: un inédit de Jaurès, 1891", in *Annales.* 1961.

J.-J. Fiechter, *Le Socialisme français de l'affaire Dreyfus à la Grande Guerre.* 1965.

C. Willard, *Les Guesdistes: le mouvement socialiste en France, 1893–1905.* 1965.

Index

Action française 135, 158, 170
Allier, Raoul 141
"Americanism" 107f
Amette, Léon-Adolphe, *abbé*, aft. Card.
　Abp of Paris 28
anticlericals 7, 9, 13–19, 55–60, 74,
　121, 123, 125, 130f, 140, 143, 155,
　157, 175 and *passim*
antisemitism 95f, 98, 122f
Association Catholique de la Jeunesse
　Française (ACJF) 90, 99, 111, 170,
　174
associations canoniques et légales 163,
　164
associations cultuelles 148, 149, 150
　155, 156, 161–5, 166

Ballu, Louis, *abbé* 168
Barrès, Maurice 116, 166
Bazire, Henri 90
Belcastel, Gabriel de 40
Benoist, Charles 153
Bert, Paul 47, 48, 59, 141
Birot, L., *abbé* 160, 161
Bismarck, Otto von, *Fürst* 37, 43
Bloy, Léon 92f, 113, 115
Bonapartists 34, 38, 42
Bonnechose, Henri Marie Gaston de,
　Card. Abp of Rouen 43f
Bougaud, Louis-Emile, *abbé* 27; Abp
　of Laval 136
Boulanger, Georges - Ernest - Jean -
　Marie, General
Bourgeois, Leon 77
Bourget, Paul 33, 113f

Brenier de Montmorand, Maxime,
　vicomte 110
Briand, Aristide 80, 136, 142, 147,
　149, 150, 156, 164, 168
Broglie, Jacques Victor Albert de, *duc*
　19, 34, 38, 42. 43
Broglie, Paul de, *abbé* 7f
Brunetière, Ferdinand 111, 113, 116f,
　151, 162
budget des cultes 4, 49, 140, 152, 168
Buisson, Ferdinand 141, 142
Buisson, Henri 47, 48

Cabrières, François-Marie-Anatole de,
　Bp of Montpellier, aft. Card. 74 &
　n, 152, 159, 167
Calippe, Charles, *abbé* 111
Cambon, Paul 45
Cassagnac, Paul de 66, 74, 152
Catholicism 10f, 14, 19, 46
Cercle Montparnasse 81f
"Cercles d'Études" 100f
Chambord, Henri de, *comte* 34ff, 40
Charity Bazaar fire 93, 124
Charost, Alexis Armand, Abp of Lille
　173
Charpin, Pierre Charles, *chanoine* 7
Chesnelong, Pierre Charles 35f
Christian Democracy (*la Démocratie
　Chrétienne*) 94–9, 109, 151
classe dirigeante, la 82, 85, 92, 96, 103
Claudel, Paul Louis Charles Marie
　112, 113, 115
Clemenceau, Georges 11, 21, 117,
　118, 142, 149, 155, 156, 165, 166,
　173

187

188

Index

harper ✦ torchbooks

American Studies: General

HENRY ADAMS Degradation of the Democratic Dogma. ‡ *Introduction by Charles Hirschfeld.* TB/1450

LOUIS D. BRANDEIS: Other People's Money, *and How the Bankers Use It. Ed. with Intro, by Richard M. Abrams* TB/3081

HENRY STEELE COMMAGER, Ed.: The Struggle for Racial Equality TB/1300

CARL N. DEGLER: Out of Our Past: *The Forces that Shaped Modern America* CN/2

CARL N. DEGLER, Ed.: Pivotal Interpretations of American History
Vol. I TB/1240; Vol. II TB/1241

LAWRENCE H. FUCHS, Ed.: American Ethnic Politics TB/1368

ROBERT L. HEILBRONER: The Limits of American Capitalism TB/1305

JOHN HIGHAM, Ed.: The Reconstruction of American History TB/1068

ROBERT H. JACKSON: The Supreme Court in the American System of Government TB/1106

JOHN F. KENNEDY: A Nation of Immigrants. *Illus. Revised and Enlarged. Introduction by Robert F. Kennedy* TB/1118

RICHARD B. MORRIS: Fair Trial: *Fourteen Who Stood Accused, from Anne Hutchinson to Alger Hiss* TB/1335

GUNNAR MYRDAL: An American Dilemma: *The Negro Problem and Modern Democracy. Introduction by the Author.*
Vol. I TB/1443; Vol. II TB/1444

GILBERT OSOFSKY, Ed.: The Burden of Race: *A Documentary History of Negro-White Relations in America* TB/1405

ARNOLD ROSE: The Negro in America: *The Condensed Version of Gunnar Myrdal's* An American Dilemma. *Second Edition* TB/3048

JOHN E. SMITH: Themes in American Philosophy: *Purpose, Experience and Community* TB/1466

WILLIAM R. TAYLOR: Cavalier and Yankee: *The Old South and American National Character* TB/1474

American Studies: Colonial

BERNARD BAILYN: The New England Merchants in the Seventeenth Century TB/1149

ROBERT E. BROWN: Middle-Class Democracy and Revolution in Massachusetts, 1691–1780. *New Introduction by Author* TB/1413

JOSEPH CHARLES: The Origins of the American Party System TB/1049

WESLEY FRANK CRAVEN: The Colonies in Transition: 1660-1712† TB/3084

CHARLES GIBSON: Spain in America † TB/3077

CHARLES GIBSON, Ed.: The Spanish Tradition in America + HR/1351

LAWRENCE HENRY GIPSON: The Coming of the Revolution: 1763-1775. † *Illus.* TB/3007

JACK P. GREENE, Ed.: Great Britain and the American Colonies: 1606-1763. + *Introduction by the Author* HR/1477

AUBREY C. LAND, Ed.: Bases of the Plantation Society + HR/1429

PERRY MILLER: Errand Into the Wilderness TB/1139

PERRY MILLER & T. H. JOHNSON, Ed.: The Puritans: *A Sourcebook of Their Writings*
Vol. I TB/1093; Vol. II TB/1094

EDMUND S. MORGAN: The Puritan Family: *Religion and Domestic Relations in Seventeenth Century New England* TB/1227

WALLACE NOTESTEIN: The English People on the Eve of Colonization: 1603-1630. † *Illus.* TB/3006

LOUIS B. WRIGHT: The Cultural Life of the American Colonies: 1607-1763. † *Illus.* TB/3005

YVES F. ZOLTVANY, Ed.: The French Tradition in America + HR/1425

American Studies: The Revolution to 1860

JOHN R. ALDEN: The American Revolution: 1775-1783. † *Illus.* TB/3011

RAY A. BILLINGTON: The Far Western Frontier: 1830-1860. † *Illus.* TB/3012

STUART BRUCHEY: The Roots of American Economic Growth, 1607-1861: *An Essay in Social Causation. New Introduction by the Author.* TB/1350

NOBLE E. CUNNINGHAM, JR., Ed.: The Early Republic, 1789-1828 + HR/1394

GEORGE DANGERFIELD: The Awakening of American Nationalism, 1815-1828. † *Illus.* TB/3061

---

† The New American Nation Series, edited by Henry Steele Commager and Richard B. Morris.
‡ American Perspectives series, edited by Bernard Wishy and William E. Leuchtenburg.
a History of Europe series, edited by J. H. Plumb.
§ The Library of Religion and Culture, edited by Benjamin Nelson.
‖ Researches in the Social, Cultural, and Behavioral Sciences, edited by Benjamin Nelson.
Σ Harper Modern Science Series, edited by James A. Newman.
° Not for sale in Canada.
+ Documentary History of the United States series, edited by Richard B. Morris.
# Documentary History of Western Civilization series, edited by Eugene C. Black and Leonard W. Levy.
Λ The Economic History of the United States series, edited by Henry David et al.
¶ European Perspectives series, edited by Eugene C. Black.
** Contemporary Essays series, edited by Leonard W. Levy.
* The Stratum Series, edited by John Hale.

CLEMENT EATON: The Freedom-of-Thought Struggle in the Old South. *Revised and Enlarged. Illus.* TB/1150

CLEMENT EATON: The Growth of Southern Civilization, 1790-1860. † *Illus.* TB/3040

ROBERT H. FERRELL, Ed.: Foundations of American Diplomacy, 1775-1872 + HR/1393

LOUIS FILLER: The Crusade against Slavery: 1830-1860. † *Illus.* TB/3029

WILLIM W. FREEHLING: Prelude to Civil War: *The Nullification Controversy in South Carolina, 1816-1836* TB/1359

PAUL W. GATES: The Farmer's Age: *Agriculture, 1815-1860* ∆ TB/1398

THOMAS JEFFERSON: Notes on the State of Virginia. ‡ *Edited by Thomas P. Abernethy* TB/3052

FORREST MCDONALD, Ed.: Confederation and Constitution, 1781-1789 + HR/1396

JOHN C. MILLER: The Federalist Era: 1789-1801. † *Illus.* TB/3027

RICHARD B. MORRIS: The American Revolution Reconsidered TB/1363

CURTIS P. NETTELS: The Emergence of a National Economy, 1775-1815 ∆ TB/1438

DOUGLASS C. NORTH & ROBERT PAUL THOMAS, Eds.: *The Growth of the American Economy ot 1860* + HR/1352

R. B. NYE: The Cultural Life of the New Nation: 1776-1830. † *Illus.* TB/3026

GILBERT OSOFSKY, Ed.: Puttin' On Ole Massa: *The Slave Narratives of Henry Bibb, William Wells Brown, and Solomon Northup* ‡ TB/1432

JAMES PARTON: The Presidency of Andrew Jackson. *From Volume III of the* Life of Andrew Jackson. *Ed. with Intro. by Robert V. Remini* TB/3080

FRANCIS S. PHILBRICK: The Rise of the West, 1754-1830. † *Illus.* TB/3067

MARSHALL SMELSER: The Democratic Republic, 1801-1815 † TB/1406

JACK M. SOSIN, Ed.: The Opening of the West + HR/1424

GEORGE ROGERS TAYLOR: The Transportation Revolution, 1815-1860 ∆ TB/1347

A. F. TYLER: Freedom's Ferment: *Phases of American Social History from the Revolution to the Outbreak of the Civil War. Illus.* TB/1074

GLYNDON G. VAN DEUSEN: The Jacksonian Era: 1828-1848. † *Illus.* TB/3028

LOUIS B. WRIGHT: Culture on the Moving Frontier TB/1053

American Studies: The Civil War to 1900

W. R. BROCK: An American Crisis: *Congress and Reconstruction, 1865-67* ° TB/1283

T. C. COCHRAN & WILLIAM MILLER: The Age of Enterprise: *A Social History of Industrial America* TB/1054

W. A. DUNNING: Reconstruction, Political and Economic: 1865-1877 TB/1073

HAROLD U. FAULKNER: Politics, Reform and Expansion: 1890-1900. † *Illus.* TB/3020

GEORGE M. FREDRICKSON: The Inner Civil War: *Northern Intellectuals and the Crisis of the Union* TB/1358

JOHN A. GARRATY: The New Commonwealth, 1877-1890 † TB/1410

JOHN A. GARRATY, Ed.: The Transformation of American Society, 1870-1890 + HR/1395

HELEN HUNT JACKSON: A Century of Dishonor: *The Early Crusade for Indian Reform.* † *Edited by Andrew F. Rolle* TB/3063

WILLIAM G. MCLOUGHLIN, Ed.: The American Evangelicals, 1800-1900: An Anthology ‡ TB/1382

JAMES S. PIKE: The Prostrate State: *South Carolina under Negro Government.* ‡ *Intro. by Robert F. Durden* TB/3085

FRED A. SHANNON: The Farmer's Last Frontier: *Agriculture, 1860-1897* TB/1348

VERNON LANE WHARTON: The Negro in Mississippi, 1865-1890 TB/1178

American Studies: The Twentieth Century

RICHARD M. ABRAMS, Ed.: The Issues of the Populist and Progressive Eras, 1892-1912 + HR/1428

RAY STANNARD BAKER: Following the Color Line: *American Negro Citizenship in Progressive Era.* ‡ *Edited by Dewey W. Grantham, Jr. Illus.* TB/3053

RANDOLPH S. BOURNE: War and the Intellectuals: *Collected Essays, 1915-1919.* ‡ *Edited by Carl Resek* TB/3043

A. RUSSELL BUCHANAN: The United States and World War II. † *Illus.*
Vol. I TB/3044; Vol. II TB/3045

THOMAS C. COCHRAN: The American Business System: *A Historical Perspective, 1900-1955* TB/1080

FOSTER RHEA DULLES: America's Rise to World Power: 1898-1954. † *Illus.* TB/3021

HAROLD U. FAULKNER: The Decline of Laissez Faire, 1897-1917 TB/1397

JOHN D. HICKS: Republican Ascendancy: 1921-1933. † *Illus.* TB/3041

WILLIAM E. LEUCHTENBURG: Franklin D. Roosevelt and the New Deal: 1932-1940. † *Illus.* TB/3025

WILLIAM E. LEUCHTENBURG, Ed.: The New Deal: *A Documentary History* + HR/1354

ARTHUR S. LINK: Woodrow Wilson and the Progressive Era: 1910-1917. † *Illus.* TB/3023

BROADUS MITCHELL: Depression Decade: *From New Era through New Deal, 1929-1941* ∆ TB/1439

GEORGE E. MOWRY: The Era of Theodore Roosevelt and the Birth of Modern America: 1900-1912. † *Illus.* TB/3022

GEORGE SOULE: Prosperity Decade: *From War to Depression, 1917-1929* ∆ TB/1349

TWELVE SOUTHERNERS: I'll Take My Stand: *The South and the Agrarian Tradition. Intro. by Louis D. Rubin, Jr.; Biographical Essays by Virginia Rock* TB/1072

Art, Art History, Aesthetics

ERWIN PANOFSKY: Renaissance and Renascences in Western Art. *Illus.* TB/1447

ERWIN PANOFSKY: Studies in Iconology: *Humanistic Themes in the Art of the Renaissance. 180 illus.* TB/1077

OTTO VON SIMSON: The Gothic Cathedral: *Origins of Gothic Architecture and the Medieval Concept of Order. 58 illus.* TB/2018

HEINRICH ZIMMER: Myths and Symbols in Indian Art and Civilization. *70 illus.* TB/2005

Asian Studies

WOLFGANG FRANKE: China and the West: *The Cultural Encounter, 13th to 20th Centuries. Trans. by R. A. Wilson* TB/1326

L. CARRINGTON GOODRICH: A Short History of the Chinese People. *Illus.* TB/3015

Economics & Economic History

C. E. BLACK: The Dynamics of Modernization: A Study in Comparative History   TB/1321
GILBERT BURCK & EDITOR OF Fortune: The Computer Age: And its Potential for Management   TB/1179
SHEPARD B. CLOUGH, THOMAS MOODIE & CAROL MOODIE, Eds.: Economic History of Europe: Twentieth Century #   HR/1388
THOMAS C. COCHRAN: The American Business System: A Historical Perspective, 1900-1955   TB/1180
HAROLD U. FAULKNER: The Decline of Laissez Faire, 1897-1917 △   TB/1397
PAUL W. GATES: The Farmer's Age: Agriculture, 1815-1860 △   TB/1398
WILLIAM GREENLEAF, Ed.: American Economic Development Since 1860 +   HR/1353
ROBERT L. HEILBRONER: The Future as History: The Historic Currents of Our Time and the Direction in Which They Are Taking America   TB/1386
ROBERT L. HEILBRONER: The Great Ascent: The Struggle for Economic Development in Our Time   TB/3030
DAVID S. LANDES: Bankers and Pashas: International Finance and Economic Imperialism in Egypt. New Preface by the Author   TB/1412
ROBERT LATOUCHE: The Birth of Western Economy: Economic Aspects of the Dark Ages   TB/1290
W. ARTHUR LEWIS: The Principles of Economic Planning. New Introduction by the Author°   TB/1436
ROBERT GREEN MC CLOSKEY: American Conservatism in the Age of Enterprise   TB/1137
WILLIAM MILLER, Ed.: Men in Business: Essays on the Historical Role of the Entrepreneur   TB/1081
HERBERT A. SIMON: The Shape of Automation: For Men and Management   TB/1245

Historiography and History of Ideas

J. BRONOWSKI & BRUCE MAZLISH: The Western Intellectual Tradition: From Leonardo to Hegel   TB/3001
WILHELM DILTHEY: Pattern and Meaning in History: Thoughts on History and Society.° Edited with an Intro. by H. P. Rickman   TB/1075
J. H. HEXTER: More's Utopia: The Biography of an Idea. Epilogue by the Author   TB/1195
H. STUART HUGHES: History as Art and as Science: Twin Vistas on the Past   TB/1207
ARTHUR O. LOVEJOY: The Great Chain of Being: A Study of the History of an Idea   TB/1009
RICHARD H. POPKIN: The History of Scepticism from Erasmus to Descartes. Revised Edition   TB/1391
MASSIMO SALVADORI, Ed.: Modern Socialism #   HR/1374
BRUNO SNELL: The Discovery of the Mind: The Greek Origins of European Thought   TB/1018

History: General

HANS KOHN: The Age of Nationalism: The First Era of Global History   TB/1380
BERNARD LEWIS: The Arabs in History   TB/1029
BERNARD LEWIS: The Middle East and the West °   TB/1274

History: Ancient

A. ANDREWS: The Greek Tyrants   TB/1103

THEODOR H. GASTER: Thespis: Ritual Myth and Drama in the Ancient Near East   TB/1281
MICHAEL GRANT: Ancient History °   TB/1190

History: Medieval

NORMAN COHN: The Pursuit of the Millennium: Revolutionary Messianism in Medieval and Reformation Europe   TB/1037
F. L. GANSHOF: Feudalism   TB/1058
F. L. GANSHOF: The Middle Ages: A History of International Relations. Translated by Rémy Hall   TB/1411
ROBERT LATOUCHE: The Birth of Western Economy: Economic Aspects of the Dark Ages °   TB/1290
HENRY CHARLES LEA: The Inquisition of the Middle Ages. || Introduction by Walter Ullmann   TB/1456

History: Renaissance & Reformation

JACOB BURCKHARDT: The Civilization of the Renaissance in Italy. Introduction by Benjamin Nelson and Charles Trinkaus. Illus. Vol. I TB/40; Vol. II TB/41
JOHN CALVIN & JACOPO SADOLETO: A Reformation Debate. Edited by John C. Olin   TB/1239
FEDERICO CHABOD: Machiavelli and the Renaissance   TB/1193
THOMAS CROMWELL: Thomas Cromwell: Selected Letters on Church and Commonwealth, 1523-1540. ¶ Ed. with an Intro. by Arthur J. Slavin   TB/1462
FRANCESCO GUICCIARDINI: History of Florence. Translated with an Introduction and Notes by Mario Domandi   TB/1470
WERNER L. GUNDERSHEIMER, Ed.: French Humanism, 1470-1600. * Illus.   TB/1473
HANS J. HILLERBRAND, Ed., The Protestant Reformation #   HR/1342
JOHAN HUIZINGA: Erasmus and the Age of Reformation. Illus.   TB/19
JOEL HURSTFIELD: The Elizabethan Nation   TB/1312
JOEL HURSTFIELD, Ed.: The Reformation Crisis   TB/1267
PAUL OSKAR KRISTELLER: Renaissance Thought: The Classic, Scholastic, and Humanist Strains   TB/1048
PAUL OSKAR KRISTELLER: Renaissance Thought II: Papers on Humanism and the Arts   TB/1163
PAUL O. KRISTELLER & PHILIP P. WIENER, Eds.: Renaissance Essays   TB/1392
DAVID LITTLE: Religion, Order and Law: A Study in Pre-Revolutionary England. § Preface by R. Bellah   TB/1418
NICCOLO MACHIAVELLI: History of Florence and of the Affairs of Italy: From the Earliest Times to the Death of Lorenzo the Magnificent. Introduction by Felix Gilbert   TB/1027
ALFRED VON MARTIN: Sociology of the Renaissance. ° Introduction by W. K. Ferguson   TB/1099
GARRETT MATTINGLY et al.: Renaissance Profiles. Edited by J. H. Plumb   TB/1162
J. H. PARRY: The Establishment of the European Hegemony: 1415-1715: Trade and Exploration in the Age of the Renaissance   TB/1045
PAOLO ROSSI: Philosophy, Technology, and the Arts, in the Early Modern Era 1400-1700. || Edited by Benjamin Nelson. Translated by Salvator Attanasio   TB/1458
R. H. TAWNEY: The Agrarian Problem in the Sixteenth Century. Intro. by Lawrence Stone   TB/1315

H. R. TREVOR-ROPER: The European Witch-craze of the Sixteenth and Seventeenth Centuries and Other Essays °   TB/1416
VESPASIANO: Rennaissance Princes, Popes, and XVth Century: The Vespasiano Memoirs. Introduction by Myron P. Gilmore. Illus.
                                               TB/1111

History: Modern European

MAX BELOFF: The Age of Absolutism, 1660-1815
                                               TB/1062
D. W. BROGAN: The Development of Modern France ° Vol. I: From the Fall of the Empire to the Dreyfus Affair   TB/1184
Vol. II: The Shadow of War, World War I, Between the Two Wars   TB/1185
ALAN BULLOCK: Hitler, A Study in Tyranny. ° Revised Edition. Illus.   TB/1123
JOHANN GOTTLIEB FICHTE: Addresses to the German Nation. Ed. with Intro. by George A. Kelly ¶   TB/1366
ALBERT GOODWIN: The French Revolution
                                               TB/1064
H. STUART HUGHES: The Obstructed Path: French Social Thought in the Years of Desperation   TB/1451
JOHAN HUIZINGA: Dutch Civilization in the 17th Century and Other Essays   TB/1453
JOHN MCMANNERS: European History, 1789-1914: Men, Machines and Freedom   TB/1419
FRANZ NEUMANN: Behemoth: The Structure and Practice of National Socialism, 1933-1944
                                               TB/1289
DAVID OGG: Europe of the Ancien Régime, 1715-1783 ° α   TB/1271
ALBERT SOREL: Europe Under the Old Regime. Translated by Francis H. Herrick   TB/1121
A. J. P. TAYLOR: From Napoleon to Lenin: Historical Essays °   TB/1268
A. J. P. TAYLOR: The Habsburg Monarchy, 1809-1918: A History of the Austrian Empire and Austria-Hungary °   TB/1187
J. M. THOMPSON: European History, 1494-1789
                                               TB/1431
H. R. TREVOR-ROPER: Historical Essays   TB/1269

Literature & Literary Criticism

JACQUES BARZUN: The House of Intellect
                                               TB/1051
W. J. BATE: From Classic to Romantic: Premises of Taste in Eighteenth Century England
                                               TB/1036
VAN WYCK BROOKS: Van Wyck Brooks: The Early Years: A Selection from his Works, 1908-1921 Ed. with Intro. by Claire Sprague
                                               TB/3082
RICHMOND LATTIMORE, Translator: The Odyssey of Homer   TB/1389

Philosophy

HENRI BERGSON: Time and Free Will: An Essay on the Immediate Data of Consciousness °
                                               TB/1021
H. J. BLACKHAM: Six Existentialist Thinkers: Kierkegaard, Nietzsche, Jaspers, Marcel, Heidegger, Sartre °   TB/1002
J. M. BOCHENSKI: The Methods of Contemporary Thought. Trans by Peter Caws TB/1377
CRANE BRINTON: Nietzsche. Preface, Bibliography, and Epilogue by the Author TB/1197
ERNST CASSIRER: Rousseau, Kant and Goethe. Intro by Peter Gay   TB/1092
WILFRID DESAN: The Tragic Finale: An Essay on the Philosophy of Jean-Paul Sartre TB/1030

MARVIN FARBER: The Aims of Phenomenology: The Motives, Methods, and Impact of Husserl's Thought   TB/1291
PAUL FRIEDLANDER: Plato: An Introduction
                                               TB/2017
MICHAEL GELVEN: A Commentary on Heidegger's "Being and Time"   TB/1464
G. W. F. HEGEL: On Art, Religion Philosophy: Introductory Lectures to the Realm of Absolute Spirit. || Edited with an Introduction by J. Glenn Gray   TB/1463
G. W. F. HEGEL: Phenomenology of Mind. ° || Introduction by eGorge Lichtheim TB/1303
MARTIN HEIDEGGER: Discourse on Thinking. Translated with a Preface by John M. Anderson and E. Hans Freund. Introduction by John M. Anderson   TB/1459
F. H. HEINEMANN: Existentialism and the Modern Predicament   TB/28
WERER HEISENBERG: Physics and Philosophy: The Revolution in Modern Science. Intro. by F. S. C. Northrop   TB/549
EDMUND HUSSERL: Phenomenology and the Crisis of Philosophy. § Translated with an Introduction by Quentin Lauer TB/1170
IMMANUEL KANT: Groundwork of the Metaphysic of Morals. Translated and Analyzed by H. J. Paton   TB/1159
IMMANUEL KANT: Lectures on Ethics. § Introduction by Lewis White Beck TB/105
QUENTIN LAUER: Phenomenology: Its Genesis and Prospect. Preface by Aron Gurwitsch
                                               TB/1169
GEORGE A. MORGAN: What Nietzsche Means
                                               TB/1198
H. J. PATON: The Categorical Imperative: A Study in Kant's Moral Philosophy TB/1325
MICHAEL POLANYI: Personal Knowledge: Towards a Post-Critical Philosophy TB/1158
WILLARD VAN ORMAN QUINE: Elementary Logic Revised Edition   TB/577
JOHN E. SMITH: Themes in American Philosophy: Purpose, Experience and Community
                                               TB/1466
MORTON WHITE: Foundations of Historical Knowledge   TB/1440
WILHELM WINDELBAND: A History of Philosophy Vol. I: Greek, Roman, Medieval   TB/38
Vol. II: Renaissance, Enlightenment, Modern
                                               TB/39
LUDWIG WITTGENSTEIN: The Blue and Brown Books °   TB/1211
LUDWIG WITTGENSTEIN: Notebooks, 1914-1916
                                               TB/1441

Political Science & Government

C. E. BLACK: The Dynamics of Modernization: A Study in Comparative History TB/1321
KENNETH E. BOULDING: Conflict and Defense: A General Theory of Action TB/3024
DENIS W. BROGAN: Politics in America. New Introduction by the Author TB/1469
LEWIS COSER, Ed.: Political Sociology TB/1293
ROBERT A. DAHL & CHARLES E. LINDBLOM: Politics, Economics, and Welfare: Planning and Politico-Economic Systems Resolved into Basic Social Processes   TB/3037
ROY C. MACRIDIS, Ed.: Political Parties: Contemporary Trends and Ideas ** TB/1322
ROBERT GREEN MC CLOSKEY: American Conservatism in the Age of Enterprise, 1865-1910
                                               TB/1137
JOHN B. MORRALL: Political Thought in Medieval Times   TB/1076

KARL R. POPPER: The Open Society and Its Enemies *Vol. I: The Spell of Plato* TB/1101 *Vol. II: The High Tide of Prophecy: Hegel, Marx, and the Aftermath* TB/1102
HENRI DE SAINT-SIMON: Social Organization, The Science of Man, and Other Writings. || *Edited and Translated with an Introduction by Felix Markham* TB/1152
JOSEPH A. SCHUMPETER: Capitalism, Socialism and Democracy TB/3008

Psychology

LUDWIG BINSWANGER: Being-in-the-World: *Selected Papers.* || *Trans. with Intro. by Jacob Needleman* TB/1365
HADLEY CANTRIL: The Invasion from Mars: *A Study in the Psychology of Panic* || TB/1282
MIRCEA ELIADE: Cosmos and History: *The Myth of the Eternal Return* § TB/2050
MIRCEA ELIADE: Myth and Reality TB/1369
MIRCEA ELIADE: Myths, Dreams and Mysteries: *The Encounter Between Contemporary Faiths and Archaic Realities* § TB/1320
MIRCEA ELIADE: Rites and Symbols of Initiation: *The Mysteries of Birth and Rebirth* § TB/1236
SIGMUND FREUD: On Creativity and the Unconscious: *Papers on the Psychology of Art, Literature, Love, Religion.* § *Intro. by Benjamin Nelson* TB/45
J. GLENN GRAY: The Warriors: *Reflections on Men in Battle. Introduction by Hannah Arendt* TB/1294
WILLIAM JAMES: Psychology: *The Briefer Course. Edited with an Intro. by Gordon Allport* TB/1034
KARL MENNINGER, M.D.: Theory of Psychoanalytic Technique TB/1144

Religion: Ancient and Classical, Biblical and Judaic Traditions

MARTIN BUBER: Eclipse of God: *Studies in the Relation Between Religion and Philosophy* TB/12
MARTIN BUBER: Hasidism and Modern Man. *Edited and Translated by Maurice Friedman* TB/839
MARTIN BUBER: The Knowledge of Man. *Edited with an Introduction by Maurice Friedman. Translated by Maurice Friedman and Ronald Gregor Smith* TB/135
MARTIN BUBER: Moses. *The Revelation and the Covenant* TB/837
MARTIN BUBER: The Origin and Meaning of Hasidism. *Edited and Translated by Maurice Friedman* TB/835
MARTIN BUBER: The Prophetic Faith TB/73
MARTIN BUBER: Two Types of Faith: *Interpenetration of Judaism and Christianity* ° TB/75
MALCOLM L. DIAMOND: Martin Buber: *Jewish Existentialist* TB/840
M. S. ENSLIN: Christian Beginnings TB/5
M. S. ENSLIN: The Literature of the Christian Movement TB/6
HENRI FRANKFORT: Ancient Egyptian Religion: *An Interpretation* TB/77
ABRAHAM HESCHEL: God in Search of Man: *A Philosophy of Judaism* TB/807
ABRAHAM HESCHEL: Man Is not Alone: *A Philosophy of Religion* TB/838
T. J. MEEK: Hebrew Origins TB/69
H. J. ROSE: Religion in Greece and Rome TB/55

Religion: Early Christianity Through Reformation

ANSELM OF CANTERBURY: Truth, Freedom, and Evil: *Three Philosophical Dialogues. Edited and Translated by Jasper Hopkins and Herbert Richardson* TB/317
JOHANNES ECKHART: Meister Eckhart: *A Modern Translation by R. Blakney* TB/8
EDGAR J. GOODSPEED: A Life of Jesus TB/1
ROBERT M. GRANT: Gnosticism and Early Christianity ° TB/136
ARTHUR DARBY NOCK: St. Paul ° TR/104
GORDON RUPP: Luther's Progress to the Diet of Worms ° TB/120

Religion: The Protestant Tradition

KARL BARTH: Church Dogmatics: *A Selection. Intro. by H. Gollwitzer. Ed. by G. W. Bromiley* TB/95
KARL BARTH: Dogmatics in Outline TB/56
KARL BARTH: The Word of God and the Word of Man TB/13
WILLIAM R. HUTCHISON, Ed.: American Protestant Thought: *The Liberal Era* ‡ TB/1385
SOREN KIERKEGAARD: Edifying Discourses. *Edited with an Intro. by Paul Holmer* TB/32
SOREN KIERKEGAARD: The Journals of Kierkegaard. ° *Edited with an Intro. by Alexander Dru* TB/52
SOREN KIERKEGAARD: The Point of View for My Work as an Author: *A Report to History.* § *Preface by Benjamin Nelson* TB/88
SOREN KIERKEGAARD: The Present Age. § *Translated and edited by Alexander Dru. Introduction by Walter Kaufmann* TB/94
SOREN KIERKEGAARD: Purity of Heart. *Trans. by Douglas Steere* TB/4
SOREN KIERKEGAARD: Repetition: *An Essay in Experimental Psychology* § TB/117
WOLFHART PANNENBERG, et al.: History and Hermeneutic. *Volume 4 of* Journal for Theology and the Church, *edited by Robert W. Funk and Gerhard Ebeling* TB/254
F. SCHLEIERMACHER: The Christian Faith. *Introduction by Richard R. Niebuhr.* Vol. I TB/108; Vol. II TB/109
F. SCHLEIERMACHER: On Religion: *Speeches to Its Cultured Despisers. Intro. by Rudolf Otto* TB/36
PAUL TILLICH: Dynamics of Faith TB/42
PAUL TILLICH: Morality and Beyond TB/142

Religion: The Roman & Eastern Christian Traditions

A. ROBERT CAPONIGRI, Ed.: Modern Catholic Thinkers II: *The Church and the Political Order* TB/307
G. P. FEDOTOV: The Russian Religious Mind: *Kievan Christianity, the tenth to the thirteenth Centuries* TB/370
GABRIEL MARCEL: Being and Having: *An Existential Diary. Introduction by James Collins* TB/310
GABRIEL MARCEL: Homo Viator: *Introduction to a Metaphysic of Hope* TB/397

Religion: Oriental Religions

TOR ANDRAE: Mohammed: *The Man and His Faith* § TB/62
EDWARD CONZE: Buddhism: *Its Essence and Development.* ° *Foreword by Arthur Waley* TB/58